FORGOTTEN RAILWAYS

FORGOTTEN RAILWAYS
Edited by Allan Patmore
Regional volumes so far published

H. P. WHITE

FORGOTTEN RAILWAYS

DAVID ST JOHN THOMAS

DAVID & CHARLES

To Allan Patmore
whose idea this was

(*half-title*) An express for Leeds via Dumfries and the Carlisle & Settle Line prepares to leave St. Enoch (Glasgow) behind 46117 'Welsh Guardsman'.
(*title page*) On the Fife coast. B1 4–6–0 No. 61404 enters Pittenweem while working the 08.37 Thornton Junction to Crail on 7 August 1965.

Note The description of an old railway route does not imply that there is a public right of way, and readers must obtain permission to enter private land.

British Library Cataloguing in Publication Data
White, H. P.
   Forgotten railways. – (Forgotten railways)
   1. Railways – Great Britain – Abandonment – History
   I. Title   II. Series
   385′.0941   HE3018

   ISBN 0-9469537-13-5

First published 1986 by David St John Thomas
and distributed by David & Charles Ltd

Set in 11/12½pt Sabon by
Typesetters (Birmingham) Ltd, Warley, Smethwick, West Midlands
and printed in Great Britain
by Redwood Burn Ltd, Trowbridge, Wilts
for David St John Thomas
Distributed by David & Charles (Holdings) Ltd
Brunel House Newton Abbot Devon
Published in the United States of America
by David & Charles Inc
North Pomfret Vermont 05053 USA

Contents

Down Trains. MOAT LANE Jc., LLANIDLOES, BUILTH WELLS and BRECON. Week Days.

STATIONS	B Passenger arr	B Passenger dep	B Auto arr	B Auto dep	12.45 p.m ex Hereford L.M.S. Passenger arr	dep	G Engine & Van MO RR dep	E 7.5 a.m from Bas'leg Goods arr	dep	K Pilot RR arr	dep	10.30 a.m. ex Hereford L.M.S. Goods arr	dep	A Passenger to Treherbert SO arr	dep	K Cattle Talgarth Fair days dep	B Passenger arr	dep	B Pass. dep	A Passenger to Barry SO arr	dep	B Passenger arr	dep
	p.m.	p.m.	p.m.	p.m.	p.m.	p.m.	p.m.	p.m.	p.m.	p.m.	p.m.	p.m.	p.m.	p.m.	p.m.	p.m.	p.m.	p.m.	p.m.	p.m.	p.m.	p.m.	p.m.
MOAT LANE JUNCTION	…	…	…	12 27	…	…	…	…	…	…	…	…	…	…	…	…	…	2†35	3†55	…	…	…	…
Llandinam	…	…	…	12 32	…	…	…	…	…	…	…	…	…	…	…	…	…	2 40	4 0	…	…	…	…
Dolwen	…	…	…	12 38	…	…	…	…	…	…	…	…	…	…	…	…	…	2 46	4 6	…	…	…	…
LLANIDLOES	…	12M35	12 43	X12 44	…	…	…	…	…	…	…	…	…	…	x2 6	…	2 51	2 53	4 11	…	…	…	…
Tylwch	…	…	…	12 51	…	…	…	…	…	…	…	…	…	2 20	x2 25	…	…	3 4½	…	…	…	…	…
Glan-yr-afon Halt	…	…	…	12 55½	…	…	…	…	…	…	…	…	…	…	…	…	…	…	…	…	…	…	…
Glan-yr-afon Siding	…	…	…	…	…	…	…	…	…	…	…	…	…	…	…	…	…	…	…	…	…	…	…
Pantydwr	…	…	…	1 4½	…	…	…	…	…	…	…	…	…	…	…	…	…	…	…	…	…	…	…
St. Harmons	…	…	…	…	…	…	…	…	…	…	…	…	…	…	…	…	3 9½	X3 12	…	…	…	…	…
Marteg Halt	…	…	…	1 1	…	…	…	…	…	…	…	…	…	…	…	…	…	3 16	…	…	…	…	…
Rhayader	…	…	1 16	X1 19	…	…	…	…	…	…	…	…	…	2 50	x2 54	…	3 28	3 32	…	…	…	5 0	4 57
Stop Board	…	…	…	…	…	…	…	…	…	…	…	…	…	…	…	…	…	3 22½	…	…	…	…	…
Cerrig Gwynion Siding	…	…	…	…	…	…	…	…	…	…	…	…	…	…	…	…	…	…	…	…	…	…	…
Doldowlod	…	…	1 26	X1 27	…	…	…	…	…	…	…	…	…	…	3 09X	…	…	3 40	…	…	…	…	…
Newbridge-on-Wye	…	…	1 35	X1 37	…	…	…	…	…	…	…	…	…	…	3813	…	…	3 49	…	…	…	…	…
Thomas' Siding	…	…	…	…	…	…	…	…	…	…	…	…	…	…	…	…	…	…	…	…	…	…	…
Builth Road	…	…	1 44	1 45	…	…	2†35	…	…	…	…	…	…	3 20	x3 21	…	3 56	3 57	…	Z4 36	4 37	…	…
BUILTH WELLS	12X53	1C10	1 48	…	1 50	X1 55	2†40	…	2 33	…	…	…	…	3 24	x3 28	…	4 0	x4 8	…	4 40	4 41	…	…
Llanelwydd Quarry Siding	…	…	…	…	…	…	…	…	…	…	…	…	…	…	…	…	…	…	…	…	…	…	…
Llanfaredd Halt	…	1 14½	…	…	2 0	X2 2	…	…	…	…	…	…	…	…	…	…	…	4 12½	…	…	…	…	…
Aberedw	…	1 19	…	…	…	X7	…	…	…	…	…	…	…	…	…	…	…	4 17	…	…	…	…	…
Erwood	…	1 25	…	…	…	…	…	…	…	…	…	…	…	…	…	…	…	4 23	…	…	…	…	…
Llanstephan Halt	…	1 31	…	…	…	…	…	…	…	…	…	…	…	…	…	…	…	4 29	…	…	…	…	…
Boughrood and Llyswen	…	1 37	…	…	…	…	…	…	…	…	2 55	2 30	2 55	…	3 53	…	…	4 33½	…	…	…	…	…
Three Cocks	1 35T	1 43	…	…	…	2X13	…	…	…	…	…	3 4	3 17	…	X	…	4 38½	4 40	…	5 11	x5 12	…	…
Talgarth	1 42X	1 50	…	…	…	2T21	…	…	…	3 15	X3‖43	3 27	3 30	…	7 J	4 10	4 45	4 46	…	…	6	…	…
Trefeinon	1 48X	X1 57	…	…	…	W2	…	…	…	…	…	…	…	…	…	4§28	…	4 53	…	…	…	…	…
Talyllyn Junction North	1 56	2 1	…	…	…	…	…	…	…	…	…	3 40	X3 55	…	…	…	…	S	…	…	…	…	…
Talyllyn	2X 4	T2 11	…	…	…	…	…	…	…	…	…	…	…	…	…	4J47	…	…	…	…	6 22 J	…	…
Llangorse Lake Halt	…	…	…	…	…	…	…	…	…	…	…	…	…	…	…	…	…	…	…	…	…	…	…
Greenway Siding	…	…	…	…	…	…	…	…	…	…	…	…	…	…	…	…	…	…	…	…	…	…	…
Groesffordd Halt	…	2 16	…	…	…	…	…	…	…	…	…	…	…	…	…	…	…	5x 0	…	…	…	…	…
Brecon Yard G. Frame	…	…	…	…	…	…	…	…	…	…	…	…	…	…	…	…	…	…	…	…	…	…	…
BRECON	2 20	…	…	…	2 29	…	…	…	2 45	3‖55	…	4 7	…	…	…	…	5 7½	…	…	…	…	…	…

C—Will leave Builth Wells at 1.15 p.m. on Saturdays, July 15th, to September 2nd, inclusive.
J—Via Talyllyn Loop. M—On Mondays only from Newbridge-on-Wye to Builth Road.
S—Calls on Saturdays only: not advertised.
W—Calls at Trefeinon on Wednesdays only.
§—Arrives Trefeinon 4.20 p.m.

Z—Through Train from Llandrindod Wells, worked by G.W. engine, etc.

Llandrindod Wells		dep. 4.15 p.m.
Builth Rd. L.M.S. No. 2 Box	arr. 4.25 p.m.	dep. 4.27 p.m.
Builth Rd. G.W. Junction	arr. 4.30 p.m.	dep. 4.35 p.m.

A page from the GW working timetable dated 3 July 1939. The variety of trains on this relatively minor cross-country line is interesting. The 2.35pm from Moat Lane is the one that figures in Chapter 1

Introduction

A Dream in Mid Wales

The early summer sunshine is beginning to lengthen the afternoon shadows across the valley floor where the Wye meanders deeply through the round green hills of Mid Wales. Following the river closely is a single-track railway and along it bustles a green 0–6–0 locomotive hauling a short train of three very miscellaneous corridor coaches in their characteristic Great Western colours of chocolate and cream. The train had left the isolated Moat Lane Junction on the ex-Cambrian line to Aberystwyth at 14.35, carrying a handful of passengers changing from the coast-bound main-line train, for Moat Lane has no local traffic. It had followed the valley of the Upper Severn to Llanidloes, the first important station, with its extensive buildings, large goods yard and loco-motive depot. It had then climbed steeply the narrowing Tylwch Valley and over open high country before descending the Marteg gorge to gain the Wye Valley, which it had followed through Rhayader and Newbridge.

Ahead, another railway on a high embankment crosses over the line and on the bridge a very noisy ex London & North Western Super D 0–8–0 loco-motive is starting to move a long and heavy southbound freight train, to begin the long climb up to Sugar Loaf Summit en route for Swansea. The GW passenger train enters the passing loop where a connecting spur rises to join the other line, passes under the bridge and comes to a stop on time at 15.56 at the Low Level station of Builth Road, a two-platform station with a modest two-storey station house on the southbound platform.

The train soon pulls out for Builth Wells and Brecon. There is an advertised connection with the next southbound London Midland & Scottish train from the High Level station, but no-one is making it this afternoon. The forecourts of the two stations adjoin, but there is also a connecting path up the embank-ment and a luggage lift. In contrast with the 'cottage' effect of the Low Level station, the High Level building on the southbound platform is an ugly two-storey stone building with bow windows. At the north end of the station is a small goods yard and to the south is a single-road engine shed off the connect-ing spur.

The next LMS train, the 14.40 from Shrewsbury, is not due until 16.32, but the wait is enlivened by a short northbound GW goods train of a dozen or so wagons, the 14.20 from Talyllyn Junction to Moat Lane Junction, timed to stop in the Low Level from 16.11 to 16.21. This afternoon there are no wagons to be attached or detached. The goods train is followed by a passenger train made up of a single brake-composite coach, hauled by another 0–6–0. It has come from Builth Wells, 1½ miles down the valley bringing half a dozen passengers for the 16.32. The locomotive runs round the coach and places it at the other platform.

A few minutes late the train from Shrewsbury appears round the bend from the north. The Black Five 4–6–0 heads a six-coach train; the red LMS coaches are much more uniform in outline than the miscellaneous GW ones, but they have an extraordinary variety of origins. Behind the engine is a refreshment car which has been picked up at Craven Arms, where it was detached from the 10.25 from Swansea, calling at Craven Arms at 13.40. Of the other coaches, one has come from Euston via Stafford, where two more originated, while one coach from Manchester and one from Liverpool have been added at Shrewsbury.

The waiting passengers entrain and the handful of descending passengers make their way down the path to the one-coach train, which will leave at 16.57 on its 3min journey to Builth Wells. The Black Five gives a deep and prolonged hoot on its siren as the driver gets the right away and, the fireman leaning out to collect the staff, blasts off for Garth, the next crossing station, where it will pass the northbound train from Swansea.

There is a deep-toned whistle from the GW locomotive below, but on turning round from watching the disappearing Swansea train there is no train to be seen. From the Low Level station house there is a curl of smoke from a chimney, but two or three cars and vans are parked where once rails passed between the platforms. On turning back again, there are two lines of rail along-side the platforms of the High Level station, but no longer is there a goods yard to the north or a small locomotive depot to the south. Recovering from the shock, there comes from the Garth direction the sound of a two-tone air horn. A two-car diesel multiple unit appears and comes to a stand in the station at 16.54.

For the year is 1982 and the vision just described is an echo of everyday events in 1938. It is all but twenty years since the last passenger train made its way over the Mid Wales line of the old Cambrian Railways, straggling for 56 miles of memorable beauty from Moat Lane Junction to Talyllyn Junction. At the same time all freight traffic ceased south of Llanidloes, though cement for the Clywedog Dam arrived there until 1967. The Central Wales line of the LNW never had many passenger trains, though it was possible to travel from Swansea to Euston in a through coach for the same fare as that to Paddington. But as late as 1950 eighteen heavy freights struggled daily over the long gradients. Its fate at one time hung in the balance and it seemed likely that it too would become, like the Mid Wales, a forgotten railway. That fate was avoided, but there are now no freight trains, while, apart from occasional excursion trains, there are only five scheduled passenger trains each way on weekdays, formed by two-car DMUs.

Builth Road in August 1959

(*above*) The Low Level Station. A BR Class 2 locomotive on a Moat Lane–Brecon train. A Swansea bound train waits at the High Level for passengers making for the connecting footpath. (*below*) The High Level platforms with a Shrewsbury–Swansea train hauled by LMS Class 4 2–6–4T

An East Anglian Scene

Such trips into re-creative imagination can be made in hundreds of places up and down the country. Traversing the new King's Lynn by-pass I recalled with surprise that the last time I had been along the route was by train. It was in September 1958, shortly before closure, that I had my one and only journey over the metals of the former Midland & Great Northern Joint line. The train was the 10.35 from Peterborough, itself now rebuilt out of all recognition from its dingy Great Northern incarnation. This had a roof over the two main platforms and double-track main line. Behind a BR Standard class 4 Mogul, No 43090, a strong contender for victory in the ugliest locomotive competition, was an ex-GW 'Syphon' bogie van and three miscellaneous corridor coaches, ample accommodation for the half-dozen passengers.

In brilliant sunshine the cavalcade trundled at 30mph across the limitless Fenland landscape, all sky and cornfields. A freight train was passed on the double line before the token was picked up from the exchange apparatus at Thorney, at the entrance to the single-track section. Away in the distance a long goods train on the March–Spalding line crossed our bows while we were held at a colour-light signal protecting the Murrow level-crossing of the two lines. Two or three passengers joined at Murrow (M&GN), the first stop.

The line passed into the fruit-growing country centred on Wisbech. The station, like all on the line, was small and unpretentious, but like the others it was well cared for. Nowhere was paint brush or broom neglected and the whole line was apparently in first-class condition. Here a number of passengers, most with cycles, were picked up. In the goods yards two class 4 2–6–0s were shunting and, beyond, sidings served the prosperous-looking river port.

The train now ran alongside the River Nene between its high embankments, pausing at Tydd station, where yet another 2–6–0 was shunting a pick-up freight. The line from Bourne and Spalding was joined before the train drew up alongside the island platform of Sutton Bridge, 27½ miles and 65min from Peterborough. Here the passengers from Wisbech left after retrieving their cycles. The combined road–rail swing bridge over the Nene is still there, now of course road only. At Walpole a westbound passenger train was passed. Here and at the adjoining stations the goods yards were very large, designed to deal with agricultural traffic, which even then was declining.

The bridge over the Ouse was crossed and the train pulled up at South Lynn, 2 miles from the town. In a few minutes the connecting train from King's Lynn arrived at the other face of the island platform, a two-coach pull-and-push unit hauled by an ex Great Eastern 0–6–2T. Meanwhile 43090 had been uncoupled and run forward to the locomotive shed. While a sister loco, 43160, backed on, about a dozen passengers and a mountain of luggage in advance were transferred from the King's Lynn train.

After a 15min stop, the train set off and in a couple of miles began to climb out of the Fens into low, rolling sandy country of woods with occasional fields carved out of them. From Gayton Road, the first station, wagon-loads of sand

A journey on the M&GN on 29 September 1958
(*above*) The 11.11 Peterborough–Yarmouth entering Sutton Bridge. The bridge is still in use for road traffic. (*below*) At Aylsham the 11.11 waits to cross the 12.54 Yarmouth–Peterborough.

were being despatched, and here a three-coach passenger train was passed. From now on the stations seemed more remote than those in Fenland, but the scene had again changed as the line passed into the 'Good Sands', the land of wheat, sugar beet and fat cattle. It was low-lying country, never more than 150ft high. But the line was built on the surface, and grades and curves were severe where it wound through the low hills. Massingham was doing a flourishing trade loading bulk grain wagons; East Rudham was also dealing with this traffic, while a line of box wagons was being unloaded for the nearby RAF station. In contrast, Raynham Park yard was devoid of wagons.

Fakenham (West), 58½ miles from Peterborough, was reached at 13.05. The goods yard was large and well filled, and in it yet another pick-up freight was shunting. Eight passengers joined and six left. Now came a long climb at 1 in 100 to the summit of the line at 294ft just short of Melton Constable, reached at 13.23.

Here at the M&GN's 'Crewe' were two connecting DMUS, in those days relatively unfamiliar, one for Norwich, the other for Cromer. Most of the passengers leaving our train joined the latter, while the mountain of luggage was transferred to it. Boarding schools were beginning their new year. At Aylsham we waited patiently in the crossing loop for the next westbound train, which was the normal formation for a passenger train, three corridor coaches behind a Mogul loco. North Walsham (North) station lay alongside North Walsham (Main), the ex-GE station on the Cromer line. Apart from coal the freight traffic had already been concentrated at the latter. At Honing came another long wait to cross a westbound train. In due course it came fast round the curve, a Mogul-hauled parcels train of eight vans, which went through the station without slackening speed, taking the new token from the tablet exchanger.

It was now flat country, Broadland. At Stalham, portable buildings were being loaded in the busy goods yard. Potter Heigham, 97 miles from Peterborough, was and is the centre of Broadland, and beyond the train rumbled over the yacht-filled River Thurne. So it arrived at Martham, where the westbound loop was occupied by a Yarmouth-bound freight waiting for us to overtake. At California the coastal sand dunes were reached and the substantial halt serving Butlin's holiday camp was passed. At Caister, just outside Yarmouth, about a dozen passengers were waiting with as many prams. And so at 15.02 the train finally reached its terminus, Yarmouth Beach station.

This was 109¾ miles from Peterborough. The 4hr 27min spent on the journey with its thirty-one intermediate stops, representing a very sedate progress of less than 25mph, was far too long to encourage the normal passenger, and it is doubtful whether, apart from two rail fans, anyone else had survived the whole distance. But for the connoisseur of rail travel it was to be enjoyed at the time and savoured in the memory. For it is a memory of a journey in a distant past which cannot be repeated. Not only was it made over a long forgotten line, the methods of operation and the traffic carried cannot be recalled even by a journey over our remaining lines. In 1984 it was possible to travel from Peterborough to Yarmouth at 12.42 (Saturdays excepted), though via Ely and Norwich (where a change was needed), in 5min under 3hr. But not only was the journey by a different route, the railway and its traffic had changed almost out of all recognition.

A Wealth of Memories

Memories can be expanded indefinitely, to the trains themselves as centre-pieces, the locomotives and the coaches or wagons; the scenery through which they ran; the people and things they carried and the railwaymen who ran them. And what endless variety these provide. On the one hand the up 'Thames–Forth' express, a heavy train of ten or more corridor coaches and A3 Pacific-hauled, climbing from Hawick, up the glen of the Slitrig Water into the bare, green tangle of the Border Hills to the final 1 in 75 and the far-off Whitrope Summit. On the other is the 1930s memory of the 1868 vintage 0–6–0 *Carlisle* of the Bishop's Castle Railway, with its short mixed train of an aged four- or six-wheeled coach with leaking roof and a handful of wagons, creeping along a track so neglected and overgrown 'you could reach out of the windows and pick hazel-nuts, wild roses and honeysuckle' through the idyllic sylvan glades of the deserted Onny Valley. And not forgetting Southern Region electric multiple units clattering through the large wooded gardens of highly desirable South London suburbs on their way to the vast barn of Crystal Palace High Level . . .

Then there are memories of operating methods, sometimes eccentric in the extreme, of interest to the transport historian but doubtless a cause of dislike and irritation for the passengers. The line over Romney Marsh from Appledore led to two terminals, Dungeness and New Romney. In South Eastern & Chatham days the train would decant New Romney passengers at Lydd before proceeding to Dungeness, taking with it the station-master to sell tickets there. Its return put an end to the vigil of the New Romney contingent, but they were replaced by those coming from Dungeness who in turn had to await the return of the train from New Romney. Beneath the high arch of the summer sky it might have been tolerable, but it would have been less so with a winter wind blowing across the bleak Marsh. History is silent as to why passengers could not remain on board or whether there was ever a mutiny. Or was the Lydd waiting room at least warmer than the carriages?

Railwaymen

Stories of the railwaymen who worked those forgotten railways and of their exploits are legion. There were many personalities on every line. Sam Waldron, a guard on the Hayling Island line (Hants), would delay the departure of the last train until he was sure all his regular passengers were aboard, going out into the station forecourt to urge on the laggards. At Harpenden East, on the ex-Great Northern Luton branch, Stanley Munt was signalman from 1926 to

Whether a station is closed or remains open, the once familiar figure of the Stationmaster is now forgotten. In 1962 the Rhydymwyn official meets a Denbigh–Chester train.

1958. On Sundays he would open the box for the first train before going to chapel. He conducted Sunday school after dealing with the afternoon train. Evening service was long over when he would signal the 22.00 cattle train from Luton and close the box.

Long service was a feature on many forgotten branch lines. On the Bunting-ford branch (Herts) James Ketley spent seventeen years as station-master, at West Mill. In 1920 he transferred to Rye House on the 'main line' to Hertford East. But after five months he was back on the branch at Braughing, where he remained for ten years. His brother George was station-master at Widford for sixteen years. But even this pales before the record of Fred Sibthorpe, who was porter/signalman on the branch for forty-six years, at Mardock and Widford.

Railwaymen who staffed rural lines were also countrymen. On the Great Western Malmesbury branch locomotive crews would set rabbit snares on the outward trip, picking up the catch on the return. The line from Brent to Kingsbridge in South Devon ran along the banks of the Avon, a noted salmon river. A local poacher had an arrangement with the enginemen to inform him of the whereabouts of the water-bailiff. A code of whistle signals was worked out and the train crews were duly rewarded in kind. Walter Waterman, for many years a driver on the Bordon Branch (Hants), always hung a horseshoe on the cab of his regular engine. He cultivated an allotment at Bordon which was within easy reach of the platform, so that the time waiting for the right away could be usefully employed.

In the latter years of the Cleobury & Ditton Priors Light Railway young BR drivers of freight trains were determined to lower existing speed records. David L. Smith tells a story of speed put to useful purpose. Between 1880 and 1935 steamer excursions to the Isle of Man were run from the tiny and shallow port of Garlieston in south-west Scotland. This was served by a mile-long branch off the long-forgotten line from Newton Stewart to Whithorn. On one occasion the driver of the connecting train from Carlisle for the steamer found the platform at Newton Stewart 'black with people' and not even standing room on the train. Calling on the assembled multitude to wait, he ran down the 16 miles to Garlieston as quickly as possible. The last two coaches were cut off and he returned to Newton Stewart with them. The waiting passengers were bundled

(*left*) Conversation piece at Buildwas Junction; (*right*) Token exchange at Bodfari on the Chester–Denbigh Line, closed in 1962.

on board and the return began. As they approached Garlieston clouds of black smoke could be seen and the steamer's siren heard. As the train ran into the terminus the train crew shouted to the passengers to run for it. As the last one boarded the steamer, the gangplank was raised and the vessel hauled away from the quay amid boiling mud. Another minute and the steamer would have grounded for twelve hours.

Nor should the managers of forgotten systems be forgotten. One often hears of the enigmatic Col Stephens, collecting semi-derelict railways at the time bus pioneers such as the Chester-based Crosland-Taylor family were building their empire with an eye on the motorised future. But he was only one. The young Sam Fay, cutting his managerial teeth on the bankrupt Midland & South Western Junction before going on to higher Great Central things, was reputed to follow the first train of the day in a light engine to collect the takings from the stations to enable the wages to be paid. Between 1891 and 1898 John Parton was Superintendent of the Line of the 18¾ mile Golden Valley Railway in Herefordshire, his office apparently lapsing when the line closed for some years due to its financial troubles. A ticket-collector at Hereford's Barrs Court station, he joined the company as Permanent Way Inspector as well as superintendent. Afterwards he became Platform Inspector at Oxford. From 1893 to 1925 the secretary and manager of the 2½ mile Easingwold Railway in the Vale of York doubled up as Medical Officer of the town as well as having a general practice.

The Theme of the Book
In spite of all these forgotten railways, it is by no means the case that railways have everywhere and inevitably entered a period of final decline and extinction. In many parts of the world heavy-haul railways for coal, iron ore and other minerals have been built in recent years; forty-two cities were provided with a new 'metro' system between 1954 and 1981; in China and Africa many miles of general carrier lines are opened each year; and in many other countries the capacities of main lines are being increased to accommodate growing traffic. Even in Great Britain, Inter-City passenger services are at a level of speed and frequency undreamed of in 1963.

However, there is no question that the railway no longer has the near universal role in transport it had before the Motor Age. Its technology and the consequent structure of its costs are such that for relatively light traffic flows over relatively short distances it can no longer compete with the road. Thus all countries with a highly developed rail network found that, with the expansion of motor transport after 1920, it was now over-extended and that contraction was necessary and inevitable, leaving in its wake a greater or lesser mileage of forgotten lines. Great Britain was certainly no exception. In 1923 some 23,000 route miles of line carried regular scheduled passenger services. By 1970 this passenger network had contracted by 14,500 miles.

Inevitably therefore large areas of the country are now without any railways at all. Inevitably too debate has raged on the definition of what functions are suitable for rail; on what are the 'real' as opposed to the 'accounting' costs and benefits of railways as opposed to road transport, particularly if consideration is taken of the social costs and the environmental consequences; and on the extent to which changes in operating methods and commercial policies could encourage traffic and increase rail's competitiveness.

In addition, and perhaps surprisingly, as the closed lines fade into history and as their physical remains are increasingly obliterated, so interest in them increases as more and more people become aware of their vanished heritage. Interest grows, not only in the locomotives and rolling stock, but in station architecture and furnishings, in the services the lines provided and the traffic they carried, as well as the relationships between the lines and their trains and the landscapes through which they ran.

It is this growing interest which has called into being the 'Forgotten Railways' series, to which this book is intended as an introduction, and books such as David Thomas's *The Country Railway*, which are evocations of the *ethos* of the forgotten lines in their heyday. Photographic records are also becoming more widely available; these include the 'Railway History in Pictures' series as well as many detailed studies of individual lines.

The whole question of forgotten railways is important because of its immense scale; is relevant because successive governments periodically hanker after even more line closures; and is of interest to an ever increasing number of people, fascinated by the past appearance and role of the railways. This book

An Essex byway. A diminutive 0–6–0T towers over the ex-Wisbech & Upwell Tramway coaches forming the train for Kelvedon at Tollesbury in July 1938.

therefore attempts an overall view of forgotten railways, drawing together the themes given detailed consideration on a regional basis in the other volumes in the 'Forgotten Railways' series.

The first task is therefore to trace the pattern of closures right through from 1840 to the massive programme of the 1960s, considering particularly the regional context of differing patterns of closure in different parts of the country. The second is to look critically at the closure process, particularly as revealed in a number of fiercely fought closure battles, and as revealed through case studies of selected forgotten main lines and branch lines, both rural and urban. In this connection too it is necessary to look at the changing policies which eventually (at least up to the time of writing) brought the closure programme to a halt. The third task is to look at the forgotten railway in the landscape, to review the physical remains of those railways and to examine the alternative uses to which the land and buildings can be put.

Closure Trends

The period between 1830 and 1914 has come to be known as the Railway Age. For this was when the rail was the almost unchallenged mode of land transport, especially in Great Britain, the land of its birth, where it was perhaps only challenged by coastal shipping. Economic historians point to the tremendous surges of investment in the British railway system during the nineteenth century. Between 1830 and 1850 alone, over 6,000 route miles of line were opened to traffic. With the vastly greater technological resources and engineering expertise available, it took about the same time to complete the first thousand miles of the motorway system.

When the Liverpool & Manchester, usually thought of as the first 'modern' railway, was opened in 1830 and thus ushered in the Railway Age, some 375 miles of line had been built under parliamentary powers since 1801. By 1866 9,701 route miles were open. The financial crisis of that year was a very severe check to investment. But thereafter, until 1912, most years saw some 100–200 route miles of line opened, to bring the system to 23,440 miles. But this was the peak and the opening of a line became increasingly rare, the only significant mileage being provided by extensions to London's Underground.

Some lines had closed between 1830 and 1914, but thereafter the rate of closure exceeded the rate of opening and then began to accelerate, leading to constant contraction of the system, though the rate of contraction has varied. During World War I, for economy reasons, a number of lines lost their passenger service or were closed entirely and many of these never re-opened.

While some urban lines suffered from tramway competition, after 1920 road haulage rapidly developed and by 1938 there were nearly 350,000 commercial motor vehicles registered. In the same period the network of rural bus services became established, long-distance coach services came into being, and urban motor buses, established prior to 1914, greatly increased their carryings. Between 1920 and 1929 the railways' passenger carryings remained virtually

The train at Easingwold, the terminus of the short independent line in North Yorks. The company kept running by hiring BR motive power.

stationary at about 19,000 million passenger miles, but traffic by bus and coach grew from 3,457 million to 11,307 million passenger miles. The rate of rail closures therefore grew with increasing competition. Though 1930 was the peak year of inter-war closures, lines were closed continuously through the 1930s, affecting not only those of the four new 'Groups', but leading to the extinction of most of the remaining independent companies. Between 1923 and 1939 about 3,500 route miles were closed to passengers.

World War II and the consequent government policy of diverting as much traffic as possible to coal-burning rail to conserve precious imported petroleum for military purposes led to a virtual halt to closures over the decade after 1940.

(*overleaf*) The place is Dulverton on the Exmoor/Devon border, the date 15 June 1963. Even ten years earlier the scene would have been considerably livelier, with groups of passengers on the up and down main platforms, and the station bus that would have brought some of them from the village parked outside along with other motor vehicles. The Taunton-Barnstaple line and the Exe Valley up from Exeter were now living on borrowed time. The 17.15 'motor train' to Exeter, propelled by No 1421, usually carried only a taxiful of passengers, at least as far as Tiverton, and was to be withdrawn totally a few months later. No 6372 cautiously enters the up platform with the signal ahead at danger, the crew as watchful as ever. This 16.10 from Barnstaple to Taunton was once a busy train carrying local and long distance passengers and mountains of parcels and seasonal traffic including rabbits when there was not sufficient to run a special up from South Molton just for them – the only rabbit special in Britain. Very soon the time-honoured steam trains, usually with three coaches, sometimes four or five, were to be replaced by single-car diesel units, total closure being only three and a half years away.

In 1948 the newly nationalised British Railways were operating some 20,000 route miles of passenger services. Improved living standards and increasing disposable incomes have been a feature of post-war society and this has led to an expansion in the demand for passenger transport. But competition from the bus and coach industry continued to grow after the War. By 1953 there were 16,000 million passenger journeys on this sector. In addition between 1952 and 1970 ton-miles of freight carried by road increased at an average rate of 5.8 per cent a year, which was twice the rate of growth of total freight carryings.

But after 1952, with the ending of petrol rationing and the increasing availability of vehicles, private cars, which had already reached 2 million in 1938, resumed their dramatic rise to number 14.4 million in 1978. The increase in car ownership was even greater in rural areas than in the inner suburban areas of large towns. All this meant that the increased demand for travel was satisfied by private, at the expense of public, transport. Rail travel declined from 1,266 million journeys in 1946 to 724 million in 1978. It must be remembered that in the long run stage-carriage bus travel was even harder hit. Peaking at 13,520 passenger journeys in 1955, patronage declined to 7,305 million in 1978.

The cost structure of rail, which becomes most unfavourable in face of falling traffic, meant that the railway system was the first to suffer from the growth of car ownership and, until about 1965, suffered much more severely and spectacularly. So, from 1950 closures began again and soon reached large proportions, affecting not only branches and other minor lines, but more and more affecting lines regarded as 'main', closure of which had been hitherto unthinkable.

Then, in 1963, came the British Railways Board's publication *The Reshaping of British Railways*, which will always be known as the 'Beeching Report'. It is rightly regarded as a landmark in the story of rail closures, but probably for the wrong reason. It is not generally realised that while the Beeching Report recommended the closure of some 5,000 route miles of passenger services, it did not initiate the closure programme. Between 1950 and 1962 4,236 route miles had already been closed. What was important was that, for the first time, the approach was a planned one. There was also for the first time a coherent accounting procedure, even though the data on which it was based was, as we shall see, often regarded as suspect.

The period 1962–70 saw the network carrying passengers contract by a further 5,700 route miles to some 9,500. Two years after the Beeching Report came another major report, *The Development of the Major Trunk Routes*, often called 'Beeching II'. Overtly those main lines on which investment was justified were picked out. Though it was not admitted officially, it was plain the routes not identified were regarded as having no long-term future, even if immediate closure was not necessarily proposed.

But soon after, in 1967, Mrs Barbara Castle, then Minister of Transport, in her turn identified a 'Basic Railway' of some 11,000 route miles (9,500 carrying passengers and the remaining 1,500 freight only) as being the minimum network to meet long-term national needs. This policy survived with remarkably little questioning and the 1970–80 decade saw a drastic reduction in the rate of closure.

Reaction to Closure

In contrast with the previous 'one-off' procedure, the Beeching Report provided for the first time a comprehensive list of closures, so public bodies and private individuals alike could get to know what was planned for the lines in their own area. In addition, most of the little-used lines serving unimportant places and routes had already been closed. While the loss of services to the Isle of Axholme (Lincs), along the Elham Valley (Kent), or between Uxbridge and Denham (Middlesex) aroused little interest, the withdrawal of services between Dumfries and Stranraer, Scarborough and Whitby, or on all routes to Mansfield (Notts) was a different matter.

So resistance to closure proposals increased and efforts to prevent their implementation became more widespread. Protests came even from those who had deserted the threatened lines and thus hastened their closure. Throughout the 1960s rail closures became national news, with much attention focussed on the consequent hardships, real and imagined, the ever longer drawn-out closure procedures and the ceremonies accompanying the last train. These latter were indicative of increased interest. On 28 September 1935 six men and a dog travelled on the last train to Lee-on-the-Solent (Hants). In 1961, during the last week of their operation, trains on the Hawkhurst branch (Kent) were strengthened and carried unheard of passenger loads, while the last train on Saturday 12 June attracted hundreds to the lineside.

But each line's subsequent fate was largely ignored; eventual closure to freight, lifting of the rails, withdrawal in its turn of the substitute bus service, and sale of the right-of-way, all went unrecorded by the media. As the physical remains of the line disappeared into the landscape, for most people the line rapidly became a forgotten railway.

The urge to forget also seemed to afflict the railway authorities. Gerard Fiennes describes how, as the newly appointed Eastern Region general manager, he arrived at Liverpool Street to find BR management the only group in favour of closing the East Suffolk line, which happily is still working, and even receiving an injection of capital investment at the time of writing. The authorities seemed bent not only on reducing the system to as small a mileage as possible, but on ridding whole regions of any memory of the railway.

In some countries, notably West Germany, buses replace lighter-loaded early and late trains, enabling a rail line to be staffed only for a single daily shift. No such halfway house has ever even been suggested in this country, it must be all or nothing. In County Donegal (Republic of Ireland) buses and lorries ran in the liveries of the County Donegal and the Londonderry & Lough Swilly railways long after the county had lost its last railway line. Only in 1980 did BR inaugurate a feeder bus service between Peterborough and Kettering with

National Bus Company buses in BR colours, ironically on a route that never did have a through rail service.

When travellers discovered in the 1930s that buses were both cheaper and ran to the town centre and then, after 1950, bought their own cars and light motor cycles, patronage of branch-line services and of stopping trains on main lines declined. To try and match declining revenue, costs were reduced, though not by the adoption of more economic working methods, but by the running down of services, which in turn led to reduced competitiveness and thence to even further loss of patronage.

Sometimes it seemed standards were worsened deliberately. David Thomas, in his evocative *The Country Railway*, tells of management turning a deaf ear to pleas by a station-master to allow cheap-day-return tickets on a train leaving at 09.52 in order to compete with a market bus. Before the service to the Cheshire commuter town of Lymm was withdrawn, the next train to leave Oxford Road (Manchester) after the 16.07 was the 18.55. It must also be remembered that for the ordinary passenger, before 1960 branch-line trains were in general slow and wayward and formed of elderly, uncomfortable stock.

Many people have enjoyed W. A. Camwell's delightful film shows of branch-line scenes in the 1950s. But close examination shows that at station after station more railwaymen are visible than boarding and alighting passengers. The Beeching Report confirmed the impression of many observers, that the cost simply of keeping open hundreds of stations far exceeded the total revenue taken at them. Diesel units, 'bus-stop' stations, conductor-guards and minimal signalling were all in the future. But there is little doubt that had the policies and standards of the 1970s been applied much earlier, some, though by no means even the majority, of the lines closed in the 1950–70 period could have been saved.

So the majority of short-distance passengers had deserted the lines before closure. But still there was a residue of hardship, aggravated by the fact there was never any real alternative for those unable to acquire their own personal transport. For one thing, replacement buses did not provide accommodation for luggage and prams. Edwin Course, describing a journey from Rugby to Leicester shortly before the ex-Midland line closed in 1962, noticed that most of the passengers were 'small women with large prams'. The buses were also much slower. The branch trains ambled up the 11½ miles to Hawkhurst in 30min, but the 'replacement' buses, for the short time before they too disappeared, took twice as long. A study published in 1980 (M. Hillman and A. Whalley, *The Social Consequences of Rail Closures*, Policy Studies Institute), which looked at the effects of closing ten lines at various dates up to eleven years previously, concluded all the areas previously served had been and still were adversely affected. 'Most [local officials and representatives] agreed access had been reduced but that this had led to a curtailment of activity by only relatively few people – a supposition not borne out by the survey findings.'

No wonder few direct-replacement bus services survived for long. One of the

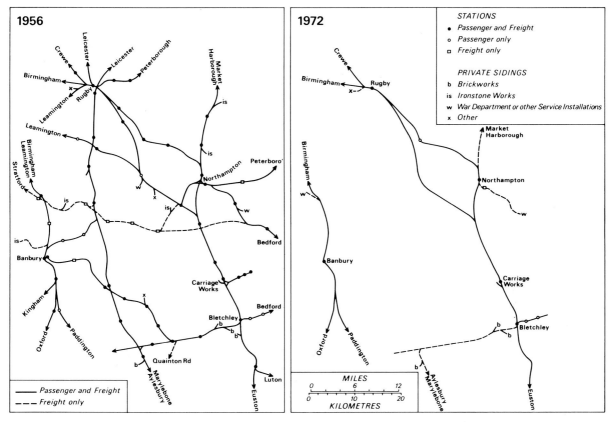

Fig. 1 Decline of the railway system in the South Midlands.

few exceptions is the Cambridge–Bletchley–Oxford bus, but this provides a better service than the railway ever did.

Thus, in the mid 1980s very large areas of the country have been deprived of access to rail transport. Our interest here is in forgotten railways, but it must be remembered there have been extensive closures of intermediate stations on those main lines which remain open. There are now no stations on the 24 miles between Didcot and Swindon; only four on the 97 miles between Huntingdon and Doncaster; and only Lockerbie on the 73½ miles from Carlisle to Carstairs. Only four passenger stations remain open in the county of Gloucester. Figure 1 shows the extent of the decline of the railway system in the south Midlands. Inevitably in many areas railways have indeed been forgotten by the traveller.

The Nostalgia Boom
But the more lines that have been closed, the more interest in forgotten railways has increased. The success of this 'Forgotten Railways' series shows the extent they are still remembered. This revival of interest is part of the increasing interest in and nostalgia for the history of the more recent past and the rapidly

25

vanishing physical remains of that history. Interest in railways, and especially the steam railway, is an essential part of a movement embracing old cars, steam road vehicles, canals and Victorian furniture.

While there have been rail fans almost as long as there have been railways, including famous names such as Ahrons, Budden and Perkins, their interest was mainly in main-line working and particularly in main-line locomotives. It was only with the passing of the branch-line scene, first with the disappearance of the queer, quaint and outrageous, such as the Wantage, Lynton & Barnstable, Manifold Valley, and Bishop's Castle, then, after 1950, with that of the orthodox, outmoded, steam-worked branches, that interest in the whole branch-line network became widespread. Nor is this interest confined to those with memories of those lines. There are numerous railway enthusiasts taking an intelligent interest in long-gone lines who were unborn when those lines were working.

One reason for all this may be that the whole railway scene has changed fundamentally and irrevocably. One has only to see the classic documentary film of the 1930s, *Night Mail*, recording a journey of the 'down special' travelling post-office from Euston to Glasgow to realise that as great a revolution has overtaken the railways as that affecting any other aspect of life over the last half century. No longer does the wayside station exist on main or

A Tavistock–Plymouth auto-train leaves Bickleigh (Devon) propelled by a 55XX 2–6–2T. Close inspection reveals it carries a single passenger.

branch line in its remembered form: the station house often of aesthetic merit; a signal-box to the standard design of a pre-Grouping company controlling semaphore signals; a couple of freight sidings with a goods shed and a few wagons; a station sometimes bowered in flowers tended by the staff in the long intervals between trains. If a wayside station does still exist, its buildings have probably been demolished and a 'bus shelter' substituted; sidings have disappeared and far down the line a colour-light signal glows, controlled from a power-box 20 miles away.

But there are other reasons for this quickening interest. Increased mobility allows more people to visit remoter sites. Again, the proliferation of preserved lines has enabled the past to be re-created. This proliferation has itself been made possible both by increasing leisure-time and by that increased mobility brought about by the spread of car-ownership that led to so many railways becoming forgotten lines.

Some Definitions

So far we have talked of 'closures' and of 'forgotten railways' without any attempt to define them. Though most lines in Great Britain were built to carry both goods and passengers, a significant mileage of freight-only lines was constructed. These have been chiefly associated with the coalfields, but have also been provided in areas of heavy industry and mineral extraction. (The Cromford & High Peak line offers a particularly interesting example.)

Before 1960 it was common practice to withdraw passenger services, but to retain the line for freight. Total closures were more rare. Thus the 9 mile, 2ft 6in Welshpool & Llanfair remained open for freight for twenty-five years after it lost its passenger trains in 1931. On the other hand, withdrawal of freight services before closure to passengers was very uncommon. It seemed strange when the Abergavenny & Merthyr line suffered this fate, freight services over most of the mileage going in 1954, but the passenger service lingering on to 1958.

In the years after 1960 total closure became the order of the day, more and more lines being completely abandoned. In addition an increasing number of freight-only lines were completely closed, especially if they were short branches in rural areas. In 1980 many lines with a passenger service have no freight facilities.

This book considers a railway 'forgotten' if it has lost its passenger service, either temporarily or permanently. This means that in many cases where the date of closure to passengers is given, total closure followed later, while a few lines will still have rails laid for freight trains.

The justification is that with passenger closure it becomes impossible for the casual observer to travel the line, unless it is possible to join the occasional rail fans' excursion. Without passenger stations and the trains serving them, a line tends to become forgotten by everyone.

In this book the intention is to provide a general introduction to the whole question of forgotten railways and not to study the details of individual lines. The reader wishing to follow up the history and ultimate fate of any specific line is referred to the regional volumes in this series and the 'Regional History of the Railways of Great Britain' series.

Here, too, we are only concerned with 'public' railways. These are lines built under either the authority of a 'private' Act of parliament (just to confuse!) or Orders made under enabling 'public' Acts, notably the Railway Construction Facilities Act (1864) and, more commonly, the Light Railways Act (1896). Of course, there are many forgotten private lines of great interest, among them systems serving estates, such as the Sand Hutton (Yorks) and the Eaton Hall (Cheshire), or such independent lines as the Whittingham, which served a mental hospital near Preston (Lancs). But space forbids doing them justice.

One problem of definition is the question of when a 'railway' becomes a tramway. Lines on their own right-of-way solely or primarily concerned with passengers and operated by 'orthodox' electric tramcars, and lines with the same characteristics along rural roadsides, have a limited history in this country. But they include such well-known examples as the Llandudno & Colwyn Bay, the Portsmouth & Horndean, the Burton & Ashby and the Grimsby & Immingham, the two last being in fact railway owned. These have been ignored, even though they may have been built under Light Railway Orders. Again the reader is referred to the extensive literature on tramway development. On the other hand the few steam-operated roadside lines which carried both passengers and freight, such as the Wisbech & Upwell and the Glyn Valley, are classified as railways.

It must be remembered the Liverpool & Manchester and the other 'new' post-1830 railways themselves superseded the horse-powered waggonways, using either flangeless or flanged wheels. These lines were for the most part either canal feeders (or distributors) or for short-distance carriage in the older coalfields, especially in the North East and South Wales. But some of the later examples were general carriers with long routes, for example the Surrey Iron Railway, the Hay and the Cheltenham & Gloucester, as well as the Oystermouth, which ended its days as the electrified Swansea & Mumbles. Bertram Baxter considered that a minimum estimate of waggonway route mileage was 1,600 and study of this subject is of great interest. But there is insufficient space here to deal with it, even in outline. The interested reader is referred to Baxter's classic work, *Stone Blocks and Iron Rails*.

Finally, since the Bluebell Railway opened in 1961, 'revived' lines have proliferated and this has meant a number of closed lines are again in operation. These 'preserved' lines, as they are usually known, can recapture to some extent what branch lines used to look like, though of course they do not serve the local community as they once did. They will be referred to again in Chapter 11.

It is now time to look more closely at the pattern of change.

PART I
THE PATTERN OF CHANGE

Liverpool Central in 1964.

CHAPTER 2

Early Days: Closures Prior to 1948

The purpose for which a line of railway was built varied, and indeed there was usually a variety of overlapping objectives. During the nineteenth century the prime purpose was to obtain a better return on investment than would have been possible in other enterprises. Lines were built to tap new sources of traffic, in order to maximise return on investment either directly, or indirectly by bringing increased traffic to the main system. Competition might be another element in the motivation, with lines being built either to obtain a share of traffic considered lucrative or as 'blocking' lines to prevent invasion of territory by other companies.

For these reasons, some lines were promoted as trunk routes connecting major centres, lines such as the Great Western (connecting London and Bristol) and the London & Birmingham; some were built to connect ports with their hinterlands, such as the London & South Western to Southampton; while others reached rapidly growing seaside resorts, for example the London & Brighton and the York & North Midland (going to Scarborough). Some lines were built to reach deposits of coal, the Taff Vale and the Barry among them, or iron ore, such as the Furness and other smaller railways of Cumbria. Though, in contrast with Switzerland, purely tourist lines, such as the Snowdon Mountain, were very rare in this country, promoters of lines like the West Highland had their eyes on this source of traffic. Of competing lines we may cite the case of the Midland, GN and GC main lines northward from Nottingham crossing and recrossing each other as they traversed the coalfield, while a good example of 'blocking' lines is those in East Sussex promoted by the LB&SC to keep the SE and the London Chatham & Dover away from Brighton.

But numerous lines were promoted with the intention of developing rural areas disadvantaged economically and socially by lack of low-cost transport for coal and fertilisers inward and livestock, grain and root crops outward, with passenger facilities usually a secondary consideration. D. I. Gordon (in *The Eastern Counties*, Vol 5 of the 'Regional History of the Railways of Great Britain' series) records that in pre-railway days coal was sold at King's Lynn for the equivalent of 80–90p per ton and at East Dereham, 26½ miles inland and without water transport, for £1.50.

However, had there been any alternative mode of transport then available, many of these lines would never have been built. Because of the heavy invest-

A Stirling R Class 0–4–4T No. 822 on the 14.22 Basford–Nottingham local train enters Thorneywood Station. A 1911 view of the GN Nottingham Suburban Line, closed to passengers in 1916.

ment needed, and consequently of the high fixed costs, though low direct movement costs, the railway is well suited to volume traffics, but particularly unfitted to be a general carrier serving a rural area offering only limited traffic potential. These rural lines were therefore the first casualties of closure policies and they provide the bulk of forgotten railways.

The financial history of most of these lines is similar. The larger companies were reluctant to promote lines they did not expect to be profitable and which were outside their strategic plans. Small independent companies were therefore inaugurated, the capital being put up by local landowners and businessmen, who were looking not so much to dividends from the line, but to increased rents and turnover from an improved local economy. The main-line company would agree to work the line for such proportion of the receipts as they calculated would be certain to bring in sufficient revenue to meet the operating costs. They would later buy out the local company, by now on its way to bankruptcy, at a greatly reduced price, and thus acquire a line the capital cost of which had already been written down. The South Eastern was particularly adept at extending its system at least cost to itself, but it was by no means alone in this practice.

In this way the rural areas of Great Britain obtained a remarkably dense rail network at almost no charge on public funds. However in Ireland, the whole of which was then part of the United Kingdom, there was a much more restricted supply of capital from this source. The reluctance to invest in local lines was due to scattered and declining population, rural poverty and lack of economic resources in country areas. In belated response to pressure for government intervention, the 1883 Tramways and Public Enterprises (Ireland) Act required the baronies (the predecessors of the district councils) to guarantee all or part of the capital of lines approved by the Grand Juries, the Treasury refunding some, but not all of their outgoings. In this way six narrow-gauge lines, including the Schull & Skibbereen, the Cavan & Leitrim and the Clogher Valley, were built.

Acts of 1889 and 1896 empowered the government in Ireland to finance a light railway declared to be necessary to develop agriculture, fisheries, etc. But with the experience of inefficient and bankrupt companies floated under the 1883 Act, the grants would only be given to existing companies. The best-known line built as a result of the new legislation was the 50 mile Letterkenny & Burtonport Extension, worked by the narrow-gauge Londonderry & Lough Swilly.

In continental Europe much of the capital for secondary lines came from regional and local government sources, such as the French *départements* and the Swiss *cantons*.

Factors in Closure

Such were the ways in which the system was extended. But, as we have seen, many lines were financial failures, even though they might have contributed indirectly to the well-being of the areas they served. But some failed to do even that and, sooner or later, they were closed. There were, of course, other reasons for closure.

Allan Patmore, whose maps are reproduced here and on whose work this chapter and the following one greatly depend, has identified a number of reasons for closure. The following classification is based on those reasons.

1. Closure resulting from diversions built to modernise the route. That is, closure for technical reasons. There are a number of early examples, but in 1908 4¾ miles of the GW main line between Wearde (Saltash) and St Germans were abandoned in favour of a new inland route selected to avoid rebuilding four life-expired wooden viaducts.

2. Closure in favour of new routes in locations more convenient for encouraging traffic. That is, diversions for commercial rather than technical reasons. Both these reasons obviously declined in importance as the system reached its maximum extent. But even as late as 1980 the inconveniently sited Bolton Street station at Bury together with ¾ mile of the approach line closed, trains being diverted over a new line to the more centrally located bus–rail Interchange provided by the Greater Manchester Passenger Transport Executive.

3. Closure resulting from changes in commercial relationships. These could come about either as a result of changes in working relationships or following amalgamation. As an example of the first kind of change, on 2 February 1850 a 3½ mile line was opened by the LNW, as successor to the Liverpool & Manchester, from Patricroft to Molyneux Junction, on the former Manchester, Bury & Rossendale Company's line via Wigan. The reason for the line was to complete a route from Liverpool to Bury which would compete with the Liverpool & Bury's rival route via Wigan. But by the time the new line was opened, the L&B had been absorbed into the Lancashire & Yorkshire and the L&M into the LNW. Both the big companies were on excellent terms, so passenger services lasted on the connecting line only until June 1850, though local goods traffic passed until 1953, being brought to an end by the collapse of a tunnel.

An early example of amalgamation leading to closure is from Harrogate. In 1854 the York & North Midland and the Leeds Northern were absorbed into the North Eastern. Both companies had lines leading to the spa town. The LN followed the low ground to a badly sited station at Starbeck. The Y&NM's branch from Church Fenton was at a high level and reached the town centre. The NER extended from the latter's dead end north eastward to Starbeck and to the south-east laid in a connection where the two lines crossed at the Crimple Viaduct. These measures allowed LN trains to reach the town centre. Eventually the Pannal–Starbeck section of the LN line was closed to passengers, but not until 1931.

4. Closure resulting from the over-provision of railway facilities. That is, closure of lines promoted to serve areas lacking potential traffic. Not all seaside resorts were little Blackpools and some embryonic resorts never achieved 'take-off'. Littlestone (Kent), Burnham (Somerset) and Sutton (Lincs), all '-on-Sea', not to mention Westward Ho! (Devon) are all such. Each was served by a wayward branch line and all these are now forgotten. Other forgotten branches were built to ports that failed or that never came into being, among them the lines to Port Patrick, Neyland and Dungeness. The East Kent Railway was promoted to develop a coalfield that failed to fulfil expectations.

In many cases branch-line traffic remained disappointingly low, but in a few cases it was so low that facilities were soon withdrawn. On 1 December 1892 the East & West Junction Railway inaugurated a passenger service on the 10½ miles between Towcester and the Midland's Northampton branch at Ravenstone Wood Junction. Though the area is traversed by through trunk routes, the West Coast main line and the M1, they have had very little effect on it and it is still sparsely populated. The very name of one of the two intermediate stations, Salcey Forest, would scarcely indicate good traffic potential. The new passenger service lasted precisely four months, to 1 April 1893.

5. Closure resulting from changed social and economic conditions. This is a very common cause of closure. A coalfield may become worked out, as did the Forest of Dean; an agricultural area may change to dependency on car and lorry, while the holidaymakers bringing late prosperity to many a minor resort

The Kent & East Sussex scene. Robertsbridge in August 1939. Passengers board the 15.50 (SO) for Headcorn. A 'Terrier' 0–6–0T heads an ex-LSW brake composite.

arrive by car and coach. If the operator of the line cannot or will not adapt to change, then sooner or later the line will be closed. In rural areas throughout the country, at least between 1920 and 1970 operators were in general slow to adapt and the list of forgotten lines lengthened inordinately. It was the achievement of the Southern Railway Company that it met the challenge of the inter-war housing explosion and the onset of the motor age head-on by modernising its whole system, branch lines as well as main lines, so that even in 1980 there were fewer forgotten railways in South East England than in other parts of the country.

Closures Before 1914
Closure to passengers for the reasons just listed began from the very earliest times of the steam railway. Indeed it began even before, though as a general rule the pre-existing waggonways did not carry passengers. Nevertheless the horse-drawn passenger service on the ¾ mile Yarm branch of the Stockton & Darlington, inaugurated in October 1826, was withdrawn on 7 September 1833. The horse-operated Stratford & Moreton Tramway carried passengers between 1853 and 1859, but in that year the southern section from Moreton to Shipston-on-Stour was converted to a normal railway and the northern section thence to Stratford-on-Avon closed to passengers.

When the horse-drawn Whitby & Pickering was converted to locomotive haulage, 4½ miles of the formation were abandoned in 1865 because of steep gradients, and this can easily be seen from trains on the North York Moors Railway. When the standard-gauge Hayle Railway of 1843 was incorporated into the route of the broad-gauge West Cornwall's main line, two sections, totalling 3¾ miles, were abandoned because they included two rope-worked inclines.

A frequent occurrence was the extension of the line from a point short of the original terminus, leading to the latter's closure to passengers together with the now redundant approach line. In 1830 Crown Street was opened as the Liverpool terminus of the L&M. But the site was peripheral and six years later it was closed, having been replaced by the more central Lime Street. In Manchester, Victoria station was opened in 1844 on a through line linking the L&M, the Manchester, Bury & Bolton and the Manchester & Leeds lines, each of which had hitherto led to a dead-end terminus. This meant that Liverpool Road and Oldham Road stations, belonging to the L&M and the M&L respectively, were closed to passengers, together with their approach lines. Salford, however, became a through station and still survives.

The terminus of the Edinburgh, Leith & Granton, opened in 1847, was Canal Street, which lay at right angles to and immediately north of Waverley station. When the line from the latter was opened through to Leith Walk in 1868, Canal Street became redundant and it and the 1½ mile rope-worked approach line through Scotland Street Tunnel were closed to passengers. There are numerous other examples, for instance at Lancaster, Whitehaven, Redcar and Braintree.

Occasionally when new lines to more convenient locations were opened, the line thus replaced would lose its main-line traffic and eventually be closed when it also lost its local functions. The 1½ mile branch from the Southampton & Dorchester line (known as 'Castleman's Corkscrew') to Hamworthy was opened in 1847. Hamworthy was the station for Poole and later for the nascent resort of Bournemouth. But after 1870 Bournemouth could be reached by a branch from Ringwood on the 'Corkscrew' via Christchurch, and in 1872 Poole acquired another branch, from Broadstone. A passenger service to Hamworthy continued, but ceased on 1 July 1896.

In the north-east of Scotland the Morayshire Railway opened in 1858 a branch from Orton to Craigellachie. Orton was on the Inverness & Aberdeen Junction, which had built westward from Keith after the financially embarrassed Great North of Scotland, with which the Morayshire had excellent relationships, had abandoned its powers. Relations between the Morayshire and the I&AJ became so bad the former opened a direct line from Rothes to Elgin to join its other line, to Lossiemouth, and eventually, in conjunction with the GNS, to complete a Craigellachie–Keith line. The 3½ miles between Orton and Rothes were thus rendered redundant and were closed by the GNS without notice on 1 August 1866, the day after they had signed a working agreement with the Morayshire.

There is another example of closure resulting from change in working relationship, this time from East Anglia. In 1848 the Newmarket & Chesterford Company opened a 16¾ mile line from Great Chesterford – on the Eastern Counties main line to Cambridge – to Newmarket. The ECR, hoping for an early collapse and a chance to acquire the line cheaply, were totally uncooperative, eventually forcing amalgamation on their own terms. One of these was the completion of a proposed branch from Six Mile Bottom – on the Newmarket–Great Chesterford line – to Cambridge. This became the main line and on the day of opening, 9 October 1851, the 11½ miles on from Six Mile Bottom to Chesterford were closed altogether.

In the North East, cradle of the early railway system, 28¾ route miles had lost passenger services by 1850 and a further 27¼ did so between 1850 and 1870. Many of the sections closed to passengers were very short, a mile or less, and the services were abandoned as new spurs and alternative routes developed. The passenger service over the 6¼ miles between Stillington and Simpasture Junctions, which later became part of the pioneer NER freight electrification of 1915, lasted only from 30 November 1841 to 12 February 1842. This formed part of an abortive attempt by the S&D to enter north–south carrying with a Darlington–Coxhoe service. Services on the route of the very early Tanfield Wagonway, converted to a steam railway in 1836 by the Brandling Junction Company, lasted over the 7 miles from 18 June 1842 to August 1844. Those on the 6 mile Waskerley–Crawley section of the Stanhope & Tyne Railway, in the lonely hill country of West Durham, lasted for fifteen months until withdrawal in December 1846.

In some cases closure was not permanent; lines were re-opened when circumstances took a favourable turn. Some very interesting examples from this early period are worth recalling. On 27 May 1844 the West London Company opened a 2½ mile single line of mixed gauge from West London Junction (Willesden) on the LNWR, across the GWR on the level at Wormwood Scrubs to the basin of the Kensington Canal, where Kensington Olympia station now stands. The line ran through open country of farms and market gardens. *Punch* lampooned it as running from nowhere to nowhere and it became known as 'Mr Punch's Railway'. There was a lavish service, though the only passenger on the inaugural train was reputed to have been a winkle-seller. So exiguous was the traffic, the service lasted only until 30 November.

But after nearly twenty years the line came into its own in 1863 with the opening of the West London Extension, which continued the WLR to Clapham Junction. Thus was created the important connection between the northern and the southern lines. But at the same time the streets of large, well-to-do terrace houses were rapidly spreading westward and so the line assumed unforeseen suburban functions. Kensington, with a single platform until 1869, became the greatly enlarged Addison Road. It became the centre of an intensive suburban service carrying top-hatted commuters Cityward over strange-sounding routes. Typical of these was the North London's 'Outer Circle' which traversed the WLR en route from Broad Street to Mansion House via Willesden Junction and Earls Court.

The subsequent decline of these steam, and later electric, services (the 4.1 million passengers using Addison Road in 1903 had shrunk to 1.3 million in 1938) is traced in detail in this author's *Greater London* volume of the 'Regional History of the Railways of Great Britain' series, and in 1940 the last of them ceased. But the line has refused to become quite forgotten and in 1984 it was possible to traverse most of it by scheduled service, the twice daily one between Manchester, Gatwick and Brighton. In 1986 more trains were put on.

In complete contrast, running through the lush pasture-lands of the Severn Valley westward from Shrewsbury is the overgrown right-of-way of the Shropshire & Montgomeryshire line of the Col Stephens Group. It epitomises much of what has been said and written of forgotten railways. Along its length are numerous relics to recall the past, and the countryside is among the most attractive in England. The Abbey station, tucked away in a remote part of Shrewsbury, survives and, at the time of writing, its yard is in use as a rail-served petroleum depot. The remains of Kinnerley Junction, the hub of the system, are surprisingly extensive and the tiny roadside station of Melverley remains untouched. Melverley Viaduct over the Severn is used by a public road. The half-mile approach from the north along the embankment previously occupied by the railway is narrow with passing places, demonstrating that conversion of railways to roads is not so simple as crank protagonists would have us think.

But this is not the first time vegetation has taken over the right-of-way. Originally promoted as part of a trunk route from Stoke-on-Trent to a new port on the Welsh coast, it was built by the Shrewsbury & North Wales, which in 1866 amalgamated with the Shrewsbury & Potteries Junction to become the Potteries, Shrewsbury & North Wales, known with exasperated affection as 'The Potts'. Double-tracked with hopeless optimism, the 17 mile line was opened on 13 August 1866. Bankruptcy immediately supervened, bailiffs took possession and trains ceased on 21 December. A little money was obtained by sale of locomotives and wagons and by singling the line. The service restarted in December 1868 and on 2 June 1871 the 5 mile Criggion branch opened.

Financial disaster, never far away, returned in 1877, when a receiver was appointed. In 1880 the Railways Inspector of the Board of Trade condemned the line. There was no money to restore it, so it closed, except for the Cambrian-worked Llanymynech–Nantmawr section.

This time it did not re-open until 13 April 1911 under the Shropshire & Montgomeryshire Light Railway Order and the direction of Col Stephens. On opening day the train, with its immaculate blue ex-LSW 0–6–0 and three smart ex-Midland bogie coaches, was scarcely in accord with our image of a Col Stephens railway in the 1930s.

The condition of the Melverley Viaduct prevented the re-opening of the Criggion branch until August 1912, and even then only the tiny *Gazelle* (happily preserved in the National Railway Museum at York) and an ex-London County Council horse tramcar were able to provide the passenger service, reduced to two trips on Saturdays in 1928. On the 'main line' an exiguous service was maintained by decaying superannuated second-hand coaches or the rattletrap three-car Ford-engined set until 6 November 1933.

But the years of glory were still to come. World War II saw a takeover by the

37

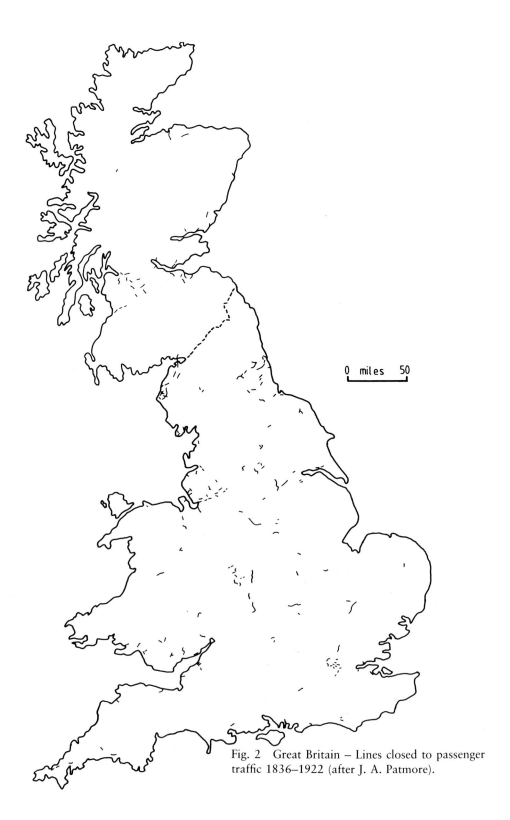

0 miles 50

Fig. 2   Great Britain – Lines closed to passenger
traffic 1836–1922 (after J. A. Patmore).

War Department, a new locomotive shed at Kinnerley and traffic undreamed of by the line's promotors. War Department 2–8–0 locos hauled long trains to and from the ammunition dumps lining the route. But, finally, in 1961 the line was handed over to BR for demolition.

Another temporary closure was that between 1912 and 1914 of the Fort Augustus branch, which ran through the Great Glen from a junction with the West Highland at Spean Bridge. John Thomas, in his *Scotland* volume of the 'Forgotten Railways' series, gives an entertaining and detailed account of the fierce and complex fight which ended in re-opening. But of course it was a re-opening which allowed the line to drag out an unprofitable existence until its inevitable end in 1933.

Even more bizarre was the passenger service on the Cromford & High Peak, of course only a short chapter in the strange story of that unique line. From 1856 to 1877 an irregular and somewhat illegal service was operated across the bare, stone-walled, limestone heights of Derbyshire's High Peak, isolated even in this motor age. A 'fly' coach was attached to a goods train and passengers walked up the inclines. Six hours from Cromford, the service terminated at Ladmanlow, 2 miles from and high above Buxton. Ahrons described walking up Middleton Incline, to find a coach at the top with a young woman and a baby as fellow passengers, and the guard saying that an engine might come for them in the next few hours.

Apart from the exceptions we have just considered, closures before 1900 tended to be of short stretches of line and for a wide variety of reasons. The pattern is therefore random, though perhaps two groups of areas can be distinguished: the major cities and coalfields on the one hand, and the remoter rural areas on the other. In the former subsequent openings tended to render the closed lines redundant, while in the latter insufficient traffic failed to justify any service at all.

After 1900 the railways began to suffer competition from other modes, and in the early years of the century the electric tramway came to be a formidable rival. Some lines, including the South London line of the London Brighton & South Coast, were saved by electrification, but others such as the 1½ mile LSW&LBSC Joint line from Fratton to East Southsea (closed 1904) succumbed.

War-time (1915–1922)

World War I brought increased traffic to the railways as a whole, but a number of lines were closed to passengers, either temporarily or permanently. We can distinguish two groups of lines.

In London a number of short lines which had lost their traffic to tram, tube and bus had their passenger services withdrawn, the companies taking the opportunity of economising. Some, such as the Crystal Palace High Level branch and the Woodside and Selsdon section, were eventually re-opened, even if after many years. But for others closure was permanent. Though a very short

Soon after 1900 a SE & CR train for the Oxted Line traverses the Woodside & S Croydon near Coombe Rd.

length of line, the most significant permanent closure was the ¼ mile from Ludgate Hill down to Snow Hill, for this brought to an end the last vestige of the once extensive services over the LCD's link with the City Widened Lines and on to the northern suburbs. Other closures included the Greenwich Park Branch of the LCD and the LSW's access to Addison Road from Studland Junction (Hammersmith). In other urban areas closures were of less signi-ficance, but among them were the 3 miles between Holmfirth and Halifax (GN and L&Y Joint) and the 1¼ mile GW branch to Oldbury (West Midlands).

In the rural areas there were also temporary closures. Among them was the Basingstoke & Alton Light Railway. But re-opening was only after a struggle by local interests and against the better judgement of the new owners, the Southern Railway. However, 58 miles of route in all (rural and urban) were permanently closed in the 1915–22 period. As in the urban areas some of the rural closures involved 'tidying up' of lines which had outlived their usefulness. One such was a quondam main line, which had lost that function and, in turn, lost its local function. With the withdrawal of the one-coach once-daily train, the 6½ miles of the Midland's branch from Whitacre to Hampton-in-Arden through the water meadows of the River Blythe, a rare stretch of rurality in the West Midlands, was closed on 1 January 1917. It had been opened in 1839 by the Birmingham & Derby Junction as an outlet to the London & Birmingham, but when the former became part of the Midland in 1844 the traffic had gone by Rugby. There were also lines such as the Highland's Keith and Portressie, which had so little traffic it was not worth keeping open. Finally, there were lines such as the independent and physically isolated Bideford, Westward Ho! & Appledore which were teetering on bankruptcy and which took the opportunity of cutting their losses.

The Grouping Era (1923–48)

On 1 January 1923 the 'Big Four' took over 123 railway companies. But many were not included. Some, such as London Electric Railways, the Metropolitan and the Mersey, were of considerable importance; others were very short and very minor. The North Sunderland had 4 route miles of single track and the Easingwold 2½ miles.

In the inter-war years, though long-distance and outer-suburban passenger traffic remained faithful to rail and grew significantly, there was increasing loss of short-distance traffic, both urban and rural. Trams and buses continued to drain off passengers, especially from the inner areas of the large cities and from short inter-urban routes in the industrial areas and coalfields. During the 1920s the network of rural bus services was laid, a network which came to connect virtually every market town and every village with at least one market town. During the 1930s car ownership expanded and, especially in rural areas, began to cast its shadow.

As can be seen from Figure 4, the rate of closure remained low until 1926, in which year 79¼ route miles lost passenger services. Then, in the five years 1929–33 services were withdrawn from 903 route miles, the peak year being 1930, when 323 miles were lost. It was a rate of closure hitherto unheard of, and more reminiscent of the Beeching era than is generally realised.

But, unlike the Beeching era, the closures were not regarded as important. We read little significant comment in either the railway or the local press. This

The Kent & East Sussex scene. Near Rolvenden on 21 September 1935. The track is in surprisingly good condition.

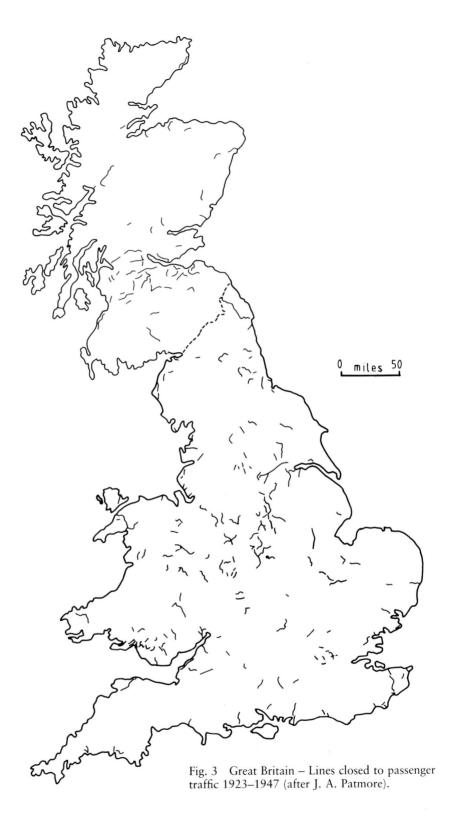

Fig. 3   Great Britain – Lines closed to passenger
traffic 1923–1947 (after J. A. Patmore).

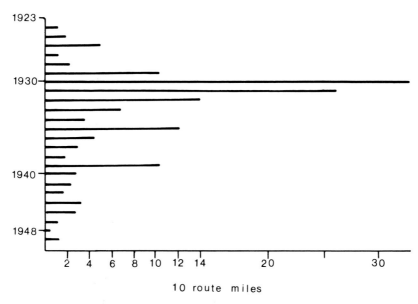

Fig. 4 Annual totals of mileage closed to passengers 1923–1949.

was perhaps because the future of the railway system in its contemporary form was not in doubt, and because closures affected unimportant and often dead-end branches, from all of which passenger traffic had almost disappeared. As for the enthusiasts, for the most part the closed lines were orthodox branch lines and, in contrast with the 1960s, there were plenty of those remaining to be travelled over and enjoyed. A few old friends among the queer and quaint were however mourned. In 1937 T. R. Perkins wrote a splendid obituary of the Bishop's Castle entitled 'Farewell to a plucky fighter', while another author accused the harsh broad-gauge bureaucrats of Exeter Division (not Waterloo it should be noted) of killing off the Lynton & Barnstaple.

Undoubtedly, had this 1ft 11½in gauge line through the beautiful edge of Exmoor lasted into the 'preservation era', it would still be operating. But before we join in the condemnation of the 'broad-gauge bureaucrats' let us imagine going on holiday to Lynmouth with children and luggage and rolling for 100min over the 19¼ mile line in carriages better suited to a museum. As a means of transport as opposed to an enjoyable day out, many of these early-closed lines left much to be desired.

In all 1,264½ route miles lost their passenger services between 1 January 1923 and 31 December 1938. There were of course no legal procedures to be undergone. The companies announced their plans and sometimes there might be protest. The Canterbury Chamber of Trade sent a deputation to Waterloo in 1931 to protest against the closure of the Canterbury & Whitstable, but they were silenced by the production of the traffic figures. In the same year Winsford UDC (Cheshire) took the Cheshire Lines Committee to the Railway & Canal Commission to try and enforce the retention of services over the Winsford

43

(*left*) The forgotten Junction. Over thirty years before the photo of Shackerstone Junction (Leicestershire) was taken in 1964 the LMS had withdrawn passenger services from Nuneaton to Gresley (left) and Loughborough (right). But it remained fully signalled for the occasional freight train. (*right*) The station that never was? Bala Junction, here seen from a Ruabon bound train in 1962, was not mentioned in public time tables and had no public access. It served as an interchange for the branch to Bala and Ffestiniog.

Branch. They relied on a judgement of 1891 enjoining the CLC to afford all due and reasonable facilities on the line. But the Commission ruled it was not 'a reasonable facility' if it meant the continuance of an unprofitable service. Obviously this judgement was of great significance.

In the course of the case revealing evidence was given. Between 1924 and 1930 passengers had fallen from 99,000 to 68,000 (about 240 per working day), while passenger receipts were down 54 per cent. Expenses had been reduced by using a Sentinel Cammell steam railcar, but signalmen and station staff were still employed. Col Stephens could reduce his lines to the basic railway, but not, it would seem, the major companies.

We can distinguish three groups of closed lines, the urban, the rural, and the independent. London was little affected, apart from a few inner suburban lines, their traffic lost to trams and buses. Among them was the historic Blackwall line. Dating from 1840, this 3½ mile line has seen amazing changes in both its operating methods and in the area it served. Westward from Stepney (East) 25kV electric trains on the London, Tilbury & Southend line thunder towards Fenchurch Street. Eastward the line closed to passengers in 1926, even then having outlived its usefulness by many years. The Blackwall Railway started as a 5ft gauge cable-operated line, becoming an orthodox standard-gauge steam one in 1849. Its original purpose was to connect with the steamers running downstream from Brunswick Wharf adjacent to the imposing classical-style terminus, and it never really recovered from the decline in those services. But even in 1920 there was an amazing total of fifty-seven down trains, almost empty through tram and bus competition. The strikes of 1926 were as good an excuse as any to bring the service to an end.

The line traversed a part of what can be described as the classic East End, an urban landscape which has seen such radical changes. Limehouse station served a district where ships' captains once lived, which later degenerated into evil slums and which, since 1945, has seen its terraces of houses built in the once familiar yellow London Stock brick swept away and replaced with tower blocks. Beyond were the docks, once filled with ships bringing cargoes from all over the world, now deserted and derelict. From Millwall Junction the Millwall Extension led south to the one-time ferry terminal at North Greenwich. A 1½ mile line, its ownership was complex and its service eccentric, maintained by horse-drawn cars, later superseded by diminutive locos hauling primitive coaches, and coming to an end also in 1926. Freight traffic on both lines was heavy while the docks prospered and disappeared with their closure. But by a twist of fate, as these words are written, a light rapid-transit system is being built on the rights-of-way of these lines as part of the rehabilitation of the area.

In Birmingham and the neighbouring Black Country five lines were closed in this period. One of them was the 2½ mile Harborne Railway operated by the LNWR. Opened in 1874 to serve a high-class suburban area, it was an archetype of the provincial suburban line. At one time it was the best-paying line in the Birmingham area and supported an intensive service; twenty-seven up trains left Harborne daily (Mondays to Fridays) in 1909. The trains were often hauled by the 'Coal Tanks' and took 16min to New Street, thus enabling city workers to return home for a midday meal. The line closed in 1934, its traffic lost to buses on shorter and faster routes. One trouble was that branch trains had low priority at Monument Lane, the junction with the busy main line, thus creating intolerable delays. Another line to close was the Midland Company's competing one through the Black Country from Walsall to Wolverhampton, all rail traffic being diverted onto the ex-LNW route.

Closures were also extensive on the main coalfields, in South Wales, Nottinghamshire, South Yorkshire, the North East and central Scotland. This was partly due to economic decline. Even in those days coal production was declining and this had led to long-term depression in these areas, and a consequent falling-off of workmen's and leisure passenger traffic, while there was the usual bus competition. But it was also a case of parallel and formerly competing lines becoming redundant after the Grouping. In South Wales, Maesteg lost its service in 1933 over the heavily graded 7½ miles of the former Port Talbot Company, because main-line connections were better at Bridgend, reached by the GW line direct down the valley. From Bathgate, midway between Glasgow and Edinburgh, the North British Morningside branch

45

intruded into Caledonian territory as it climbed up to the bleak moors of the Shotts plateau with its numerous small and dying coal mines and mining villages. Passenger services ceased in 1936.

In rural areas, as shown in Figure 3, a large number of short dead-end branches were closed all over the country, from the Dyke branch climbing up into the Sussex Downs from the coast at Aldrington (1939) to the Hopeman (1931) and Ellon (1932) branches in the north of Scotland. Some of the closures leave the student wondering less at why they were closed than why they came to be built in the first place.

It seems odd that the small and rather isolated Cambridgeshire market town of Ramsey, on the edge of the Fens, acquired two dead-end and unconnected branches, from Somersham on the GN&GE Joint line from St Ives to March, itself now forgotten, and from Holme on the GN main line. It was no wonder the former closed in 1930, more surprising that the latter lasted until 1947. It must have been a brave passenger who took the train across the Fens to the lonely station of Holme, there to await a train for Peterborough and a further change there, or for a southbound stopping train which would eventually reach King's Cross in anything up to three hours.

It seems even more odd that Dolphinton should have had two similar unconnected dead-end branches. For even today it is an insignificant hamlet on the A702, which runs southward from Edinburgh along the high country which lies along the eastern flank of the Pentland Hills. One branch, the Caledonian, climbed up from Carstairs round the southern end of the Pentlands, while the one belonging to the North British came across lonely country from Leadburn on their Peebles line. The strange-sounding name of one of the intermediate stations, Lamancha, was the inspiration, rather than Cervantes, for John Buchan in the naming of one of his fictional characters. Both lines ended in small stations on either side of the road in the middle of nowhere and were closed to passengers in 1932 and 1933 respectively.

Certain areas were worse hit: the Welsh Marches and the eastern slopes of the Pennines and, to some extent, southern Scotland. One of the casualties here was the 7¾ mile line that climbed away from Elvanfoot on the main line from Glasgow to Carlisle out of the green valley of the Upper Clyde into the highest of the Border hills. Leadhills station was 1,405ft above sea-level, but to reach the terminus at Wanlockhead it climbed further to a 1,498ft summit, the highest point reached by any British standard-gauge line. The hoped-for mineral traffic never appeared, but until 1939 a steam railcar made four daily trips for the benefit of locals and 'ramblers', one of which trains was 'mixed' if there was a wagon of coal to be taken up. As a wry commentary on developments over the years, John Thomas (in *Scotland: The Lowlands and the Borders*, Vol 6 in the 'Regional History of the Railways of Great Britain' series) tells of the fate of a would-be traveller to Wanlockhead in 1967. At the Glasgow bus station, 60 miles away, he was told it was not in the timetable. A helpful inspector found a four-year-old letter about a once daily trip between

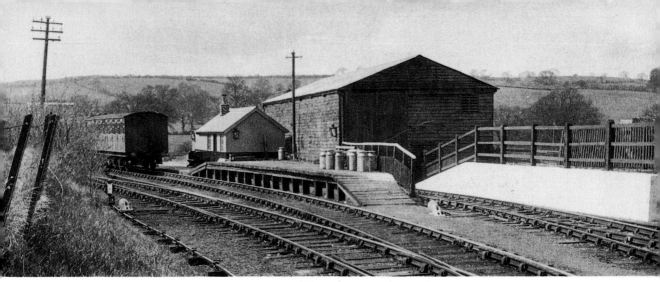

Ultima Thule of the Metropolitan. Brill Station, lonely amid the North Bucks countryside, 51¼ miles and light years from the Inner Circle.

Sanquhar and Abington. A 'phone call to the former place produced the news that the bus did not run in school holidays (which were then in progress). Thomas adds it was no comfort to the frustrated traveller that he could obtain from an adjacent travel agent a ticket for Bangkok 'at the touch of a computerised button'.

The South West, however, apart from the lamented loss of the Lynton & Barnstaple, was almost unscathed. Perhaps this was due to the fact most branches served small seaside resorts. In those days a majority of holiday visitors still reached the coast by rail, adding a summer peak to the already failing winter traffic.

The Independents (1923–48)

It was the Independents that suffered particularly heavily from the advent of Grouping. Even in 1923 the lines of the small companies were so lightly trafficked that the Groups refused to absorb them. There was no chance of cross-subsidisation from more lucrative routes. They were always under-capitalised and in their later years were starved of any form of investment. Sixteen lines owned by companies other than the four Groups were closed to passengers between 1925 and 1940, totalling 150½ route miles.

These included the 1¾ miles Gallions branch in London's dockland. This was owned by the Port of London Authority, but operated by the LNER, and closed in 1940 when it was decided not to restore the stations after bomb damage. Also there were the last rural outposts of the London Passenger Transport Board, both in remotest North Buckinghamshire. The rural branch from Quainton Road to Verney Junction was shared with the LNER. But it brought Metropolitan 4–4–4T locos and six-coach sets, the latter having started from Baker Street, out to the wilds of Verney Junction. The two termini of the service could scarcely present a more violent contrast. The other, the Brill branch, was even more individualistic. On it the trains were of stock surviving

47

from the steam-operated Inner Circle. They were formed of a Beyer Peacock outside-cylinder 4–4–0T and a single brake-composite rigid eight-wheeled coach. An occasional goods wagon or two would be added as the train called at the primitive and remote stations. In sylvan glades the guard, attired in London Transport uniform, would operate level-crossing gates. In its last year, 1935, the line carried an average of fifty-eight passengers and 34 tons of goods daily. Fortunately the line was so photogenic that pictorial records are extensive and appear in some excellent publications.

The small company lines included the West Sussex (1935), Shropshire & Montgomeryshire (1933) and Weston, Clevedon & Portishead (1940), all of which were in the Col Stephens Group. There was also the Derwent Valley (1926), running from the outskirts of York southward through the rich farmlands, which survived at least in part as a freight line into the 1980s, and the unique Bishop's Castle (1935), in receivership since 1867 and which never had telegraph or telephone.

But equally idiosyncratic was the Wantage (1925) which started in the station forecourt of Wantage Road station and ran along the verge of the A338 road for 2½ miles to end in a wooden shed near the centre of Wantage town. In the 1920s passenger trains consisted of one or more single-deck tramcars. Of the locomotive stock, No 5, *Shannon*, was an 0–4–0 well tank built in 1857 by George England for the Sandy & Potton Railway (Bedfordshire), bought by the tramway company in 1878 and happily preserved after freight traffic ceased in 1945. No 7, a 0–4–0 saddle tank, started life as a contractor's loco building the Manchester Ship Canal.

S. H. Pearce Higgins (*The Wantage Tramway*, Abbey Press 1958) gives a revealing account of a day's work in the 1920s. Two locos, 'the Goods' and 'the

Independents were often characterised by simpler equipment and layout. Here is the Wantage Town terminus of the Wantage Tramway.

The 1ft 11½in Ashover Light had only eleven years of passenger life. Opened in 1925 to bring limestone to the Clay Cross Iron Works, the occasional passenger was catered for on mixed trains such as this, though specials were run at holiday times.

Passenger' were prepared, and at 07.00 the first down car went off to Wantage Road, to be followed at 08.10 by the second. The two cars returned behind the passenger engine bringing up mail and parcels as well as any passengers. The goods loco shunted the GW yard and brought back the wagons from Bristol. It waited in a passing loop for the 09.30 down car if it could not get back by the time the latter started. The 09.30 had to turn round quickly at Wantage Road to be back in time for the 10.15 working. This was followed by a freight working, mainly for returning empty wagons. At Wantage Road the goods engine collected wagons from London. Sometimes it had to help out the GW by fetching the 'slip' if the guard misjudged the braking distance or by detaching a horse-box from a stopping passenger train. It brought up the wagons in time for the driver's lunch. In all the passenger engine made eleven trips, another driver taking over when the 13.00 from Wantage Road arrived. The goods engine pottered about the Upper and Lower yards during the afternoon, its final duty was to make a trip to Wantage Road and back before the 17.30 down car. The passenger loco's day ended with the arrival of the 20.40 departure from Wantage Road.

Many of the Independents were narrow gauge. The eight independent narrow-gauge lines closed totalled 69½ route miles and to these must be added 43 route miles of narrow gauge owned by three of the four Groups. It would require a whole book on each line to do them justice. But mention must be

Reality and myth at Southwold. (*above*) Train and staff at the Southwold terminus of the 3ft gauge line from Halesworth which closed in 1929. (*below*) A typical postcard lampooning the line.

THE SOUTHWOLD EXPRESS   THE DRIVER DOES A ROARING TRADE OWING TO A DELAY CAUSED BY THE PORTER OVERESTIMATING HIS STRENGTH - THE GUARD MAKES THE MOST OF THIS, AND TRIES TO SPOT A WINNER - THE STATIONMASTER DOES ALL IN HIS POWER TO GET THE TRAIN AWAY.

made of the Southwold (1929). This was England's only 3ft gauge public rail-way. Its primitive rolling stock and unreliable service led to constant lampoon-ing and gave rise to a comic-picture-postcard industry which still flourishes in the pleasant old-fashioned East Coast resort. A visit to Halesworth, the junction with the Great Eastern, in 1984 revealed a wooded glade as the site of the terminus. Then there was the 2ft Ashover Light (1936), only opened in 1925, to bring limestone down from the Peak District to Clay Cross ironworks. But the Amber Valley, with its attractive scenery, gave access to the beauties of the Peak and for a brief period its passenger trains were crowded at holiday times. There were no less than eleven stations and halts on the 7¼ miles, apart from the termini, and at Ashover the whole train was turned on a triangle. Six Baldwin-built 4–6–0Ts of North American appearance had been obtained as war surplus after service on the Western Front.

The Welsh narrow gauge was more extensive. There was the Welsh Highland (1936) and the Festiniog (1939). Neither lacks records and recorders and the Festiniog is happily restored throughout its length not only to its former glory, but to glories hitherto unknown. The Welsh Highland as a through 21½ mile route across Snowdonia dated only from 1923 and the kindest thing to be said for its promoters was that they showed considerable optimism. At no time were more than two or three daily round trips made through the Aberglaslyn Pass, which through the long winters was a traffic desert. P. B. Whitehouse gives a graphic account of a footplate trip on the Fairlie 0–6–4T: '. . . this schoolboy, comparatively tall, found his hair giving the cab a cleaning it never had for years. *Moel Tryfan* leaked steam from everywhere and outside it was raining hard so there was not much scenery to see . . .' There was also the roadside Glyn Valley, with its unique gauge of 2ft 4½in, which threaded the narrowing Ceiriog Valley up from Chirk GW station to the small slate-quarrying town of Glyn Ceiriog.

Scotland had only one narrow-gauge public line, the Campbeltown & Machrihanish. Its 6 mile route crossed the long, narrow peninsula of the Mull of Kintyre from Campbeltown harbour, the *ultima Thule* of the Clyde steamers, to the sandy, Atlantic-beaten beaches of Machrihanish. Rebuilt in 1906 from a coal tramway, which in turn had replaced a canal, the 2ft 3in line was extended to the then new resort. Arriving steamer passengers would find a train of six brown (or was it green?) coaches drawn up on the quay, which was also Hall Street, to take them over to Machrihanish. On the shorter local trains tickets were sold by a conductress. The superintendent was 'Wee McCabe'. Like the other employees his job involved much versatility and he would often have been found carrying out adjustments under the Andrew Barclay 0–6–2T. He used his growing family to supplement the regular staff, which dwindled after the closure of the coal mine. His son recalls as a boy riding on the buffer beam of the locomotive banking the steamer express out of Campbeltown in order to pull out the coupling pin when the summit was reached.

Narrow-gauge lines under main-line ownership included the LMS-owned

Manifold Valley (1935), like the Ashover a Peak District line; the two Welsh lines of the GW, the Corris and the Welshpool & Llanfair, which both lost their passenger services in 1931; and the Southern's Lynton & Barnstaple (1935). By the outbreak of war in 1939 the narrow-gauge public passenger railway had become extinct in England and Scotland, with the well-known 15in exceptions of the Romney, Hythe & Dymchurch and the Ravenglass & Eskdale, and more arguably the 4ft Glasgow Underground. In Wales only the GW's Vale of Rheidol and the independent Snowdon Mountain offered seasonal tourist services, while the Tal-y-Llyn had a sparse but regular train service provided by Sir Haydn Jones as a social service for the residents of the isolated valley.

The Irish Parallel

This book deals with forgotten railways of Great Britain, but there are useful parallels to be drawn from the closure theme across the water in Ireland. Here, in the years after 1920 there was the same loss of passenger and freight traffic in the rural areas due to road competition. But in the far West the roads were so awful that some lines lingered until their rivals were rebuilt. The broad-gauge lines to Clifden and to Achill were closed in 1935 and 1937 respectively after the parallel roads were metalled. The Londonderry & Lough Swilly, in spite of its policy of diverting traffic from rail to its buses and lorries, was forced to keep the line open to Burtonport after a disastrous attempt in 1931 to run a bus service over unmetalled roads resulting in demands from the county council for consequent repairs.

In addition political events affected the system to an extent unknown in Great Britain. The 'Troubles' of 1916–21 which ended in partition, together with the subsequent civil war in the South, resulted in much damage and sealed the fate of some lines. In the North the unfortunate railway strike of 1933 gave the LMS the opportunity of withdrawing the passenger service on the narrow-gauge line from Larne to Ballymena.

Partition resulted in the emergence of three groups of lines and in the survival of a number of small independents. In the South, on the British model, all lines, strong and weak, orthodox or quaint, broad or narrow, were absorbed into the new Great Southern Group set up in 1924. In the North the two major companies, the Northern Counties Committee which had come into the possession of the Midland and thence into that of the LMS, and the Belfast & County Down, together with independents such as the Clogher Valley, were all left alone to live or die. Finally there were the cross-border lines, which again were left either to prosper as did the GNR(I) or to suffer as did the broad Sligo,

(*opposite*) (*top*) Closure ceremonials were matched by opening ones such as that on the Manifold Valley in 1904. (*centre*) Hulme End, the remote terminus and locomotive depot of the Manifold Valley, closed in 1934. Note standard gauge open wagons and 'colonial' van. (*bottom*) Transshipment was the downfall of the narrow gauge. The transporters on the Manifold Valley were an attempted solution. A scene at Waterhouses.

Leitrim & Northern Counties (locally Slow, Late & Never Certain) and the narrow Londonderry & Lough Swilly.

New Trends

During this inter-war period there were two new developments. First, until 1923 very few closures involved lines exceeding 10 miles in length. The 11½ miles of the Newmarket & Chesterford (1850) was exceptional. But the inter-war closures included, for example, 25¾ miles of line between Alnwick and Coldstream (1930). This served an area of good grassy farmland, but sparse population, in northern Northumberland, with only the small market town of Wooler of any size or importance. The places many of the stations were named after are not shown on the 1:250,000 Ordnance map. It was the sort of area that could be served better by bus from a very early date.

In eastern England were two lines across the low, flat and fertile farmlands. In north Lincolnshire was the 22 mile Isle of Axholme Joint (LMS&LNE) (1933). Its 'main line' ran south from Goole to join the Doncaster–Gainsborough line at Haxey. The Fockerby branch in 1930 saw only one trip a day (two on Wednesdays). Since the turnround time at Fockerby was only some twenty minutes, who the owning companies expected to use the advertised service is a matter for speculation. The other was the 15 mile ex-GE line in the Isle of Ely between Sutton Branch Junction (Ely) and Needingworth Junction (St Ives). The stations, admittedly some way from the villages whose name they optimistically bore, never saw a lavish service. But the villages are large ones, and it is not easy to see why this East Anglian line was selected from a wide choice of similar lines so many years before the post-1950 slaughter. Finally, in complete contrast, scenic, climatic and cultural, to the Fens, mention must be made of the 23¼ mile branch from Spean Bridge, on the West Highland Railway, running alongside the lochs of the Great Glen to Fort Augustus. Once the line failed to reach Inverness it scarcely had any role except for limited tourism over a short summer season.

The other development was the first closure of any line that could be regarded as a main line, albeit a competing and by now redundant one. In 1932 all through passenger traffic on the former Hull & Barnsley main line ceased. A suburban service between Hull and South Howden continued, but all regular passenger traffic ceased on the 38½ miles westward to Cudworth.

In the early months of World War II there was a flurry of closures, officially to conserve fuel and rolling stock. These mainly affected the LNER and included Woodham Ferrers to Maldon (8½ miles), Forncett–Wymondham (6½ miles) and three short lines in County Durham. Otherwise the main closure was the 6½ mile GW Alcester branch in Warwickshire. But for the rest of the war closures were few, and even in 1946 only the 2½ mile ex-Highland branch to Strathpeffer was closed. Though the mileage of closures increased to 63½ in 1947, in the immediate aftermath of war there was no indication of the coming devastation.

CHAPTER 3

BR Before Beeching: Closures 1948–62

Nationalisation

The 1947 Transport Act nationalised a major part of the public transport system and set up the monolithic British Transport Commission (BTC) to take it over. The BTC was charged to provide 'an efficient, adequate, economical and properly integrated system of public inland transport', but at the time it was described by Prof Gilbert Walker as 'one of the least promising forms of business organisation yet devised by man'.

On 1 January 1948 the four railway Groups passed into BTC ownership, together with fifty-four Joint and Independent railway concerns. These fifty-four were those which came under the control of the war-time Railway Executive Committee. But this had been somewhat arbitrary, and of the independent lines still with passenger services, the two Col Stephens railways, the Kent & East Sussex and the East Kent, were nationalised, while the North Sunderland and the Corringham (Essex) remained independent.

The BTC was the policy-making body. Administrative and day-to-day control was exercised by Executives. The London Transport Executive was concerned with the railways previously owned by the London Passenger Transport Board, and the Railway Executive with all other nationalised railways, taking over 19,639 route miles. These formed a system which, as we have just seen, had not fundamentally altered in shape since 1923.

Social and Economic Trends

In the aftermath of war there was full employment and wages had risen in real terms since 1939. But there were shortages of consumer durables, especially cars, while petrol was severely rationed. Television lay in the future and the cinema still loomed large in the recreation scene. There was thus a pent-up demand for local public transport, especially in the rural areas. This was mainly satisfied by buses, but for longer local journeys, to the market town, between towns, and to the seaside for day trips, rail was still well used. Local trains carried a good share of the traffic, not only of passengers, but of passenger-rated parcels and miscellaneous traffic.

But the situation existing before 1950 rapidly changed thereafter. Car ownership accelerated particularly rapidly. In 1948 there were 2 million cars registered, the 1939 level having been regained. By 1954 there were 3.1 million and in 1962 6.6 million. The total passenger mileage was increasing, but

A hop pickers' special at Hawkhurst (Kent) in September 1953. By this time 'Hopping' traffic was in decline. But the sleepy branch still occasionally woke up, as shown by the stock for two more specials in the sidings.

entirely because of the increase in the mileage of private transport. The latter's share of the total rose from 33.78 per cent in 1952 to 69.91 per cent in 1962.

For rail the consequences were not experienced evenly. Long-distance traffic remained relatively stable, once the abnormal levels of the war years had declined. However, much holiday traffic was lost to cars, though the effect was mainly felt in short-distance rural traffic, for it was in the remoter rural areas that car ownership had the largest increases. In 1961 Montgomeryshire and Radnorshire had the highest levels of car ownership in England and Wales.

Figures for rail passenger carryings are almost impossible to disaggregate into numbers for particular traffics or lines. The overall figures remained remarkably stable. In 1960 1,069 million passenger journeys were made on BR, compared with 996 million in 1948. Any decline in short-distance journeys had been more than made up for by increases in long-distance and in outer-suburban traffics. So there is a lack of quantitative evidence of falling rural traffic. But even in the early post-war years carryings on some rural branches were at least as light as they had become in the late 1930s. To cite personal examples, in 1949 the author was in a student party returning to Wells from Cheddar. Some walked, but those who felt too tired sought the bus, to find it full. So they went to the station and travelled in an otherwise empty train. About that time the author was also the sole passenger on the 17.40 from Hatfield to St Albans for the whole of its journey.

Costs and Policies

It must be remembered that the halcyon days of the bus were coming to an end, though this was unrecognised at the time. The buses' share of the total market fell from 45 per cent in 1952 to 25 per cent in 1962, a 20 per cent loss, the rail share falling over the same period from 21 per cent to 13 per cent, an 8 per cent fall. But the bus industry was not yet in trouble — that was not to come until the late 1960s. It is a characteristic of the bus industry that costs fall more in line with declining revenue that do rail costs. In fact this is the essential problem besetting rail transport. A high proportion of costs are fixed, ie independent of variations in traffic volume. Costs of track, signalling and stations remain constant, even if the number of trains per day is halved, or doubled. Thus a decline in rail traffic is not matched by anything approaching an equivalent cost saving.

As far as branch lines were concerned, this inescapable fact was made worse by two further facts. Firstly, wages, the chief cost element, accounting at that time for some 60 per cent of total costs incurred by BR and absorbing 80 per cent of the revenue, were rising faster than fares. Between 1948 and 1961 wage costs more than doubled, and in 1961 operating costs exceeded those of 1938 by more than 300 per cent. On the other hand rates and fares had increased by only 160 per cent in this latter period, and this must be set against the stationary or declining traffic on most branch lines, which would have resulted in rapidly worsening revenue/cost ratio.

This policy of fares restraint and wage inflation, foisted by government on the BTC, inevitably led to deficit for the whole railway system. The point at which this came was deferred by the high traffic levels in the immediate post-war period. But by 1955 revenue no longer covered even operating costs. At the

The normal service on the Hawkhurst Branch was provided by pull-and-push (the Southern way round) sets powered by H Class 0–4–4Ts. Note the Col. Stephens corrugated iron station, the large SM's house and the signal box where trains never crossed.

same time the government was reluctant to face the consequences and to consider any policy of subsidy. Instead they sought the goal of a 'profitable' railway system, a goal clearly impossible but one still hankered after in 1985.

While there had been considerable investment in main and suburban lines during the Grouping era, the branch line of 1948 bore a remarkable resemblance to that of 1923 in both outward appearance and in operating methods.

The Southern Railway had electrified many secondary and branch lines, but even on the Southern Region in 1950 many steam-worked branches were being operated with pre-Grouping locomotives and coaches. On all regions signalling had remained basically unchanged in method and equipment, even if upper-quadrant semaphores were gradually replacing older signals, except on the Western Region, which still had lower-quadrants as standard. The un-modernised Victorian stations were still staffed, though on a greatly reduced scale. But in 1955 the four stations on the Hawkhurst Branch (Kent) each had a station-master, two booking porters and two signalmen. Roadside stations still dealt not only with a few passengers, but with some parcels, mail bags, sundries goods traffic and a wagon or two of coal and fertilisers. Station staff would release racing-pigeons which arrived in baskets.

Oswestry, HQ of the Cambrian, on a winter's day. The auto-train from Gobowen has just arrived.

There had been some cost-cutting developments. But, apart from the Southern's electrification policy, only on the Western Region had they been applied with anything like a consistent policy. The GWR had introduced diesel railcars widely on branch lines and on secondary main lines, such as Castle Cary to Weymouth and Princes Risborough to Oxford. They had also opened numerous unstaffed halts with what we would now call 'bus-stop' facilities.

The other Groups had done little more than flirt with such methods, and they could scarcely be said to have got beyond the experimental stage. Some halts had been opened, especially in East Anglia, while steam and internal-combustion railcars were introduced in small and scarcely cost-saving numbers. But there was no consistent policy, with the dubious exception of the use of small numbers of Sentinel-Cammell steam railcars by the LNER. On a few branches, such as that to Thaxted (Essex), tickets were sold on the train, but the practice was not general. The LNER tried a signalling system which did away with movable semaphore signals on the Pilmoor–Knaresborough branch. The LMS ran a road–rail bus for a short time in 1932 from Blisworth to Stratford-on-Avon and thence along the road to their Welcombe Hotel. But most such experiments had disappeared by 1948.

In contrast, the GNR(I) had introduced rail-buses and DMUs during the 1930s and by 1948 a significant proportion of their passenger mileage, including Belfast to Enniskillen and to Londonderry were being worked by them. Their Chief Mechanical Engineer and a colleague had also introduced the Howden–Meredith wheels with steel tyres and flanges on pneumatic tyres of a standard road bus, a method never tried in Britain. The legendary Henry Forbes of the County Donegal Railways had also dieselised virtually all their passenger services. The CDR railcars would stop anywhere on being given a hand signal from an intending passenger.

As hinted already, in many cases timetables were inconvenient. By 1939 they were based more on history than on market research. The subsequent exigencies of war had led to service reductions rather than to closure and in the post-war period the low marginal cost and marketing attraction of increasing frequency, appreciated by Sir Herbert Walker on the inter-war Southern, was apparently forgotten by the BTC. In 1952 there was an attractive day-return fare from Edinburgh to Peebles, but no train between 07.56 and 13.18.

Again, the BTC made little progress towards its statutory commitment of integration, particularly between rail and bus, before the obligation was removed by the 1952 Transport Act. The four Groups had invested heavily in the 'Territorial' bus companies, controlled by two groups, British Electric Traction and Thomas Tilling. But their nominated directors on the bus-company boards were instructed to concern themselves with bus-oriented objectives rather than rail-oriented ones. By 1948 there had been virtually no progress towards integration of the bus and rail systems in terms of fare structures and services. Bus and rail stations were usually at opposite sides of towns and where a bus route passed a station, the hourly bus often would leave five minutes before the arrival of the hourly train, as at Staplehurst on the main line to Ashford and Dover. In only a few cases, for example where mail buses connected with trains as at Achnasheen on the Kyle of Lochalsh line, or where the times of connecting buses from railway stations in the west of England were shown in Southern Railway timetables, was there any real integration.

The BTC inherited both the bus investments and the 'policy' just outlined. Holdings in Territorial companies were adjusted so that in England and Wales the Tilling Group came under BTC control, while the BET Group remained in private ownership until 1968.

There is little doubt the BTC intended setting up a Bus Executive, but made little progress towards welding the Territorial companies into a single unit with a common policy. In fact this did not happen until the setting up of the National Bus Company in 1968. The BTC did however publish a plan for integrated rail/bus transport in Northumberland.

On the Cambrian main line
Like many Cambrian stations, that at Ellesmere was substantial. (*inset*) In April 1962 a train for Whitchurch arrives from Welshpool. (*main picture*) The same scene in 1984.

The Modernisation Plan and After

Meanwhile, BR 'Standard' locomotives and coaches were becoming more common on secondary main lines and on branch lines. They had first appeared in 1951, when 177 locos, 2–6–4T, 2–6–2T and 2–6–0, and 388 non-corridor coaches went into service. By 1960 they were to be seen everywhere.

On 14 June 1954 the first of the now familiar two-car diesel multiple units (DMUs) were introduced in the Leeds area. The same innovation was made later in the year on Manchester (Victoria) suburban services and on the Carlisle–Silloth route, the first rural route to receive them. But the BTC remained wedded to steam on most lines not scheduled for electrification. This was in the face of evidence from abroad. By 1946 diesel power was responsible for 25 per cent of the then very considerable passenger mileage on US railways. Yet in 1955 steam accounted for 87 per cent of the total traction mileage on BR, 10 per cent was electrically operated, and only 3 per cent diesel, performed by shunting locos and the few ex-GWR railcars and new DMUs.

Then, in 1955 the government, recognising the need to catch up with railway investment, foregone during the war and delayed after the war, approved the 'Modernisation Plan' of the BTC. The main objectives of the plan were to overcome the investment shortfall, to reduce operating costs and to improve efficiency. This would attract the traffic resulting from the post-war revival of industry (freight) and higher living standards (passengers).

As far as we are concerned here, the main result of the plan was the substitution of diesel for steam traction. The last steam loco, *Evening Star*, was built in 1960. By 1963 diesel and electricity accounted for 63 per cent of the traction mileage, and the last steam locomotives ran in scheduled service in 1968. Ironically these services were main-line ones, for branch lines had been dieselised by then.

The DMU programme had been extensive and designed to provide the basic traction for branch and secondary main lines as well as suburban services. Some aspects were very successful. Cost reductions were considerable; among other things DMUs required only a two-man crew against the three of steam, they were more comfortable, presented a better image, and gave children and rail fans a superb view of the line ahead. The Southern Region's 'Hampshire' D/EMUs were particularly cost-effective. The initial 1957 diagrams called for sixteen of the eighteen units to be in daily use.

But the Modernisation Plan was a technical one. It was not commercial in that the investment was expected to yield results without any drastic overhaul of operating methods and commercial objectives, which were still essentially pre-war. The plan therefore had no effect on the rapidly worsening finances. How it could achieve its declared objective of the railways breaking even by 1961–62 was regarded by D. H. Aldcroft as 'beyond comprehension'.

Consequently the government began to lose faith in the BTC. In 1960 the Conservative Minister of Transport (Ernest Marples) appointed the Stedeford Group to enquire into the future role of the railways. The group's report has never been made public, but there is little doubt it was adverse as far as BR was concerned. This was the first time the basic role of rail in the British transport system was really questioned. Hitherto it had been regarded as the central transport mode, and if only the organisation and financial objectives could be got right, it would attain permanent solvency without subsidy. It was only during the 1960s that the idea became respectable that the role of railways would be very restricted and that they might even have no long-term future.

Marples took up these ideas with great vigour. He was determined that BR should achieve financial viability. This would have to be attained not only by radical change in the BTC's commercial activities, but by drastic surgery. In many respects this was regarded as a good policy. What brought the minister into contention with the parliamentary opposition, local authorities, media and academics was his rigid determination that the BTC must attain profitability before any comprehensive transport plan could even be considered, even though one was desperately needed. But profitability must be reached, even if the resulting rump of the railway system would be too small for a planned national transport system.

Then, in 1962 another Transport Act received the royal assent. This represented one more stage in Conservative dismemberment of the highly (perhaps overly) centralised socialist scheme for transport and in the replacement of co-ordination through legislation and planning by competition. Any ideas for integration of public transport were firmly consigned to the shelf. The BTC was finally dissolved and the tier of Executives was replaced by Boards, including the British Railways Board (BRB), plus the Transport Holding Company, which took over the nationalised sector of the bus and road-haulage industries.

These new bodies were completely independent of each other, and there was no obligation placed on them to co-operate. In addition, as we shall see, there were clauses aimed at reducing public control over the Boards. Although these were denounced later by the Labour opposition, the latter allowed the clauses through without any real question and did little to remedy the position when they came to power.

One member of the Stedeford Group was a director of ICI with considerable experience in industrial administration. Dr Richard (later Lord) Beeching had attracted the minister's attention and in 1961 he was appointed chairman of the BTC. *Trains Illustrated* approved of his career and abilities, but waxed sarcastic on the terms of his appointment:

> After an interim of meditation . . . at East Grinstead (where he lived) the Doctor is to descend on No. 222 Marylebone Road with tablets on which will be engraved all the requirements for prosperity – or at least solvency – that the practical railwayman has vainly sought . . . since the mid-1950s.

Then, in 1962 the new BRB took over the assets hitherto managed by the Railway Executive, and Dr Beeching became its first chairman.

Partial modernisation was no answer
(*above*) Steam to Amlwch (Anglesey). The 14.05 from Amlwch at Llanerchymedd on 15 August 1963. (*below*) Amlwch dieselised. The 13.05 from Gaerwen calls at Llanerchymedd in September 1963. In spite of an apparent high level of patronage, dieselisation without other cost-saving measures was not enough to save such a line.

Closures 1948–62: Analysis

We have seen that in the early years after the war there was no consistent policy towards the more lightly trafficked lines aimed either at encouraging traffic or at reducing costs. With the hindsight available in 1985, however, it can be seen that, while for many lines there was a potential, it is difficult to see how for many others there still remained any potential traffic sources to be tapped, whatever marketing package could have been devised. But certainly the prevailing high-cost operating methods, coupled with decreased service frequencies, a frozen and rigid fare structure and poor marketing, was a complete recipe for disaster. On the other hand, DMUs were rapidly introduced after 1954, which did result in substantial cost savings and increased patronage.

At first there was no suitable method of cost analysis. It was obvious that many branch lines were not even covering their operating (direct) costs, let alone making any contribution to the heavy fixed overhead costs which are characteristic of railways. The direct costs of operating the branch, especially wages and fuel, could be easily calculated. But there was no procedure for apportioning the branch's share of such costs as the provision of rolling stock, and the provision and maintenance of track, signalling and stations on any part of the main line used by the branch trains. Nor could the loss of through bookings from branch stations, should the line be closed, be calculated. Finally, there was no means of apportioning the fixed costs of the branch line between passenger and freight traffic.

Where procedures were available they were based on those of orthodox accounting, which is essentially retrospective, using as their raw data details of money already spent. The economist's approach, based on calculating 'escapable' costs, ie those costs which could be avoided by not providing the service in question, was not introduced until after 1963. However, after 1955 and particularly after 1960 'traffic studies' began to be made with greater frequency. These were cost/revenue studies of particular aspects of the system, either of services, such as the carriage of freight sundries, or of individual branch lines.

With declining, or at best static, traffic and with increasing costs, the pace of closure to passengers increased rapidly. Though at first the pace seemed deceptively slow, plans for extensive closures were being finalised. Thus in 1948 only three lines, totalling 61¼ route miles, were closed. These included the formerly independent East Kent and the still independent Easingwold, both of which trundled an elderly coach on their goods trains, presumably for the benefit of visiting rail fans. The following year was similar; only three more lines totalling 13¾ miles were closed.

Then the pace began to quicken, though casualties were still mostly of lightly used, short, dead-end branches. Eleven lines (148¾ miles) lost their passenger services in 1950 and then 38 lines (274½ miles) in 1951. Some of these were in suburban areas and included Marsh Lane to Aintree and Princes Street (Edinburgh) to Barnton and the outer suburban services from Edinburgh to

Plymouth Friary, the LSW terminus. Though the photograph was probably taken in early Southern days, locomotives and coaching stock were still all of LSW vintage.

Polton and to Penicuik; others were in industrial areas, particularly the coalfields, eg West Hartlepool to Sunderland (via Wellfield) and to Ferryhill (via Castle Eden) and the former Lancashire, Derbyshire & East Coast line from Chesterfield (Market Place) to Langwith; but above all they were in the remoter rural areas, for example Haughley to Laxfield (Mid-Suffolk Light), Much Wenlock to Craven Arms, Morpeth to Rothbury and Reedsmouth and the Alyth branch. No part of the country between east Kent and west Wales and the Scottish Highlands was immune, but the closures were still coming singly and in isolation.

But thereafter cross-country routes began to be affected. In 1952 the Stratford-on-Avon & Midland Junction line lost its always sparse passenger service between Blisworth and Stratford (38¼ miles). Then in 1958 the ex-LNW line across the Heads of the Valleys from Abergavenny to Merthyr (High Street) (24¼ miles) was closed altogether, unusually for those days having already lost its freight services (1954). The 1959 closure list totalled 376¼ miles and included the St Ives–Kettering cross-country line (33 miles); while 1961, when 178½ miles were closed, saw the end of services on both the ex-Midland & South Western Junction (61½ miles) and the ex-Didcot, Newbury & Southampton (47¼ miles).

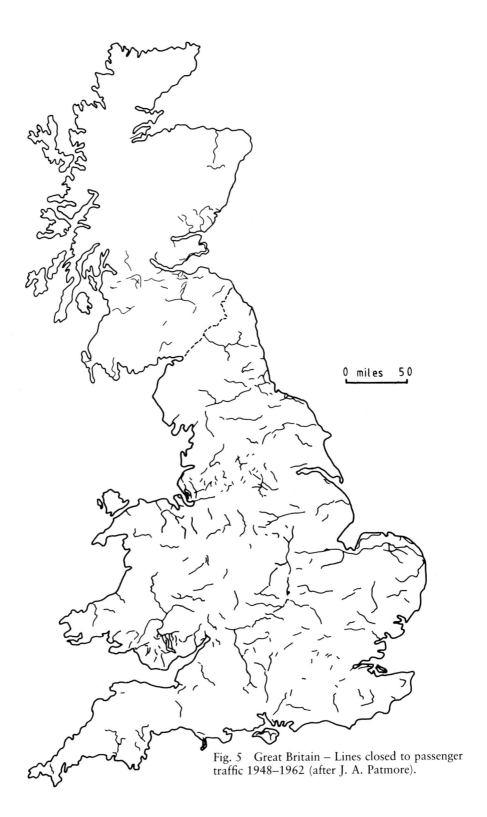

0 miles 50

Fig. 5   Great Britain – Lines closed to passenger
traffic 1948–1962 (after J. A. Patmore).

By that time secondary main lines, whose closure would have been unthinkable even ten years before, were being lost. The closure of virtually the whole of the ex Midland & Great Northern Joint system, 174¾ route miles at one fell swoop, was the real shock of 1959, while services across Stainmore Summit between Barnard Castle and Penrith ceased in 1962. By then even the Great Central north of Aylesbury was being run down at a rate presaging early closure.

The climax came in 1962 with the closure of forty-six lines totalling 794¼ route miles. There was the same apparently random scatter from the Gwinear Road–Helston branch in Cornwall to a number of lines in the Glasgow and Edinburgh areas. Closures included 162¾ miles in the Welsh Marches made up of four lines converging on Brecon; the short Keighley–Oxenhope branch which later re-opened as the Keighley & Worth Valley; and by coincidence the two lines which, in turn, were part of the Midland's early approaches to London, the Midland Counties line of 1836 to Rugby from Leicester, and the Bedford–Hitchin line.

In all 3,318 route miles had been closed to passengers by the BTC between its inception on 1 January 1948 and 31 December 1962, a space of fifteen years. The pace then slowed temporarily in the early part of 1963. There were a large number of proposals in the pipeline, but final closures were deferred until the publication of the Beeching Report and subsequent parliamentary debate.

It is hard to say what part of the country suffered most. As to length of lines closed, reference to the map (Figure 5) shows the closures spread right across the country, though it must be remembered that in some of the remoter areas the original network was not a dense one. So in proportion to mileage in 1948, closures in the Welsh border country were more extensive than those in the coalfield to the south.

The map shows that between 1948 and 1962 Greater London and the inner parts of the Home Counties suffered the loss of only thirteen short branches totalling some twenty miles. In relation to the mileage still remaining open, the South and South West also suffered comparatively little.

On the other hand the cumulative effect of closures was beginning to be felt in a wide zone from north Norfolk across the east Midlands to the shores of the Severn estuary. The loss of the four lines to Brecon and those centred on Leominster had deprived a large area of the southern Marches of any form of rail transport. The industrial areas of South Wales, south Lancashire and west Yorkshire also were concentrations of closed lines. On the other hand the West Midlands industrial area escaped almost unscathed. In northern England both rural and industrial areas suffered heavily. In Scotland closures were extensive in the central area and in the rural areas of the Border country.

As to the social consequences, in the case of the M&GN at least, the heavy through holiday traffic had been diverted without undue damage. In the more urbanised areas bus services were still of a high standard. In most of the rural areas population was sparse and car ownership high. But there was hardship

One face of the Brecon & Merthyr. In spite of the railway's name, Bassaleg (near Newport) was its starting point. As always, in 1961 coal was more important than passengers. Note the parcels delivery vehicle on the platform.

for the minority still dependent on public transport for longer journeys, especially with luggage, for it is this sector of transport in which the British stage-carriage bus system has never been a wholly satisfactory substitute for rail.

The point has already been made (page 23) that there has always been a reluctance in Great Britain, as opposed to the Continent and Ireland, for railway administrators to think in other than railway terms. They have very rarely considered combining bus and train in such a way as to exploit the favourable features of each. There has of course been a history of road services being developed as feeder and connecting services, even though efforts in this direction can only be described as intermittent, but parallel bus services have always been thought of as competing or, in later years, as complete replacements.

This view has been supported and later enforced by legislation. Many railway companies, notably the GW, developed feeder bus services using their own vehicles in the same way as they used their own vans and lorries for collecting and delivering goods. But the 1930 Road Traffic Act, in return for allowing the railway companies to become shareholders in bus companies, deprived them of 'operating rights', that is they could no longer use their own vehicles.

Thus, subsequently, if railways did consider partial substitution or augmentation of a train service with buses, they would have to think in terms of employing an existing operator, who of course would be reluctant to assist his rival in this way. But on the other hand there is no evidence that such a policy was ever seriously contemplated.

In contrast, in 1984 the author travelled by rail from Marseille to Digne in Provence. The latter town is the terminus of a short branch from the main line to Briançon, but this has only two trains a day. The other trips are made by a bus hired from a local firm by the national railways (SNCF). The bus not only connects with trains at the nearby junction of St Auban, but occasionally continues to the more important rail centre of Veynes. This is a reasonably common practice on secondary and branch lines in West Germany and Denmark, as reference to timetables will show. In this way buses are substituted for trains at certain times of day, when the demand is limited and is within the capacity of the road vehicle. This can be done on Sundays to save opening up the line, or on early and/or late services to allow the line to be operated on a single shift.

From Dowlais Top the B&M descended vertiguously the scarp of the Brecon Beacons to reach the rural delights of Talybont-on-Usk. The Stephenson Locomotive Society's last train paused for water on 2 May 1964.

In Ireland the railways in both South and North were early in developing co-ordinated road services for both passengers and goods. The Great Southern was particularly assiduous in this respect, though the GNR(I) was also active. But unfortunately co-ordination eventually came to grief. In 1944 the Coras Iompair Eireann (CIE) was set up, its logo with more than a nod at London Transport, but unkindly dubbed 'the flying snail'. Although a private company, the government guaranteed debenture interest. Once motor fuel became more plentiful a pro-road policy emerged. Under the chairmanship of C. S. Andrews a 'Marples-Beeching' closure programme ensued.

In Northern Ireland the government was more consistently anti-rail. In 1935 it set up the Northern Ireland Road Transport Board, a monopoly of all road passenger and freight operations, including those of the GNR(I) wholly within the Province. Promises of co-ordination soon faded. Then in 1948 the Ulster Transport Authority, a mini-counterpart of the BTC, was created to nationalise all public transport. Once again promises of integration were replaced by an intensive rail closure programme, including the Province's share of the GNR(I), apportioned between the two governments when it finally failed financially. In fairness, however, with the longest haul the hundred miles from Belfast to Londonderry, lack of minerals or other bulk freight traffic, and the consequences of road improvements on passenger traffic, there was a very limited role for rail.

Reaction to an Accelerating Closure Rate

The rate of closure rapidly gathered momentum after 1950 so that by the end of 1959 nearly 2,000 route miles had lost their passenger services. At first public reaction was limited and muted. But who could complain of personal hardship or of damage to the local economy if the one-coach train which ambled through deepest rural Northamptonshire between Banbury and Blisworth was withdrawn, thus depriving the small villages of Helmdon and Wappenham of a scarcely used service; if it were no longer possible to take the auto-train from Faringdon to Uffington, there to wait for up to an hour for the main line 'connection' to Swindon, when the bus went direct in a fraction of the time; or if it were no longer possible to travel from Coatbridge Central to Bothwell, threading the complex of formerly competing lines through the decaying industrial area east of Glasgow?

But as the decade unfolded, more heavily used lines began to disappear from the timetables and because of this opposition built up. At their meeting on 9 September 1954 the South West Area Transport Users' Consultative Committee recommended that the Princetown branch up on to Dartmoor should be retained owing to the general inability to provide suitable alternative services. Then in 1955 there was a *cause célèbre* when an action was brought against the BTC by local residents led by a Miss Bessimer. This forced the authority to restore a service on the recently closed line between East Grinstead and Lewes. The closure was declared illegal on the grounds of a clause in the agreement for operating the line between the LBSCR and the nominally independent Lewes & East Grinstead Company which guaranteed the original four stations four daily trains each way.

The BTC reacted with characteristic bad grace. Four and only four round trips were made when nobody wanted to travel and Barcombe station remained closed. It had developed into the busiest station, but as a later addition was not named in the agreement. The farce was played out until an enabling Act could be obtained and the line was closed once more in 1958. But part of the line was again re-opened in 1960 as the Bluebell Railway.

Proposals to close the 9¼ mile Coniston branch in the Lake District were published in 1957. BR stated that on a summer Saturday an average of 711 passengers joined and alighted from trains at the four branch stations, and 432 on a typical winter weekday. David Thomas in his *The Rural Transport Problem* (1963) recorded that the local authorities, the Friends of the Lake District and prominent members of the general public submitted evidence that persuaded the majority of independent members of the North Western Transport Users' Consultative Committee to ask BR to continue the service on the grounds of its general value to the area. BR had calculated closure would lead to a net saving of £16,679 per year (£1,803 per mile). There was no parallel bus service and the road was unsuitable. The county council was not prepared to spend the money on widening (which would have been greater than many years of savings put together). But the votes of BR members gave a majority in favour of closure. Subsequent criticism of the handling of this case led to BR members of TUCs being instructed not to vote on closure proposals.

Even in 1962 double-headed holiday trains steamed over the doomed Somerset & Dorset. Here a southbound train climbs out of Bath between Devonshire and Coombe Down Tunnels.

Cross-country lines existed for freight as well as passengers. A goods train is captured by the camera on one of the most photographed spots on the S&D. Wellow Church is in the background.

So on the anti-closure side were ranged the parliamentary opposition and those Conservative backbenchers with slender majorities and constituencies affected by closures; the majority of the national, technical and the local press; more and more local authorities; and increasing numbers of individuals. They formed a multitude of bodies and individuals of the most diverse opinions and political outlooks. But a cynic might have said they were at least united in one respect: had they been able to persuade the minister to retain their particular loss-making local service, they would not have expected to provide it themselves with financial support through subsidy or higher fares. Regional aspects of opposition too were soon to emerge. But that is for the next chapter.

On the other side was the BTC. Faced with constant nagging instructions to break even and with equally constant refusals by the government to introduce overt subsidies, it had no option but to cut costs where it could. One direction open was the withdrawal of those passenger and freight services it considered loss-makers. In its annual report for 1954 the Central Transport Consultative Committee (CTCC) stated it had considered 102 closure proposals during the year. In July 1959 it was reported the London Midland Region had 26 lines under consideration for closure by the December.

Behind the BTC was the Ministry of Transport. The minister, Ernest Marples, one of the few Ministers of Transport with a strong charisma, had the ear and unquestioning support of the cabinet. He and his ministry became more and more obdurate, particularly after the passage of the 1962 Transport Act. In the debate on its second reading, the lack of co-ordination between the nationalised road and rail services, constantly stressed by the technical press and experienced by users, was emphasised by G. R. Strauss, the opposition spokesman for transport. The parliamentary secretary to the Minister of Transport insisted there *was* 'practical day-to-day' co-ordination. 'When did he last travel by bus or train?' commented the *Daily Telegraph*. In 1961 the CTCC recommended the Westerham (Kent) branch should be retained in view of its importance to commuters. Immediately the minister rejected their advice.

The Attitude of the BTC

It is difficult to understand the attitude of the BTC in all this. Charged with the maintenance and operation of the greater part of the nation's transport system and faced with a directive to break even financially, it had three options: to reduce the costs of providing the services; to increase the revenue from them; or to abandon them altogether. It appears to have chosen the latter in preference to the other choices, and to have made little or no attempt to evolve policies to save on operating costs and to attract more traffic. Again, instead of attempting to enlist as allies those opposed to closures, it chose to fight them in a series of increasingly bitter battles.

In the first place, as we have already seen, there was a reprehensible reluctance to introduce operating economies. The 'basic railway', sketched out by G. Fiennes in the 1960s after most closures had taken place, did not finally emerge as a policy for a further ten years. The basic railway is single track with minimum signalling and unstaffed, 'bus-stop' stations and operated with light diesel railcars used as intensively as possible.

During twelve months in 1961–2 the Western Region produced a number of economy plans for the South West, which included closure to passengers of eight branch lines. David Thomas showed that, while the net annual savings from these schemes were estimated at £248,643, over £1 million annually could have been saved throughout the area without having to close any line, by economies of much the same sort as were later introduced.

He looked in detail at a number of the schemes, including the proposal to withdraw passenger services from the Helston branch, but to maintain it for freight. The net annual savings for this 8¾ mile line were calculated to be £9,077, or £1,037 per mile, a modest sum even at 1960 prices. However the movement costs of diesel units 'operated under the cheapest working methods possible' were put at £16,700 and their use was therefore rejected. The comparable figure for the Exe Valley line, 24¾ miles, was £19,000, which was puzzling. But assuming the figure to be correct, the loss would have been reduced to only £5,000. But this was basing the calculation on the existing timetable which needed two trains. Suitable revision, without loss of convenience for the majority of passengers, would have meant the use of only one train and a reduction of the loss to under £2,000. When this sum is set against the inconvenience of closure, David Thomas questioned whether the TUCC would have recommended, or the minister accepted, the closure proposal had these figures been produced.

Nor was there a consistent policy on cost savings. Thus the London Midland Region refused to allow unstaffed stations. There is also the story then current of an officer of the Manchester Division saying, after consent had been given to withdrawal of a certain service, that it could now be operated more economically until final closure (the implication being that cost savings that could easily have been made were deferred in order to strengthen the closure case). Examples of wastage could be multiplied indefinitely.

Naturally there would have been union resistance to economies, which would have had to be directed mainly to savings in labour costs. But the introduction of the new technology becoming available was essential to the survival of the railways. It would result in greater productivity and thus the unions would in any event have to be faced sooner or later. Productivity would have to be increased also as a result of the Guillebrand award of high wage increases.

The BTC's approach to the outside was often heavy-handed. There was a closure procedure (described in greater detail in Chapter 5), and once a proposal was advertised the regional TUCC concerned had to consider the case at a public inquiry should any objection be received. Yet routes scheduled for closure but not yet considered by the TUCC or formally endorsed by the minister were deliberately omitted from new timetables. Again, preparation of cases for presentation to the TUCCs was sometimes slipshod. In 1960 the CTCC reported that, though contentious cases were few in number, one case was unduly complicated by the BR officer proving to be incapable of preparing a report, while yet other presentations had to be returned for clarification. One is left with the impression the BTC was just not bothered about public relations.

On occasion, as we have seen already, the costings were open to doubt. In its report on the case for closure of the East Grinstead and Lewes service (the Bluebell Line) the CTCC criticised the BTC for the way it applied average costs derived on a system-wide basis to individual lines. Such a procedure was extremely questionable as local circumstances could cause wide divergences from the national average. They were also critical of the way savings on interest charges were included. The BTC was in the habit of calculating a nominal capital value for the line to be closed and then claiming that closure would enable savings to be made of the interest on that capital. This they justified on the ground that closure would render a sinking fund for renewals unnecessary. In practice nothing was set aside for this purpose, so the CTCC considered interest savings to be an improper figure to use in support of a closure case.

In the heyday of the Midland & South Western Junction. In 1923 the 10.24 from Southampton, including through carriages for Liverpool, drifts through Charlton Kings on its way down to Cheltenham behind loco No. 7.

In some cases savings were claimed twice over, when a line was closed to passengers and then again later when withdrawal of the freight service was proposed. After closure to passengers the Coniston branch was maintained at a much higher standard than needed for a thrice weekly freight trip – so high that the occasional excursion was run at speeds of 40mph or more. Yet those costs which should have been escaped by withdrawing passenger trains were listed a second time as being saved by complete closure.

It was normal practice to overestimate savings at the junction station. Thus, if the branch service slated for closure accounted for 30 per cent of the movements at the junction with the main line, 30 per cent of all signalling and station costs would be claimed as being saved. But obviously such a high level would not be achieved. For example the signal-box and booking office would still be manned to deal with the main-line trains.

These malpractices were maintained even when the art of costing gained greater precision as the 1960s progressed. In 1963 BR's case for closing the Buntingford branch (Essex) claimed a net annual saving of £35,000. But it was claimed that the cost of nine permanent-way men would be saved, though time spent on the branch was only the equivalent of two full-time men. Again, six

(*left*) St. James was the GW's principal Cheltenham station for both passengers and goods. But diversion of the MSWJ trains in 1960 from Lansdown was part of the planned run-down of the line. (*right*) A train from Cambridge arrives at the dying junction of St. Ives in 1969.

signalmen had been made redundant in 1960, but the case listed their wages as savings through closure. The whole cost of repairs to the diesel multiple units used on the branch were also listed as savings, though they were only rostered on the branch for half their daily mileage. Local authority objectors stated annual savings would in fact be nearer £10,000. Incidentally, the TUCC thought hardship could be alleviated by introducing through rail/bus season tickets available on the replacement bus, but BR had objected.

Sometimes too the public suspected the BTC of deliberately running down services in order to discourage traffic and thus strengthen the closure case. It is difficult for the most impartial student to disagree in the case of the Midland & South Western Junction line. The latter's function was always that indicated by

its title. Trains originated at Cheltenham's Lansdown station where connections were made with trains on the ex-Midland Birmingham–Bristol line, and ran to Andover Junction on the ex-LSW main line, some of them going on to Southampton. Even though the majority of passengers using the service were changing at Cheltenham, in 1959 trains were diverted to the ex-GW station of St James, thus severing the connections. At the same time the three through trains to Andover Junction were reduced to a single one. Small wonder there were few passengers left to complain of inconvenience when closure proposals were published in 1961. Yet there was no procedure to prevent BR running down the service in this way.

Finally, it also seemed that the BTC and its successor, the BRB, took any advantage they could of accident. In the Border country, after flood damage in 1948 the Reston–Duns passenger service was never restored, though the freight-only Lauder branch was repaired. On the other hand it was true the Brightlingsea (Essex) branch was eventually fully restored after heavy damage

Table 115 CHELTENHAM SPA, CIRENCESTER, SWINDON, MARLBOROUGH and ANDOVER JUNCTION

Miles		Week Days am (Except Saturdays)	am	am	am	pm (Saturdays only)	am	pm (TC Cheltenham Spa (St. James') to Southampton (Central and Terminus) Saturdays only)	pm (TC Cheltenham Spa (St. James') to Southampton (Central and Terminus) Except Saturdays)	pm	pm (Except Saturdays)	pm (Saturdays only)	pm (Except Saturdays)	pm	pm (Except Saturdays)	pm	Sundays am		pm
	Cheltenham Spa																		
—	St. James' .. .. dep	..	**6 30**	..	**9 50**	..	**1050**	**1 48**	**1 52**	**2 25**	..	..	..	**5 50**	..	**6 28**	..	..	..
½	Malvern Road	..	..	..	**9 52**	..	**1052**	**1 50**	**1 55**	**2 27**	..	..	..	**5 52**	..	**6 30**	..	..	..
3	Cheltenham Leckhampton ..		6 37	..	9 59	..	1058	1 57	2 1	2 33	..	..	..	5 58	..	6 36	..	..	..
4¼	Charlton Kings Halt		6 42	..	10 4	..	11 3	..	..	2 38	..	..	..	6 3	..	6 41	..	..	..
8	Andoversford		6 52	..	1012	..	1112	2 10	2 14	2 47	..	..	..	6 12	..	6 50	..	..	..
11	Withington (Glos.) Halt		..	..	—	..	..	2 17	2 20	..	..	..	..	..	..	..	..	..	..
14½	Chedworth Halt.		..	..	Stop	..	..	2 27	2 30	..	..	..	..	..	..	..	..	..	..
15¾	Foss Cross		..	..	..	..	..	2 31	2 33	..	..	..	..	..	..	..	..	..	..
22	**Cirencester** (Watermoor) ..	**6 34**	..	..	..	..	..	**2 45**	**2 45**	..	..	..		..	**7 10**	..	..	..	..
25	South Cerney	6 40	..	..	..	..	..	2 52	2 52	..	..	..		..	7 17	..	..	..	..
28½	Cricklade	6 49	..	..	..	..	..	3 0	3 0	..	..	..		..	7 24	..	..	..	..
36¾	**Swindon Town** arr	**7 3**	..	..	..	..	..	**3 15**	**3 15**	..				..	**7 38**	..	..	..	..
39¾	**Swindon** .. .. .. arr	**7 15**	..	..	..	..	..	..	..	..				..		..	..	..	..
—	Mls **Swindon** dep	..	..	**7 4**	..	**1 5**	..	..	..	..			**5 55**	..		..	**9 35**	..	**5 45**
—	3 **Swindon Town** .. .. arr	..	..	**7 18**	am	**1 14**	..	..	..	..			**6 3**	..		..	**9 43**	..	**5 53**
—	**Swindon Town** dep	..	..	**7 22**	**8 9**	**1 15**	..	**3 19**	**3 19**	..	**4 52**	**4 52**	**6 7**	..		..	**9 50**	..	**5 55**
40	Chiseldon	..	..	7 32	8 17	1 24	..	3 27	3 27	..	5 0	5 0	6 15	..		..	9 58	..	6 3
41¼	Chiseldon Camp Halt	..	..	7 36	..	1 28	..	3 30	3 30	..	5 3	5 3	..	..	..	..	..	..	..
43½	Ogbourne	..	..	7 42	..	1 35	..	3 36	3 36	..	5 9	5 9	..	..	..	..	10 7	..	..
48	**Marlborough** arr	..	..	**7 52**	..	**1 49**	..	**3 46**	**3 46**	..	**5 19**	**5 19**	..	..	..	..	**10 16**	..	**6 22**
	dep	..	..	**7 55**	..	..	..	**3 51**	**3 48**	..	**5 20**	**5 20**	..	..	..	..	**10 18**	..	**6 23**
53	Savernake (Low Level) arr	..	..	8 7	..	..	..	4 2	3 59	..	5 31	5 31	..	..	..	..	10 29	..	6 34
	dep	..	..	8 28	..		..	4 4	4 1	..	5 32	5 32	..	..	..	..	10 31	..	6 35
55	Grafton and Burbage	..	..	8 35	..		..	4 10	4 7	..	5 38	5 38	..	..	..	..	10 37	..	6 41
58	Collingbourne Kingston Halt ..	..	..	8 41	..		..	4 15	4 12	..	5 43	5 43	..	..	..	..	10 41	..	6 45
59¼	Collingbourne	..	..	8 45	..		..	4 18	4 15	..	5 47	5 47	..	..	..	..	10 45	..	6 49
61¾	Ludgershall	..	..	8 53	..		..	4 25	4 22	..	5 53	5 53	..	..	..	..	10 52	..	6 55
65¾	Weyhill	..	..	9 1	..		..	4 33	4 30	..	6 1	6 1	..	..	..	..	11 0	..	7 3
69¼	**Andover Junction** .. .. arr	..	..	**9 8**	..		..	**4 41**	**4 38**	..	**6 9**	**6 9**	..	..	..	..	**11 8**	..	**7 12**
95½	Southampton Central .. arr	..	..	10C49	..	..	..	5 28	5 27	..	7 32	7 32	..	..	..	..	12 19	..	8 19
97¼	Southampton Terminus "	..	..	10E47	..	..	..	5 36	5 37	..	..	7 47	..	..	..	..	..	..	..
122	Portsmouth & Southsea "	..	..	11 16	..	..	..	6 16	6 14	..	8 12	8 16	..	..	..	..	12 47	..	8 53
119	Bournemouth Central. "	..	..	12 9	..	..	..	6 40	6 26	..	8F37	8 37	..	..	..	..	1 42	..	9 24
86¾	Salisbury .. .. .. "	..	..	10C 3	..	..	..	5 57	5 57	..	7 0	7 0	..	..	..	..	11 51	..	7 42
136	**London** (Waterloo) ... "	..	..	**11 8**	..	..	..	**6 13**	**6 33**	..	**8 6**	**8 15**	..	..	..	..	**3 49**	..	**9H15**

C On Saturdays arr Southampton Central 11 3 am and Salisbury 9 42 am

E Except Saturdays
F On Fridays arr 8 29 pm

H Until 10th July arr 9 8 pm
TC Through Carriages

Bradshaw of 13 June 1960 reveals how the Midland & South Western Junction line was being run down. Connections had been severed and only a single through service was left.

from the 1952 East Coast floods. The Severn Bridge, damaged by a coastal tanker colliding with it in 1960, was abandoned and demolished. P. Howard Anderson, author of the *East Midlands* volume of the 'Forgotten Railways' series), gives a lesser-known example. It was the deteriorating condition of the long tunnel under Bolsover Castle which led to the withdrawal in 1951 of the service over the ex-Lancashire, Derbyshire & East Coast line to Chesterfield and the closure of Market Place terminus.

Thus relations between the BTC and numerous bodies, groups and individuals were rapidly worsening when Dr Beeching was appointed chairman. What happened then is recorded in the next chapter.

CHAPTER 4

From Beeching to Castle:
Closures After 1962

Lord Beeching

At Henfield (Sussex) a housing development occupies the site of the station and goods yard, closed in 1966. It is called 'The Beechings'. The name of Richard (later Lord) Beeching has come to be indissolubly linked in the popular mind with the rundown and dismemberment of the British railway system, and his name tends to be invoked by the headlines whenever there is a further effort in the same direction.

In 1963 the BRB published *The Reshaping of British Railways*, which is invariably known as the Beeching Report. The railway historian is justified in pointing to the occasion as a signpost of fundamental importance. It is no exaggeration to say it signalled a basic change of direction in commercial and operating policies for the railways. Until the late 1950s these had continued essentially unchanged since 1939. Now they were to launch out in the directions with which we are now familiar. High Speed Trains are as much a consequence of these new policies as the overgrown hedges bordering the grass- and bramble-grown rights-of-way of abandoned and forgotten railway lines.

In order to fit the closure programme into the larger context of the new policies, it is useful to attempt a re-assessment of those policies and of Lord Beeching's place in recent transport history. In the first place, as we have just seen, Beeching was not the initiator of the extensive closure programme, either in terms of complete closure of branch and secondary lines or in terms of closure of wayside stations on main lines.

It is clear from the contemporary press, particularly the journals specialising in transport, that Beeching was appointed to implement a policy already formulated, namely that the railway system must be returned to 'profitability', without either overt or hidden subsidy, by the reduction of those services and lines regarded as 'unprofitable'. He was regarded as an administrator with the necessary ability to implement this policy by identifying the 'unprofitable' parts of the system and then shedding them. It was his contribution to history that he carried out the task allocated to him with great efficiency and made the whole country, for the first time in the changed conditions of the post-war world, think about and face up to the evaluation of the role of the railway in the transport system.

As a result of the association of his name solely with closures, Beeching has been seen as having a purely negative approach to his brief. But in a message to BR employees in July 1962 he expressed the hope that, having talked hitherto largely about cuts, he would soon be able to talk of growth. That he was denied the opportunity was due less to his own inclination than to government policies – or rather the lack of them. The foundations of the successful Inter-City package, the freightliner system and 'merry-go-round' trains were firmly laid in the Beeching era, to be built on in the 1970s. But these positive aspects lie outside the scope of this book.

The Beeching Report

The new chairman allowed no time for grass to grow under his feet. Extensive traffic studies were quickly initiated. Then, in March 1962, at a luncheon for industrialists in the North East, the chairman shocked his listeners by abandoning his prepared speech and threatening possible closure of the then electric Tyneside suburban lines. In this case however, according to G. Freeman Allen (in *The Eastern Region Since 1948*, pub Ian Allan), this was not based on the traffic studies but was 'a spontaneous reaction to gloomy figures which local railway officers had been bandying about over the lunch table'.

The press commented he was setting out deliberately to alarm the local authorities – and this was probably correct. It would be some time before local government would be brought to accepting the need to plan and pay for their local transport system, for which they had hitherto expected someone else to

Then and now at Allhallows-on-Sea

(*left*) On a summer evening in 1960 a train for Gravesend is ready to start. A Bulleid 0–6–0 heads a two coach pull-and-push set, while a Class 33 diesel will follow with a train of three wagons of shingle. (*right*) In 1975 the semi-derelict station survived surrounded by a caravan site.

take financial responsibility. But in view of subsequent events on Tyneside with the coming of the 'Metro' it is now rather ironic to read of these threats.

In June 1962, the annual report of the BTC for 1961, the first year of the Beeching era, underlined an operating deficit of £87 million with a further £49 million for interest and other fixed charges. Such was the scale of the economies the commission had been told to look for. No details were given as yet, but Sydney Greene, general secretary of the National Union of Railwaymen, estimated that as a result of the traffic studies 33 per cent of the network was to go. Characteristically the BTC made no comment.

Then, during the debate on the second reading of the Transport Bill, the Minister of Transport, Ernest Marples, made great play of the traffic studies. These included the soon-to-be-notorious 19.48 train from Berwick to Edinburgh. For the week 23–29 October 1961 movement costs were estimated at £164 per day for the 57 miles. Gross revenue averaged 10s (50p) from the passengers, whose number varied from two to eight per day.

These figures had come from a paper allegedly circulated to the unions to justify the economies and which had fallen into the hands of the media. Scottish Region complained of leaks. But, said *Trains Illustrated*, if these costings *were* correct, why the secrecy – surely there could be no public complaints about the disappearance of this sort of train?

But this was typical of the secrecy which was alienating the BTC (and subsequently the BRB) from the public. There were also some odd things about the costings. Why did the 07.50 Glasgow–Ayr, covering 42 miles of level track, in contrast with the hilly 57 mile Berwick road, cost £57 *more* than the 19.48? And why did revenue on the Ayr route average less than 25 per cent of movement costs if the passenger complement varied from 322 to 185? The question immediately raised was: if this train fell so far short of covering its costs, how many trains in Scotland *were* covering them? And, if there were many other similar examples, why pick on the 07.50?

In July 1962 the traffic maps which were to reappear in the Beeching Report were first published. They were based on a census week in October 1961 and for the first time there was a complete route-density map of British railways, showing passenger numbers and freight tonnage. There were few real surprises, but for all to see was the huge mileage with less than 5,000 passengers per week (though, oddly, lines open for freight only were included in this category). There was little doubt there was no future for these lines.

The *Daily Telegraph*, never noted for its support of BR, took the opportunity of summarising the whole reasoned case against the Marples–Beeching policy:

At a time when more and more cars and trucks are clogging up our roads, polluting our air, killing our children and demanding ever greater road space, many people must be wondering whether we have these matters in their right perspective. What would happen if those who caused most wear and tear, delay and pressure on road space were asked to pay the full cost of their journeys?

They are, depressingly, words equally appropriate for the mid '80s as for 1962. If road users are not expected to pay the full cost of their journeys, why expect rail users to do so?

In the autumn great strength of feeling built up, especially in Scotland following a visit by Dr Beeching. He certainly gave a 'take it or leave it' impression in his public image, and it was reported that all who spoke to him regarded his mind as already made up, though *Trains Illustrated* commented that the real target should be the government.

As the winter dragged on, government and BRB tried to keep their cards as close as possible to their chests. Their opponents speculated with increasing accuracy what the expected Beeching Report would contain. Re-reading the technical press one is surprised how their foresight matches our hindsight. Speculation then ended with the publication of the report in March 1963.

Trains Illustrated summed it up: 'Despite the staring headlines of "bombshell" which greeted it, there are few shattering surprises in the Beeching Plan.' On page 56 of the report it is stated: 'The thought underlying the whole report is that the railways should be used to meet that part of the total transport requirement of the whole country for which they offer the best available means and that they should cease to do things for which they are ill suited.' Readers were assured that only those services would be eliminated 'which by their very nature railways are ill suited to provide', and that 'to retain only those parts of the existing system which are virtually certain to be self-supporting . . . would lead to a grave risk of destroying assets which, in the event, might have proved to be of value'.

A train for Mildenhall branches from the Cambridge–Ely Line at Barnwell Junction. Unusually there were no main-line platforms at this so-called junction.

So far so good, these are excellent sentiments. But the seriousness of the situation as it affected lightly trafficked lines was then dealt with. In 1961 the route mileage of BR passenger services was 13,830, having already shrunk from over 17,000 miles in 1948. To this, of course should be added the 4,000 miles open only to freight. Of this total, 33 per cent carried 1 per cent of the traffic (no mention was made of the fact that one third of the road network carried 2 per cent of the total road traffic). It was also evident that hundreds of stations were taking less in revenue than the cost of keeping them open. Thirty-four stations produced 26 per cent of the revenue.

Details were given of margins – negative and positive – of revenue over costs and the conclusion reached was that if DMUs were used, a traffic flow of 6,000 passengers a week over any particular section would be needed to cover direct operating costs. Even more important, in the light of subsequent wholesale freight withdrawals, the system costs, that is the cost of track and signalling, would not be covered by less than 12,000 passengers per week, even if there was a reasonable flow of freight with which these costs could be shared. If there were no freight traffic, to cover the full costs a flow of at least 17,000 passengers a week would be required.

But the report gives no indication that system costs could be reduced from the levels then pertaining by the introduction of new signalling technology, 'bus-stop' stations and 'pay-trains', and the simplification of track. Yet in 1966 the East Suffolk line carried over 2,000 passengers a day (say 11,000 per week). Gerard Fiennes considered, 'we could run a lot of railway profitably on that'. He also considered that the £225,000 cost which had been given to the TUCC seemed enormous for 45 route miles and that this could be reduced to £84,000.

In the report a sample of ten lines was used to analyse costs in greater detail (Appendix 2, Table 1, of the report). All have since been closed except the service from Leeds and Bradford to Skipton via Ilkley, which still continues as far as the latter and will therefore be excluded from consideration. Of the rest, Banff–Tillynaught was still worked by steam, services on the rest being maintained by DMUs and to a lesser extent by diesel locomotives, though two battery-powered units formed some of the Aberdeen–Ballater trains. This was reflected in the 'movement expenses per train mile' which varied from 7s 7d (nearly 40p) for the steam Banff branch to 2s 6d (12½p) for the Deeside line to Ballater and 2s 4d (nearly 12p) for the Gleneagles–Crieff–Comrie service.

From the figures given in the table the net savings per mile to be achieved by withdrawal of the passenger services can be calculated. The Calne branch (Wilts) was the biggest loss-maker, with a net escapable cost of £4,800 per mile per year. Now in 1961 the gross operating deficit over the 17,830 route miles of BR then open was almost £87 million. From this we can calculate that the average system-wide operating loss was £4,879 per route mile. This is virtually equal to that of the Calne branch, and assuming the costings to be correct, it would seem reasonable to consider that line for closure. But on all the other eight lines the loss per mile was less than the system average. The

Yatton–Clevedon branch (Somerset) lost £4,475 per annum, but four of them lost less than £1,000 per mile, and Sunderland–West Hartlepool only £291. It is therefore difficult to see how closure of these lines was going to eliminate the overall deficit as quickly as the closure of a few trunk lines, say Euston–Crewe.

But the feature of the report which really captured public attention was the seemingly interminable lists of proposed line and station closures, which occupied 35 pages of the 148 page document. Even if one accepted the plan in principle, the stark reality of what it meant was brought home by seeing one's own local station on the death list.

These lists included 55 services 'under consideration for withdrawal before the formulation of this Report', of which 31 were stated to have already been implemented, including the lines to Brecon and the Didcot–Newbury. They also named a further 266 passenger services 'to be withdrawn'. In view of what has already been said of BTC/BRB attitudes, it will be noted the wording was not 'proposed for withdrawal'. Of the 266, 38 were local services, such as Crewe–Preston–Carlisle, on main lines not themselves proposed for closure.

One can find anomalies: if local services between Fort William and Mallaig were withdrawn, what would be left? On the other hand the Craigendoran–Arrochar section of the West Highland line was listed for complete closure. But the picture was there for all to see: over 200 more lines – totalling over 5,000 route miles – over and above those already closed or proposed for closure were to go, as were 2,363 passenger stations on lines which would remain open. Instead of the piecemeal approach hitherto adopted, here was an overall picture of a vast closure programme.

Passing trains in the Welsh Marches. A Brecon–Hereford train with a GW Collett 0–6–0, No. 2287, crosses a Hereford bound train at Hay-on-Wye on 28 August 1959.

The Implementation of the Plan

The report was debated in parliament. By all accounts the level of debate fell far short of the importance of the occasion. *Modern Railways* said:

> The only construction which could be put on Marples' abysmal handling of the Parliamentary Debate, repeated pre-judgements that one third of the system was to be closed and his inability to make any other answer than he would 'look into it' is that this [Conservative] Government is as dogmatic as the 1948 [Labour] one that created the BTC.

The opposition and those Conservative members of marginal constituencies were alike unable either to rise above the level of previous debates – when time and time again light rail-buses, which the BTC were said to have wilfully neglected, were triumphantly brought forward as the panacea which would bring the most lightly trafficked line into the black – or to make a reasoned case for subsidy. The Lords' debate was equally unproductive; all that was said had been said already.

So the machine rolled forward and soon the consultative committees were swamped with closure proposals. But the 1962 Transport Act had gone far to deny them any useful role. The area committees now had to submit their reports direct to the minister, thus by-passing the CTCC and preventing that body from having an overview of policies and their consequences. Nor could the TUCCs question the traffic figures and costings produced by the BRB in support of its proposals; all they could do was to make recommendations on the extent of hardship. Furthermore the BRB now only had to bring final closure proposals to them. Services could be reduced so far as the board wished, even to the extent of limiting them to one service in the small hours, without reference to the TUCC. Finally, the BRB was relieved of the duty to refer freight closures. Freight depots could be closed at will and freight traffic diverted from lines with passenger traffic which would cease to be viable once it had to carry the whole cost. The lack of public accountability of nationalised industries, a topic invoking constant Conservative criticism, was being exploited to the full with the support of a Conservative government.

At a press conference unveiling the report, Dr Beeching revealed his plans to send the first batch of closure proposals to the TUCCs in May 1963, following the April debate in parliament. He hoped the procedure would be speeded up by the consideration of the proposals in groups. He stated that the first closures would come in the autumn, and that they would reach a peak in 1964 and then taper off in 1965. But in the event, in spite of the TUCCs' reduced powers, the procedures took a long time to grind through to their almost inevitable conclusion. The pipeline became choked. By October 1963 the TUCCs had 120 proposals before them. It was not until January 1964 that the first of the proposals appearing initially in the report were finally implemented, and the lines from Harrogate to Cross Gates and to Church Fenton closed. In March Dr Beeching publicly denied he had threatened resignation over the slow progress.

But it was election year and opposition was hardening. On 12 February the minister announced no closure of lines to holiday resorts before 1 October 1964. Opposition was fuelled by the realisation that well-used and regionally important lines were now threatened, and – because of the minister's dogmatic insistence that a truncated railway system must be a prelude to and not part of any new transport policy – was focussing more and more attention on the incompleteness of the report, even among those initially welcoming it.

Nowhere was opposition stronger and more articulate than in the Highlands. The Highland lobby is traditionally powerful and this occasion was no exception. The report had slated for closure all lines north of Inverness, 231¾ route miles. In February 1964 the government-appointed Highland Panel, charged with advising the government on economic development in the Highlands, threatened resignation if the lines were closed. F. G. Thompson, a leading figure in the Scottish Vigilantes' Association, condemned the report roundly, if a trifle unfairly, but giving voice to widespread suspicions. 'No professional accountant, or back-street bookie's runner for that matter, would put his name to figures of that sort,' was his comment on the case for closure.

Then, on 12 February 1964 the minister refused closure of the Central Wales line. It was another political hot potato. In those days it carried a heavy freight traffic over the 83¼ miles between Craven Arms and Pontardulais, and in 1960 it had been announced that centralised traffic control would be installed. It was rumoured that some of the equipment had even been delivered on site. But now the BRB wanted to avoid the cost by withdrawing the lightly loaded passenger service to allow more paths for freight trains and the closure of passing loops. In June 1962 withdrawal notices were published. At the enquiry there was ample evidence of hardship and even the Western Region Commercial Officer agreed it would be considerable. But, he said, of stations north of Llandovery, only Llandrindod Wells and Knighton were taking more than £5 a day from passenger bookings.

The TUCC referred their findings on hardship to the minister, who upheld them and refused consent to closure. He had bowed to political pressure. It was election year and it was unkindly said the line ran through a number of marginal constituencies. At the time of writing, two-car DMUs still travel the line five times a day in each direction, but there are no freight trains with which to share the track costs. Cost/revenue ratios must be the worst in the country.

No doubt fortified by this decision, pressure from the Highland lobby increased and again a reprieve was won. This was just as well. North Sea oil was just over the horizon, though apparently unperceived by Beeching, who had written in the report: 'It has been assumed that the pattern [of the distribution of industry and population] will continue to be basically similar to that at present.' This was at a time when the tremendous post-war changes in that pattern were gathering momentum.

In its turn the Northern Ireland government applied pressure to ensure retention of one of the two lines to Stranraer. In the event it was the one from

Ayr via Girvan that survived. Probably, in view of subsequent traffic growth, BRB now regrets the loss of the one from Dumfries, which could have been used either as a substitute or as an additional route.

In contrast there was no orchestrated opposition from the English shires, nor any similar cases of politically inspired refusals of closure. It is hard to resist the thought that the 'grassy shires' were so solidly Conservative they could be safely ignored by Conservative and Labour governments alike. On the other hand many of the threatened lines were suburban or outer-suburban, including Broad Street–Richmond, Stockport–Buxton and New Brighton–Wrexham. These proposals were in direct conflict with the conclusions of the Buchanan Report on Traffic in Towns, also published in 1963 and also accepted by the government. This pointed to the impossibility of dealing with all urban movement by the private car, even in moderately sized towns. Many of these lines were therefore eventually spared.

During the election campaign Harold (now Lord) Wilson promised the electors of Whitby he would rescind the closure orders on the lines from Scarborough and from Malton. When Labour were victorious and he became prime minister, he was called upon to redeem his promise. It then transpired that under the 1962 Act, once the Minister of Transport had agreed to closure, it was impossible for the prime minister or anyone else to order re-opening. The two lines in question duly closed on 8 March 1965. The more the historian studies the 1962 Transport Act and its consequences, the more he is surprised by the thinking, or rather the lack of thought, behind it and the poverty of criticism and opposition.

However, the new Minister of Transport, T. Fraser, did make one sensible move. He ordered the BRB to give him prior notice of all closure proposals, so that if they were so contentious they would most probably be refused no further action need be taken. In this way some proposals, notably the suburban ones, including Broad Street–Richmond and the Buxton line, never came to the TUCCs. Otherwise the closure machine rolled on as inexorably under the new Labour government as under the old Conservative one.

Beeching II

It also began to emerge that the closure list in the Beeching Report was not the final one. In 1965 the BRB published a report entitled 'The Development of the Major Railway Trunk Routes'. This indicated which major routes the board recommended for extensive capital investment in track and signalling to permit higher speeds and increased capacity.

This report is usually known as Beeching II. Though it had perhaps even greater significance than the original Beeching Report, it received little publicity or popular attention. This was largely because, though it was intended eventually to close those lines not listed as being suitable for large-scale investment, this was not openly declared. Perhaps some lessons on diplomacy had been learned. But it was envisaged there would be no railways at all west of a line

The small town of Monmouth once boasted two stations. An auto-train is about to leave Troy Station for Chepstow. The line on which a connecting train stands leads through Mayhill Station to Ross-on-Wye.

drawn between Chester, Swansea and Plymouth.

But in addition to these outlying limbs of the system, the main target had now become 'duplicating main lines', it being held there was insufficient traffic to justify more than a single route. It was never pointed out that though there might be two routes between X and Y, one line might serve A, B and C and the other D, E and F, and so it was never established how much of this intermediate traffic would be lost. Thus it was stated that there were three routes between London and Exeter, via Bristol, via Westbury and via Salisbury, and that one of these must go. Similarly it was pointed out there were too many trans-Pennine routes.

Additionally, in the next three years there were constant hints of plans to divert long-distance Midland trains south of Leicester on to the West Coast main line and to terminate all Bedford suburban trains at Moorgate. This would allow the closure of the main line between Bedford and either Market Harborough or Leicester and of St Pancras itself.

The trouble was there seemed to be no agreement on the criteria for selecting main lines for closure. I recall a conversation with a London Midland officer in 1967. After congratulating him on the excellent loadings being enjoyed by a new morning service introduced from Manchester to Euston, I expressed the hope more trains would soon be put on. He replied there was a shortage of paths for the return services in the evening peak. I pointed out if this was the case, how would it be possible to divert the Midland trains to Euston? He then said he had been talking about path shortage if trains ran at 5 minute intervals, but the new signalling would permit 2½ minute ones. Obviously there were two official answers, one for Manchester and one for the east Midlands and he had been forced into giving them both.

Besides, the question of whether the Midland trains should be routed from Leicester to Euston via Nuneaton or via Market Harborough and Northampton, a shorter route but necessitating retention of more route mileage, was never resolved; nor was the choice between retaining the ex-GWR West of England line via Westbury or the ex-LSW one via Yeovil Junction. Again, while the original Beeching Report proposed closure of the Hope Valley line across the Pennines, the so-called 'fast' trains between Manchester and Sheffield were diverted over it in 1967 from the Woodhead line, while a pay-train service of stopping trains which extends the suburban service from Manchester to New Mills on to Sheffield is maintained in addition. Furthermore, the electrified

Trains passing at Fawley (Hereford) on 16 May 1964. The 10.30 Hereford–Gloucester enters, while the 09.48 Gloucester–Hereford waits.

Woodhead route, earmarked for investment in 1965, was finally closed to all traffic in 1981.

Fortunately many of these questions were settled by the steady growth of passenger traffic created by the new Inter-City package. This has prevented St Pancras, the Newcastle–Edinburgh line and at least one of the West of England routes from figuring further in a book on forgotten railways.

In addition, the original Beeching Report closure programme was having little effect on the BRB's deficits. The goal of reducing the system to a 'profitable core' was as elusive as ever – not surprising in view of the fact that, with the high level of fixed costs involved in running a railway, declining revenue cannot be matched by cost reductions, and also that many of the closed lines had less than average deficits.

At this point, Mrs Barbara Castle was appointed Minister of Transport, in 1965. In 1967 she announced that the rail network would be stabilised at 11,000 route miles, the point roughly attained by the closure programme at that date. Beeching II as a further closure programme was put on the shelf, and so for the purposes of this book the Beeching era could be said to have come to an end.

Analysis of the Closures

The 1950–62 period saw great inroads into the rural branch lines and the Beeching era their virtual extinction. The Beeching Report left only some dozen stub-end branches untouched, and most of these were subsequently condemned. In addition, as we have seen, inroads had begun on cross-country lines. These inroads were greatly accelerated in the report, where closure proposals included: the Somerset & Dorset; the lines from Peterborough to both Rugby and Northampton; Ruabon–Barmouth Junction; and Dumfries–Stranraer. The dividing line between a cross-country route and a secondary main line is perhaps open to argument. But there was no argument about the main-line status of the Great Central's trunk and of the Waverley route from Edinburgh to Carlisle, and both of these were among the proposed closures.

But careful examination of the Beeching Report maps reveals not only the extent of the planned closures, but, by their absence from the maps, how many closures had already taken place. It was true that lines through rural areas that were in fact outer-suburban ones were to survive, not only in the Home Counties, but provincial ones such as Altrincham to Chester. But truly rural lines with stopping trains and numerous wayside stations, such as the lines from Nottingham to Lincoln and to Grantham are now very rare indeed. Where they do exist, they have been modified out of all recognition.

As we have seen, 1963 saw a slackening of the rate of closures after a peak in 1962, due to a temporary moratorium while the Beeching plan was being debated in parliament. In 1963, closures dropped to 324 route miles, but 1964 saw the all-time peak, when 1,058 miles of line lost their passenger services. But whereas until 1960 many lines were retained for freight, total closure was now

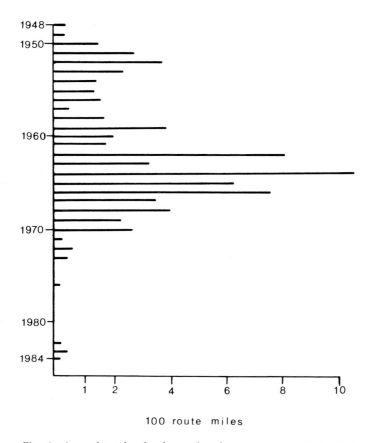

Fig. 6   Annual totals of mileage closed to passengers 1948–1984.

usual. In 1966 virtually the whole of the former Somerset & Dorset main line from Mangotsfield through Bath and Templecombe to Broadstone was totally closed, the few miles which were retained for freight being closed soon after.

The rate of closure remained high for the next few years, though gradually falling off from the 1964 peak: the figure for 1965 was 769 route miles, but 1967's total was 259, and closures in 1969 amounted to 234 route miles, with 271 in 1970. But with few new proposals now entering the pipeline, the pace of closure rapidly fell off. The next year, 1971, saw only 23 miles closed, while 1974 was the first year since 1945 in which no lines are recorded as having lost their passenger service. Paradoxically, 1977–81 inclusive was perhaps the longest period without any closures since the 1840s.

A point of interest is that the maps and the lists did not turn out to be the immutable 'tablets of stone' they appeared to be when first published. (As already hinted, one of the underlying flaws of the Beeching Report was its tone of inflexibility.) Though the overwhelming majority of threatened lines were eventually closed, a considerable mileage proposed for closure has remained open. This, as we have seen, was partly the result of political pressure applied on the government, and partly the result of changed traffic flows. On the other

91

The Warrington & Stockport's line was still busy with freight but the exiguous passenger service ceased in 1962, soon after this photograph of an Oxford Rd. (Manchester) to Warrington push-and-pull train calling at Dunham Massey was taken.

hand, some lines not proposed for closure eventually felt the axe. The best example was the greater part of the Oxford–Bletchley–Cambridge line (see page 103).

If we examine the closures on a regional basis, we find that by 1970 there are only five long-distance lines, with a few branches from them, in the whole of Wales. Principally these are the two trunk lines, from Severn Tunnel Junction to Fishguard and from Chester to Holyhead. The former has two branches in the far West, to Milford Haven and Pembroke Dock, while Cardiff is still the centre of an albeit-very-much-reduced network of local services. But all the other services in South Wales have gone. The Holyhead line has two branches, both from Llandudno Junction, but again, the network of lines in the Wrexham industrial area and the once numerous branches along the North Wales coast are no more. Though Mid Wales never did have an extensive network, it now only has the Shrewsbury–Aberystwyth/Pwllheli and the Central Wales lines. But the branches from the Shrewsbury–Hereford–Newport line which served the Marches have also all gone. Finally, the tourist line to Devil's Bridge survives as BR's only steam-worked, narrow-gauge line and a remnant to remind us of the once extensive 'queer and quaint'.

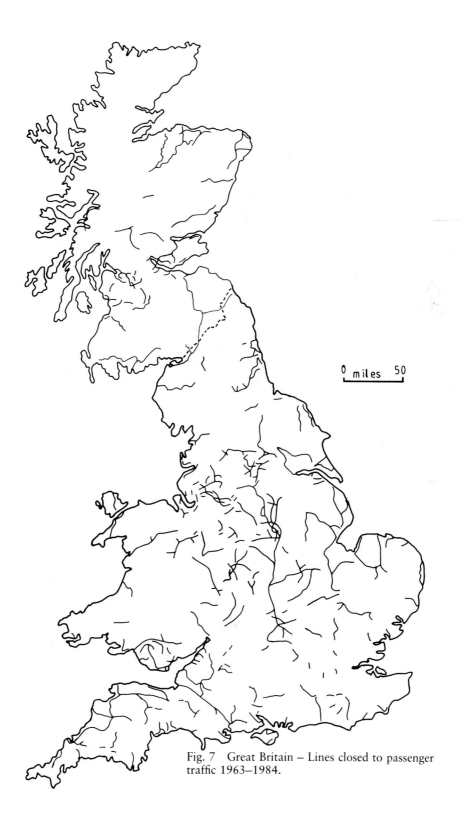

0 miles 50

Fig. 7   Great Britain – Lines closed to passenger traffic 1963–1984.

In Scotland, the southern uplands now have only the three trunk lines, two from Carlisle and one from Berwick, shorn of branches and intermediate stations, and the line from Ayr to Stranraer. In the central lowlands the Glasgow suburban network has survived as the backbone of public transport, but elsewhere the once extensive network of secondary and branch lines, together with the Edinburgh suburban services, have all been forgotten. In contrast, the never extensive network in the Highlands has survived to a remarkable extent, except that even here the short branches have all disappeared, except for that to Thurso. But the North East, beyond Aberdeen, has lost everything except a few stations on the Aberdeen–Inverness line. It is not generally appreciated what a big area this is and what a large mileage it has lost.

In the north of England an almost clean sweep has been made of rural lines, while the coalfield has also suffered heavily. On the other hand, closures have left the conurbation of West Yorkshire less affected, though here the once numerous competing lines, especially those of the GNR, have been eliminated to leave a single route between each major town. On the other side of the Pennines the heartland of the North West, the area bounded by Greater Manchester, Merseyside, Crewe and Preston, has suffered even less, though there have been a number of closures of the more lightly used lines. A number of these were closed when Central station, Manchester, closed in 1969. In the

On the 'Cuckoo'. A train for Eastbourne takes the 'Cuckoo' line at Redgate Mill Junction and starts the long hard climb to Mayfield.

Journey's end for thousands of holiday makers and with station facilities typical of the smaller resort – Hunstanton (GER). The 'East Anglian Pullman' stands at the second platform from the left.

West Midlands the principal loss was that of the ex-GWR main line from Bordesley Junction through Snow Hill and Wolverhampton to Oxley. There were also closures of all the lines, ex-GWR and ex-LNWR, to Dudley and of most of the lines to Walsall. But there have been few closures in the commuter belt south of Birmingham, as there have been in that south of Manchester.

However, it is the English lowlands which have suffered most heavily from closures. This is true whatever measure of comparison is taken: its relatively dense rural population; its numerous small and medium-sized towns, which were growing as fast or faster than in any other part of the country; or the former extent of the railway system. East Anglia and Lincolnshire now have a very reduced network, if network it can be called. North Norfolk, for example, was once quartered by a close pattern of passenger-carrying lines. Today, north of the Ely–Norwich–Yarmouth line there are only two others: one from Ely to King's Lynn; the other from Norwich to Cromer and Sheringham. Some junction stations, Dereham, Long Melford and Melton Constable among them, have been swept into complete oblivion, their sites far from any line. Others such as Bury St Edmunds and Wymondham have been shorn of their branches. On a recent visit to an unfamiliar part of Lincolnshire, now without railways, passing through towns such as Spilsby, Horncastle and Woodhall Spa brought a recollection that all once had a line serving them.

The south Midlands have also lost an enormous mileage. This large and rather amorphous area has had its formerly extensive network reduced to a few main lines, themselves denuded of intermediate stations. For the most part these radiate from London; only one west–east cross-country line survives, the one meandering from Birmingham to Peterborough through Nuneaton, Leicester and Oakham. But eastward from the run-down Oxford–Worcester line to the East Coast main line is a broad swathe of prosperous rural areas and numerous towns. Here closures have had perhaps more effect than anywhere else. Secondary and branch lines are almost non-existent (see Fig 1, p. 25).

The same story must be told for Wessex and for the counties on the Welsh border. The county of Gloucester (shorn of the southern part which went to Avon) now has six stations: Lydney, Stonehouse, Stroud, Kemble, Cheltenham and Gloucester itself. The historic county of Hereford has only three stations other than Hereford.

In the West Country the smaller seaside resorts, unless they happen to be on a main line which runs along the coast (as Dawlish and Teignmouth are), have been largely deprived of rail access. But there are some curious contrasts. In South Devon the branches to Lyme Regis, Seaton, Sidmouth, Kingswear (from Paignton) and Kingsbridge were all closed, as were the lines to the North Devon and Somerset resorts of Bude, Ilfracombe and Minehead. But the Cornish branches to Looe, Newquay and St Ives remain open. Incidentally the first two of these escaped listing in the Beeching Report.

In contrast, the network of the Home Counties has seen little change compared with other areas. Only a few branches outside the main commuter zones have been eliminated. South Hertfordshire has lost the branches from Hatfield to St Albans and from Welwyn Garden City to Luton and to Hertford. In particular the electrified lines of Southern Region survived almost intact, apart from some short oddities such as the branch from Haywards Heath to Horsted Keynes. Even the branches to Sheerness, Alton and Seaford were not considered for closure, though traffic on some of them fell well below 5,000 passengers per week and hundreds of miles of similar lines were closed elsewhere. As far as Southern Region was concerned it was the non-electrified lines served by the new diesel-electric multiple units that were involved in the final round of closures in 1965–7. This affected the Wealden lines south of East Grinstead and in West Sussex, the New Romney branch in Kent and a number of services in Hampshire.

The system map issued with the 1984–5 BR timetable bears a very close resemblance to that of 1970. But it reveals a very slim and open network when compared with that shown on a 1955 map. At that date, with the exception of the remoter highlands of Scotland and Wales, very few places were more than 5 miles from a functioning passenger station. Lynton, 17 miles from the station at Minehead and 21 miles from that at Barnstaple, was very much an exception. But today such distances are commonplace.

PART II
CLOSURE THEMES

A Barnard Castle – Tebay train among the Pennines. The locomotive is an ex-NER J21 0–6–0.

CHAPTER 5

Changing Attitudes and Policies

The echoes of the massive closure programme of 1950 to 1967 took a long time to die away. In Northumberland the single-track Alston branch diverged from the Newcastle–Carlisle line at Haltwhistle and followed the deep and narrowing valley of the South Tyne for 13 miles into the very heart of the northern Pennines to reach the small isolated market town of Alston, reputedly the highest town in the country. An obvious candidate for closure under the policies we have been examining, agreement was given by the minister in 1962, subject to improvements to the parallel road, to allow an 'adequate' bus service. When the latter was inaugurated, which was not until 1976, the line duly closed. The cost of the road improvements was not debited to the bus service, as logically it should have been. We may therefore speculate on the willingness of the operator to provide a bus service and of the patrons to use it if they had to bear the costs incurred on their behalf. Yet the railway was expected to bear its full costs and was closed because it did not.

On the other hand there were few references to the TUCCs between 1967 and the end of 1982, and none of these were of great significance. In fact, one reference, involving the closure of New Holland Pier in 1981, demonstrates the change which came about in the intervening period.

The north Lincolnshire branches from Habrough to New Holland Pier and from New Holland Town to Barton-on-Humber were listed for closure in the Beeching Report. But they survived, as they formed the only public-transport link from the southern terminal of the Humber ferry. With agreement obtained for the Humber Bridge, no-one was willing to spend money on replacing the rail link along the ramshackle pier. When the bridge was opened the ferry was closed, but the lines survived except for that along the pier. The climate had changed completely, the local authorities now had wide planning powers over public transport, and the government was willing to subsidise this vital activity. So trains now run from Cleethorpes through Habrough to Barton. Instead of reversing at New Holland on to the Barton branch, they use the direct southern spur of what was once a triangular junction. Here new platforms to serve New Holland have been erected. At Barton, connections, advertised in the BR timetables, are made with the Hull–Scunthorpe bus service, which crosses the bridge.

Barbara Castle

These examples illustrate the changes in policy which came about after 1967. The initiator of these changes was Mrs Barbara Castle. Her time in office provides a landmark of equal importance to that of the Beeching Report, and before looking in some detail at some notable closure cases it is appropriate to summarise her influence. Appointed Minister of Transport in 1965, she soon revealed she was determined to look at the country's transport as a whole – as a system. This was in stark contrast with so many of her predecessors and successors, who have confined themselves to tinkering round the edges.

For our present purpose two very significant policy changes were initiated by Mrs Castle. The first has already been referred to, her stabilisation of the network at 11,000 route miles, which we can fairly call, following the press comments of the time, 'Mrs Castle's basic railway'. The other was the acceptance of the principle of subsidy for public transport. Until at least 1963 subsidy had been a dirty word for all political parties. But the occasional refusal by the minister to sanction a closure inflicted an illogical burden on the BRB. It had been told to break even, but it now had imposed on it the duty of maintaining a service it had sought to close because it was a contributor to the losses. But through Mrs Castle the Labour government came to recognise the need for subsidy.

On 18 April 1966, speaking at a lunch to mark the inauguration of electrification to Euston, she raised the need for subsidy and for investigating what economies could be made before suggesting closure. Almost at the same time she reprieved six suburban services, including the 1,500 volt dc electric line from Manchester to Glossop, on the grounds of the need to keep commuter traffic off the roads. 'I am only prepared to agree to [rail] cuts where they will not conflict with Regional Plans or cause social or economic damage.'

The new policies were formulated in the White Paper of July 1966, 'Transport Policy' (Cmnd 3057), which stated, 'It is now widely recognised that the railway system cannot play its proper role in the economy of the country and also comply with the 1962 Act' (para 16) and, 'For the foreseeable future, the country's transport system must include a substantial rail network' (para 17). This was followed by another White Paper on 'Railway Policy' (Cmnd 3439) published in November 1967. This stated that, 'On the passenger side it is clear that there are many railway services which have little or no prospects of paying their way in a commercial sense, yet whose value to the community outweighs their accounting cost.'

These policies were implemented in the 1968 Transport Act. This provided the minister with the necessary powers to subsidise rail passenger services deemed to be 'socially necessary'. Local authorities were also empowered to subsidise passenger services, including rail, while the authorities administering the major provincial conurbations were given the duty of planning all public transport, rail as well as bus, in their areas through the Passenger Transport Authorities. The 1973 Local Government Act set up the metropolitan counties, which became the transport authorities working through the Passenger Transport Executives, and also laid on the 'shire' counties the duty of planning public transport. Another Act extended an essentially similar system to Scotland.

Sadly for the transport industry and its users Mrs Castle was moved to the Ministry of Labour and her influence was lost. Thus the amendments to the Transport Act of 1968 and above all the negative way in which it was implemented by her successor, Sir Richard Marsh, as well as by the 1979 Conservative government, undid much of her good work. But so far this has had little effect on the topic of this book.

Ireland

Interestingly, there was also a fundamental change across the water in both parts of Ireland which paralleled that in Great Britain. In the Republic the closure programme under the Andrews regime in the CIE (page 70) eventually ground to a halt, leaving a very slim network. The narrow-gauge lines and the highly individualistic broad-gauge rural lines had been eliminated, together with most of the secondary main lines. But the 1970s saw not only an end to closures, but considerable investment in diesel locomotives, passenger coaches and specialised freight wagons. This culminated in 1984 with the opening of the Dublin suburban electrification, $22\frac{1}{2}$ route miles. This included the line to Bray, which had been steadily run down during the 1950s and 1960s.

In Northern Ireland the run-down had gone even further. The much disliked Ulster Transport Authority (page 70) had come to the verge of financial collapse in 1962. After the subsequent Benson inquiry all road services were removed from the UTA and further rail closures initiated. But here too the last major closure came in 1965 with the elimination of the second route to Londonderry, that of the GNR(I) from Portadown via Omagh. Then in 1968 Northern Ireland Railways was established, the new authority actively pursuing an aggressive marketing policy. It also opened a new Central station on the long-closed line connecting the GNR(I) and the Belfast & County Down Railway. This also entailed re-opening to passengers the Lisburn–Antrim line for the Belfast Central–Londonderry trains.

Notable Closure Battles

We have seen how opposition to closures was at first very limited, but became more widespread and vocal as closures began to affect more heavily used lines. Some cases were particularly hard fought. A study of these more contentious cases can tell us much about the reasoning of the various parties and also about the decision-making processes and changing policies.

Stainmore

Rails from the east reached Barnard Castle in 1856. Westward loomed the barrier of the High Pennines and the South Durham & Lancashire Union

Company was promoted to overcome this with a 35 mile line to join the West Coast main line at Tebay. Opened in 1861, another connection from Kirkby Stephen to the LNWR, at Eden Valley Junction south of Penrith, was completed in 1862. The route was one of the most spectacular in the country. The watershed was crossed by the 1,370ft summit on the open moorland of Stainmore, with wide westward views as the trains began to descend to Kirkby Stephen. On both the steeply inclined eastern and western approaches to Stainmore the line crossed deep valleys or 'gills' over nine viaducts, the creation of Sir Thomas Bouch, designer of the ill-fated first Tay Bridge. These included the all-metal Belah (196ft high) and Deepdale (161ft) viaducts and the stone one at Mousegill (106ft).

The principal function of the line was to convey coal and coke from the West Durham field to the Cumbrian ironworks and to return with ore for those of the North East. To these traffics was added limestone from sidings in the Kirkby Stephen area. Mineral trains with locomotives front and rear struggled up to Stainmore night and day, summer and hard winter alike. In 1867 four mineral trains, with derailed engines and wagons, became stuck in the snow west of Barras on the approach to Stainmore.

In later years holiday traffic between the North East and Cumbria built up. But local passenger traffic was exiguous in the extreme. The timetable reveals that on August Saturdays in 1955 four stopping trains left Barnard Castle for

A DMU from Darlington to Tebay crosses the Lartington Viaduct, typical of the spectacular structures on the Stainmore line.

Kirkby Stephen, as did three 'expresses' to Blackpool from South Shields, Darlington and from Newcastle. But by then freight traffic had declined catastrophically with the decline of the Cumbrian steel industry and the use of imported ore by the plants of the North East.

Regular trains had been withdrawn between Kirkby Stephen and Tebay in 1952 and closure of the line over Stainmore was announced on 9 December 1959. Subsequently fifty-one objections were received, including those from three MPs, twenty-three local authorities and bodies such as the YHA and various chambers of trade. So on 24 February 1960 there was a joint hearing by the North Eastern and North Western TUCCs. The proceedings illustrate the more extensive powers vested in the TUCCs prior to the 1962 Transport Act. For example, objections to withdrawal of freight facilities could be made and Dorman Long, one of the principal freight shippers, were among the objectors.

BR claimed closure would save £103,274 annually, with £257,000 obtained from reclaimed material. Dr K. R. Ashby questioned their figures, which he would not have been allowed to do under the 1962 Act. He claimed that costings were based on twenty-two-wagon limestone trains, where the allowed limit was twenty-seven wagons, and that this had led to falsely high figures for the net savings from diverting this traffic. As for the passenger side, a proposal to extend the DMUs, which had recently taken over the stopping services from Penrith on to Carlisle and Keswick, had been vetoed by the London Midland Region. Again, since services had been reduced as an economy measure, uneconomic stock-working was at too high a level.

The area TUCCs both recommended against closure and they exhorted BR to attract more tourist traffic. The CTCC, to which the recommendations were sent, returned them with the instruction that when the area TUCCs were satisfied that the freight traffic, diverted via the Carlisle and Newcastle line, was being dealt with satisfactorily, the line should be closed.

On 9 December 1960 the TUCCs again met jointly. As a result they maintained closure would yield net savings of only £36,000 annually, very different from BR's calculations. A decision was postponed until a CTCC meeting on 16 January. Ten members voted for closure and six against, but a majority of North Eastern members were against closure. Once again the CTCC referred the matter back on the grounds of the split vote. At yet another joint meeting on 8 June 1961 the North Eastern committee announced agreement to closure. The end came quickly after ministerial approval on 7 December. The last passenger trains between Barnard Castle and Penrith ran on 20 January 1962.

A visit to Kirkby Stephen in September 1963 revealed a picture of desolation. From the main-road bridge a flight of steps led down to the island platform. An all-over roof supported on stone walls covered it and the platform lines. On either side ran two goods loops and there were a number of sidings and a four-road locomotive shed, where once banking engines simmered. It was all fully signalled, rusting and derelict, though the line was open from Eden Valley Junction to the quarries at Hartley, a mile beyond Kirkby Stephen.

Oxford and Cambridge

From the LNWR main line at Bletchley two long branches straggled for 31¼ miles westward to Oxford and eastward for 45¾ miles to Cambridge. The former traversed the pastures and hedgerow elms of the rolling Oxford Clay vale to end in a curious wooden shed, which was called Rewley Road station and which in 1983 still did duty as a garage, disfiguring the approach to what was another wooden shed, the GW station, now happily if unimaginatively rebuilt. Eastwards from Bletchley the line ran through brickfields and no less than nine intermediate stations and halts for 16 miles to Bedford. Beyond there was much agriculture but little population. Trains terminated in the Great Eastern station at Cambridge, architecturally a more worthy structure than Oxford was ever allowed.

These east–west branches crossed many of the trunk lines radiating from London, but originally there were few connections with them and they had little influence on the passenger traffic. During World War II connecting spurs were laid in at Yarnton (with the Oxford–Worcester line), Calvert (with the GC) and Sandy (with the GN). In 1955 it was scheduled for development as an 'outer circle' route round London for freight, and from this sprang the impressive but little-used Bletchley flyover.

On the Oxford–Bletchley line in LMS days. A 'Cauliflower' 0–6–0 is about to leave Verney Junction with a Bletchley train. A Metropolitan train for Quainton Rd. and Aylesbury stands at the other platform. So remote was the station it was named after a local landowner.

Throughout the life of the lines, trains were infrequent, slow and outdated, stopping at most stations and with long waits at Bletchley, even for the rare through trains. Services changed little over the years, except perhaps to deteriorate. Thus in 1906 there were nine weekday departures from Oxford for Bletchley, three continuing to Cambridge and stopping only at Bicester before Bletchley, and six from Cambridge, three through to Oxford. In 1939 there were eight trains from Oxford to Bletchley, only one through to Cambridge. From Cambridge there were six departures, but by now there was a reasonably frequent service of push-and-pull trains between Bedford and Bletchley. The writer recalls a trip that year from Bletchley to Cambridge on the 16.23, a train of three elderly corridor coaches behind an ex-LNWR 4–4–0, through a sun-drenched afternoon calling at stations miles from anywhere and devoid of traffic. In 1955 the timetable was virtually unchanged except that the through train, the 14.28 from Oxford, took 6 minutes short of 3 hours to cover the 77 miles.

In 1959 the 'Bedford Committee' of interested local authorities was established to formulate policies in the event of railway closures. Reasonably, closure of the little used Bedford–Northampton line was unopposed, but there was to be strong opposition to closure of the Oxford–Bletchley–Cambridge route, at that time under threat.

But closure was not yet official and when withdrawal of the Kettering–St Ives–Cambridge service was opposed, the TUCC stated that their acceptance of closure had been influenced by the 'reasonable alternative' available via Bedford. Furthermore the lines were not listed for closure in the Beeching Report.

Track lifting on the Bedford–Cambridge Line. Old North Road Station on 22 August 1968. The bridge carrying the Old North Road (A14) still survives, as do the buildings.

Yet on 6 December 1963 the BRB published notice of closure to passengers. This drastically reduced the west–east routes in the south Midlands at a time when the towns in the area were expanding, the New Town of Milton Keynes had been designated, and national plans envisaged further growth. The Bedford Committee claimed the BRB had ignored this growth potential. This seems likely, for it was not until the 1970s that the board took much interest in monitoring social and economic trends. The committee also made suggestions as to how the services could be improved, not a hard task, and how the lines could be upgraded into a trunk route. Certainly one has always been needed, but never provided.

The 'heads of information' (which is what the BRB called the details of traffic flows and costs they provided for the TUCCs and the objectors) claimed operating expenses of £199,700 annually against passenger revenue of £102,200. Granted that these figures were not 'loaded', but we must remember that costs were inflated by manning little-used stations and running loco-motive-hauled trains as well as DMUs, while revenue was discouraged by the appalling service.

At the East Anglian TUCC hearing on 30 July 1963 the spokesman for the Bedford Committee was allowed to question the traffic figures, pointing out that those given by the Great Eastern line manager were at variance with the heads of information. But even the latter, though less favourable, gave the number of passengers using the stations between Bedford and Bletchley inclusive during a census week as 30,511. It will be recalled (page 83) that the Beeching Report had suggested a flow of 17,000 passengers a week would cover full costs without a contribution from freight traffic. The spokesman also revealed that the details of bus services as given were very misleading. It was stated that there was a bus service between Winslow and Bletchley, but it was not stated that this ran on only one day a week. Times to be taken by the replacement buses were also far too optimistic.

In the face of all this it might have been expected that either the BRB or a Labour government wedded to regional planning would have accepted the part the lines could play in the development of the area with attention to reasonable cost-cutting, attractive service and good marketing, such as are now given to individual lines by BR and local authorities. Instead the war of attrition dragged on. There were also delays caused by inability to license replacement buses due to crew shortages. Bowing, albeit belatedly, to logic the Bletchley–Bedford local service was reprieved, but all other services ceased on 1 January 1968.

Traffic potential is probably confirmed by the fact the replacement bus service between Oxford and Cambridge is among the few to have survived, though there is no mention of it in the BR timetable. There is little doubt that had the present machinery been available in 1963, closure would not have taken place. First, since 1968 subsidies have been given for services considered socially necessary. At first, lists of services were published annually, but under the 1974 Railways Act the procedure was simplified. A Public Service Obligation (PSO) network is identified and a single block grant given, the size of the network being agreed annually between the government and the BRB. Second, the members of the Bedford Committee would have had powers under the 1973 Local Government Act to plan for public transport, and so would have included the lines in their 'strategic plan'. Thirdly, the BRB would have been keener to develop the potential for the route.

The Mid-Hants
This case is notable for the consistent and well-conducted opposition, among the few prior to the 1968 Act to be willing to put their money where their mouth was.

The rolling chalk downlands of eastern Hampshire, with their steep eastern scarp overlooking the Weald, once again became a great corn-growing area after 1939, having experienced many years of depression. Below the scarp was the market town of Alton, reached by the LSWR in 1852. In 1865 the Mid-Hants Company opened a 17 mile line to Winchester Junction on the main line to Southampton. Worked from the first by the LSWR, railwaymen have always spoken of trains on the line going 'over the Alps'. From Alton the line climbed the scarp up a wooded combe at 1 in 60 to Medstead & Four Marks station to drop at 1 in 80 into the beautiful Itchen Valley, which it followed to Winchester. In Southern Railway days a member of the head-office staff lived in the Medstead station-house and travelled daily to Waterloo. When he heard the train leave Ropley on its ten-minute climb he would sit down to breakfast and be on the platform as the train ran in.

The LSWR operated the line as a through route, running a service of stopping trains between Waterloo and Southampton. In 1930 the Southern was running six daily trains from Waterloo 'over the Alps', but electrification to Alton in 1937 brought through working to an end. But it provided a useful diversionary route when the main line via Basingstoke was closed, so much so that it was at one time included in the Bournemouth electrification scheme.

In 1957 D/EMUs replaced steam pull-and-push trains and an hourly interval service was introduced between Alton and Southampton. Passenger traffic increased steadily, while costs were reduced by de-staffing stations and removing passing loops. Subsequently, however, the policy changed. It must be presumed the Southern was expected to assume a fuller share of closures and was reluctant to eliminate electrified services, even if more lightly used than those operated by D/EMUs. In 1967 connections at Alton were, apparently gratuitously, made less convenient. Indeed the timetable did not show any connections at all. Then closure proposals were published.

About a thousand objections were received by the TUCC, who held a hearing in April 1968. Opposition was co-ordinated under the vigorous leadership of the deputy clerk of Winchester Rural District Council. There had been considerable population growth along the line, including a large housing estate

106

The Mid-Hants was one of the hardest fought of the closure battles. In steam days (1951) M7 0–4–4T 30378 takes the 13.49 from Southampton Ctl. out of Alresford on its journey 'Over the Alps'. Apart from the loco's number there is nothing to show the picture was not taken in SR or even LSW days.

near Winchester Junction. On a wider scale, industrial growth was planned for the Southampton–Portsmouth corridor. Winchester RDC were not only pressing BR to provide a new station at Kings Worthy, they had offered to subscribe £10,000 towards the cost and to provide free car-parking.

The objectors pointed to a rail schedule between Alresford and Eastleigh of 23 minutes against one of 120 minutes by bus. Electrification and commercial development of the line were also urged. BR's traffic figures were also questioned. It transpired that the Sunday census of passengers had been taken on a day when engineering work had meant trains beyond both Eastleigh and Alton had been replaced by buses. The TUCC recommended a new census and reported that there would be considerable hardship.

The minister was unable to reach a decision and ordered another inquiry. The local bus company, Aldershot and District Traction, was suffering crew shortages and the objectors seized on this. At the enquiry the TUCC accepted that buses would be able to cope with the existing level of traffic, but not with the expected increase due to population growth.

Meanwhile BR's attitude can only be described as ambivalent. Track maintenance levels were run down, but an electric unit was hauled over the line to test clearances. BR was also becoming resigned to retaining the Ashford–

Hastings service and had declared willingness to develop it. Yet the traffic potential of the Mid-Hants was at least as great.

In March 1969 a deputation from the RDC met the minister to argue that the Carrington Formula (see below) as applied to the line did not give a fair picture of cost savings, and in any case maintenance costs incurred by main-line trains diverted during electrification work had been debited to the local service. The new census was eventually taken, the RDC being allowed to take part. The council claimed that receipts had risen in real terms by 66 per cent over the years 1969–70.

All was in vain. Ministerial approval of closure came in 1971. There were further delays over licensing replacement buses, but the end came on 5 February 1973. It was not the end of the story. The efforts of the Winchester & Alton Railway have made it possible once more to travel 'over the Alps' (page 204).

The Mid-Hants case illustrates a number of points. In the first place, policies and attitudes adopted by the minister and by the BRB for the moment are over-riding, and these may change at any time. Local opposition, even if based on a very good case, can make little progress if the BRB is determined to close a line. A minister deaf to local outcry and blind to social and economic change will change his or her mind only if sufficient political pressure can be brought to bear. However, as we shall see (page 108), once the board is forced to keep a line open, efforts will be made to develop traffic, reduce costs, and even to seek the aid of local authorities.

Second, the Mid-Hants case illustrates the growing willingness of local authorities to support train services. Support has included the re-opening of a number of closed stations, among them the legendary Llanfair PG, while new stations, such as Hattersley and Brinnington in Greater Manchester, have been provided by the PTEs. In 1980 Gwynedd County Council began chartering trains for a Sunday service on the Conway Valley branch to Blaenau Ffestiniog and in 1975 the Yorkshire Dales National Park Authority obtained reinstatement on summer weekends of a local service on the Settle–Carlisle line coupled with the re-opening of Dent and Garsdale stations.

Early in 1971 the Peterborough–Spalding passenger service was withdrawn. But on 7 June that year two round trips a day were reinstated on receipt of £16,000 from three local authorities. But for delays imposed by the Ministry of Transport, there need not have been any interruption of service. In 1983 there were nine trains each way on ordinary weekdays, the line having acquired new importance in 1982 with the total closure of the direct line between March and Spalding and the diversion of trains via Peterborough.

Third, the case illustrates the widespread and not unfounded suspicion that BR concealed revenue and inflated costs in the heads of information. To allay these suspicions the minister had in 1963 appointed an accountant, Sir William Carrington, to investigate. Among his findings was the rather obvious one that the actual money taken at a station is no true guide to the earnings of the service as a whole. For example, the takings at a station serving a seaside resort may be small even if the arriving trains are well loaded with passengers who have come from other stations. The 'Carrington Formula' was used until 1968 and it was this the Winchester RDC questioned as applied to the Mid-Hants.

The Carrington Formula was replaced by the 'Cooper Formula' devised by the City firm of Cooper Brothers. It was the best effort at costing to date. But the allocation of costs to individual services or lines must always be arbitrary and therefore open to question or manipulation. Such costs are also accounting costs. Cost/benefit accounting, which includes the wider social costs involved, is used to justify road expenditure and, since 1968, has been used also for urban rail services. Successive governments have always shied away from applying it to other aspects of rail services. The system is not without fault, but it is an illogicality that what is sauce for the road goose cannot be sauce for the rail gander.

The Waverley Route

Here closure proceedings resulted in more heat than light. For the railway historian and for the rail fan the 98 mile line of the North British from Waverley to Carlisle has a fascination out of all proportion to its national importance, due partly to the interest of its operation and partly to the magnificent country through which it passed. It also served a number of textile-producing, rugby-playing towns with a sense of isolation perhaps more psychological than real.

The summit of the Waverley Route was at Whitrope, reached by A3 60097 'Bayardo' heading a typical Edinburgh–Carlisle semi-fast.

The railway from Edinburgh reached Hawick in 1849. The Border Union Railway extended the line for 43 miles to Carlisle in 1862. It has always been the 'Waverley Route', passing near Abbotsford and traversing country made famous in the Waverley Novels. At Carlisle the NB faced the unremitting enmity of the Caledonian and its LNWR ally. But after 1876 it had a friend, the Midland, which provided most of the through traffic. Grouping and nationalisation, by eliminating competition, reduced its importance.

From Portobello East Junction (Edinburgh) the line climbed through the suburbs and coal-mines and then up the narrowing valley of the Gore Water, a long drag of 15 miles mainly at 1 in 70 until gaining the crest of the Lammermuirs at Falahill Summit. Less steeply, the descent took the line down the valley of the Gala Water to Galashiels and the Tweed. It then undulated gently through the rolling farmlands, diversified by Scots pine shelterbelts, to Hawick. From the very platform end began the 14 mile climb, largely at 1 in 70, into the bare moorlands of the high Cheviots. From Whitrope Summit there was a 10 mile descent, again mostly at 1 in 70 to Newcastleton, to traverse gentler lowlands and the Solway flats to Carlisle. Two miles south of Whitrope was Riccarton Junction, where the Border Counties line diverged for the North Tyne and Hexham. Here was a shed for the bankers and a railway settlement without a road. The island platform station served as post office and village hall, with its refreshment room as public house. On Sundays special trains took residents to church alternately at Hawick and Newcastleton.

The line was costly to work, and only between Galashiels and Hawick was there much local traffic, to and from the small towns so justly famed for their tweed cloth. South of Hawick was a traffic desert. In 1920 the nine intermediate stations between Hawick and Longtown took £7,381 from passenger traffic. The line existed on through freight. The 1949 working timetable shows there were fourteen southbound express freights leaving Hawick daily, having stopped to attach an assistant loco, and two pick-up trains. On the passenger side there were only four expresses and three stopping trains to Carlisle, with three more as far as Riccarton Junction.

With declining freight traffic and increasing ability to divert what remained via Berwick or Carstairs, the writing was therefore on the wall for the Waverley route. There was considerable opposition to closure, especially from the towns of the Middle Tweed, who felt they would suffer greatly increased isolation. It must be remembered they had lost their other rail outlets, from St Boswells to Tweedmouth and to Reston, and closure of the Waverley was also to be total. But formal proposals came surprisingly late – in 1966.

Protests were voluble, but the Borders lacked the political power of the Highland and Welsh lobbies. The protestors also probably made a tactical error in concentrating on trying to keep the whole line open, for by doing so they drew attention from the less costly alternative of a 52¾ mile, DMU-operated, 'basic' railway between Hawick and Edinburgh. Under the methods of operation then pertaining, to retain the Hawick–Edinburgh section would

CARLISLE TO EDINBURGH

DOWN TRAINS   **WEEKDAYS**

		602	117	774		5072	518			594	1046	250		250
No.		602	117	774		5072	518			594	1046	250		250
Description											ECS			
Class		H	B	K		B	E			E	C	B		B
Departs from				Selkirk 4.25 p.m.		Berwick 3.28 p.m.					Carlisle No. 12, 2.40 p.m.			
Previous Times on Page				W87		W89								
		SO PM	SX PM	SX PM		HC PM	PM			PM	SO PM	SX PM		SO PM
CARLISLE (Citadel Stn.)	1										2 48	3 37		3 37
Carlisle (Canal Yard)	2						1 35			2 35				
Canal Junction	3						1 37			2 37	2 52	3 41		3 41
Brunthill	4						1 40			2 40				
Parkhouse Halt	5													
Harker	6													
Lyneside	7													
¶Fauldmoor	8													
Longtown Junction	9											3 52		3 52
Longtown Junction	10						1 51			2 51		3 54		3 54
Scotch Dyke	11													
Riddings Junction	12						2 0			3 0		4N 2		4N 2
Penton	13											4 8		4 8
Kershope Foot	14		..*									4 16		4 16
Newcastleton	15						2 22			3P29		4 23		4 23
Steele Road	16											4 33		4 33
Riccarton Junction	17						2 57			4 7		4 43		4 43
Whitrope Siding	18						3 5			4 15		▲▲		
Shankend	19											4 57		4 57
Stobs	20											5 3		5 3
Stobs Camp	21						3 50							
Hawick	22						4▼0			4▼42		5 10		5 10
Hawick	23	4 0		4 15			4 35			6 5		5 16		5 16
Hassendean	24			4 23								5 23		5 23
Belses	25			4 30								5 29		5 29
Charlesfield Halt	26													
Kelso Junction	27					4 55								
St. Boswells Junction	28		4 37			4 56						5 36		5 36
St. Boswells Junction	29	4 33					5 2			6 32		5 40		5 40
Ravenswood Junction	30													
Melrose	31											5 47		5 47
Selkirk Junction	32					4 50								
Galashiels	33					4 55						5 53		5 53
Galashiels	34	4 49					5 16			6 46		5 57		5 57
¶Paterson's No. 1 Siding	35													
¶ Do. No. 2 Siding	36													
¶Sanderson & Murray's Siding	37													
Kilnknowe Junction	38													
Bowland	39											6 6		6 6
Stow	40											6 15		6 15
Fountainhall	41											6 23		6 23
Heriot	42											6 30		6 30
Falahill	43	5 44					6 1			7 31		6 37		6 37
Tynehead	44													
Borthwick Bank	45													
Fushiebridge	46													
Gorebridge	47											6 44		6 44
Lady Victoria Pit Siding	48													
Newtongrange	49													6 50
Hardengreen Junction	50	6 18												
Hardengreen Junction	51						6 26			7 56		6 51		6 53
Eskbank	52											6 53		6 55
Glenesk Junction	53													
Millerhill Junction	54													
Niddrie South Junction	55						6 34			8 7		6 58		7 0
Niddrie West Yard	56						6 39							
Niddrie North Junction	57													
Portobello	58											7 2		7 4
EDINBURGH (Wav.)	59											7 8		7 10
Arrives at										Meadows 8.25 p.m.	Canal 2.53 p.m.			
Forward Times on Page										W55				

A typical extract from the Waverley Route working timetable of 15 September 1952 shows something of the passenger and freight activity.

From Hawick in the Tweed Valley the Waverley Route climbed along the Slitrig Water into the Border Hills. A3 Pacific 60093 takes an up local out of Shankend Station in 1957.

have required a subsidy of 11d (4½p) for every 3½d (1½p) taken in fares. Grant aid, permitted under the 1968 Act, was paid on one or two other services to be retained up to 5p. But to retain the whole line would have needed a subsidy of 100p for each journey, clearly an impossible level.

As usual BR's figures came in for criticism, but no-one could question that passenger traffic was in decline. But what could be questioned was how much of this could be attributed to the fact that BR had constantly threatened closure since 1963, three years before formally advertising the fact. A consultant was retained by the Rt Hon David Steel, whose constituency lay athwart the line. In his detailed report he claimed that on the Hawick–Edinburgh section operating costs could be reduced and revenue increased by reduction to a basic railway providing a reasonably fast interval service (i.e. with trains at regular intervals, say every hour or half-hour) of DMUS, increased traffic being attracted by aggressive marketing techniques. This was obviously true, but at this distance some of his calculations are not particularly convincing. Nor was it likely that his suggestion of financial support from the local authorities would have been received at all enthusiastically by these bodies, so vociferous in their protests against closure of a line they considered essential to the well-being of their areas.

It was pointed out that Galashiels and Hawick, with a combined population of 30,000, were to lose their rail services, while Aberystwyth, with 10,000, was going to continue enjoying the benefits of its rail link. The *Railway Gazette* pointed out that the Cambrian was a less costly line to maintain and operate and that tourism, its mainstay, was negligible in the Borders. One feels that if this last were true, for an area of such magnificent scenery and historical associations, this must have been at least in part due to a long-standing want of initiative in exploiting its railway for this purpose.

But BR wanted to get rid of the surviving through freight traffic. So the procedures dragged on to their inevitable conclusion. Late in 1968 ministerial consent was given and Saturday 4 January began the last week-end of service. It was a day of sullen public protest and the last train did not reach Carlisle until the Monday was well advanced.

Next day BR, in the presence of invited media representatives, symbolically lifted a length of rail at Riddings. They had forgotten the Churchillian wisdom: 'In victory, magnanimity'. Of more significance was that two companies successively floated to take over working the line failed to make progress. It was not simply that BR had failed to appreciate the potential of the line. Meanwhile the Borders soon discovered the railway was not basic to either their society or their economy.

Gateacre

The closure battle fought over the Gateacre service provides an urban example. The Cheshire Lines Committee's Liverpool terminus, aptly named Central, was opened in 1874. In 1879 a branch was opened from a triangular junction east of Hunt's Cross, on the main line to Manchester, through Gateacre and on to Southport. Although competition from tram and bus was strong, by 1930 there was a frequent service from Central to Hunt's Cross, with a much sparser one to Gateacre, where many trains terminated.

The Southport branch lost its passenger service in 1952, except for a skeletal one to Gateacre. This was later augmented and patronage encouraged by cheap fares. Then, in March 1964 proposals were published for the closure of Central

Newcastleton station. An Anglo-Scottish express arrives over the level crossing, scene of the last-day protest described on page 179.

and the line to Hunt's Cross, the diversion of the Manchester and Warrington trains west of Hunt's Cross up the spur to Allerton and on to Lime Street, and the end of the Gateacre service.

The TUCC enquiry was held on 23 September 1964 and revealed considerable opposition from individuals and public bodies. But a census had revealed that 400 of the 650 passengers leaving Central daily on the Gateacre service did so on three trains; most passengers got out at St Michaels; and only 23 people joined the Liverpool-bound trains daily at Gateacre. But the bus services were widely regarded as inadequate.

The minister (Barbara Castle) gave consent to the closure of Central (High Level) and the line from Hunt's Cross in April 1966. The trains from Warrington were duly diverted to Lime Street in September, when Central was due to close. But the Gateacre service continued as the City Transport Department stated they were unable to provide the replacement buses, presumably as part of the City Council's delaying tactics. The BR response was to close most of the entrances to Central, inconveniencing the numerous Mersey-line passengers using Low Level, and to post notices stating: 'All trains now run from Lime Street.' The Gateacre service was run down and patronage lost.

But plans for the Passenger Transport Authority were nearing fruition and the city planners had ideas of reinvigorating the suburban services. The city council offered to assume responsibility for the line, but their enthusiasm cooled on receipt of costings from BR and they asked their transport department to provide buses. The department was unable to comply. BR made arrangements with a private firm and on 2 April 1968 applied for and were granted licences. The city lodged an appeal, whereupon BR made the tactical mistake of announcing closure on a date before the hearing of the appeal and was forced to rescind the notice. The appeal to the Traffic Commissioners was allowed and the licences were withdrawn. The Gateacre service therefore continued, eventually to become the responsibility of the PTA.

Withdrawal came in 1972, but only temporarily. Although Central High Level was dispensed with, the approach line was connected with the electric line to Southport/Ormskirk by the new Link Line through Low Level and under the city centre. A basic 20 minute service ran out to Garston in 1978 and on to Hunt's Cross in 1983.

These events presage the increasing interest shown by planners during the 1970s in the role of rail in urban transport. This arose first from a realisation that the car can never completely replace public transport, while buses suffer car-inflicted congestion. It was a result, secondly, of the setting up of the PTEs, which brought the rail services within their areas under the local planners' control; and thirdly it arose through the willingness of the government to support urban transport under the 1968 Transport Act, and, after 1974, through the TPP system. Under this each metropolitan county had the duty to return annually to the Secretary of State for Transport its Transport Policies and Programme (TPP). This was a five-year rolling programme which included the costings both for capital expenditure and operating subsidies. When the level of each TPP was agreed the government assumed about 65 per cent of the costs. This has led not only to the reprieve of most of the suburban lines listed in the Beeching Report, but to the upgrading of many of them. At the time of writing, however, the government is preparing drastic changes to the TPP system (page 226).

The East Suffolk Line

This case has been included as it is one of the few for which we have the comments of a BR officer involved. It has also been selected to illustrate changes in BR's attitude.

The 49 mile line from Lowestoft to Ipswich, built in a somewhat piecemeal fashion, was completed as a through route in 1859. For the most part it traverses pleasant gently rolling countryside, diversified by more hedges and hedgerow trees than is usual nowadays in East Anglia, coming down briefly at Woodbridge to run along the shore of the Deben estuary. It is an area of rich agricultural land and attractive market towns, which have expanded in recent years – Beccles, Halesworth, Saxmundham, Wickham Market and Wood-bridge. In spite of the gentle topography it was built as a surface line, so gradients though short are steep, curves sharp and, above all, level-crossings numerous. There are thirty-six of them on public roads.

In the early days services were by no means lavish, but always included through expresses to and from London, especially in summer. In the 1950s BR made more use of the line than ever, providing up to twenty-five trains each way on summer Saturdays, including the 'Easterling', non-stop each way between Liverpool Street and Beccles. In November 1958 the basic down weekday service consisted of eleven departures from Ipswich, four of them through from Liverpool Street, together with two freight trains to deal with an already declining traffic.

But the usual gap between revenue and operating costs was setting in. Some economies were attempted – the introduction of DMUs on the local services, station closure and de-staffing, and in 1963 a 45mph speed limit over most of the line. But it was a typical secondary line and predictably was included in the closure list of the Beeching Report. In due course closure proposals were published, in 1965, arousing widespread opposition. On Christmas Eve the TUCC recommended retention.

We have seen that one of the features of the Beeching era was the BRB's determination to proceed with closure in the face of the strongest opposition. One is left with the impression that as time went on, with the exception of elements in the Ministry of Transport (their successors are still alive and well in Marsham Street), British Rail management was the only body who really wished to see the elimination of railways from large tracts of the country.

In his memoirs (*I Tried to Run a Railway*, 1967) G. F. Fiennes tells how, on taking up his appointment as general manager of the Eastern Region, he found the regional management ranged against 'a serried phalanx of the MPs, the TUCC, the local press, the local populace and the railway staff'. They were 'dashing at this phalanx with all the residual courage and waning enthusiasm of the last handful of Kellerman's dragoons in front of Picton's squares at Waterloo'.

Foreseeing ministerial refusal to closure, Fiennes realised that something must be done to forestall accusations that management would continue deliberately to run the service down after they were forced to keep it open, as well as doing this in the run-up to publishing closure proposals. He therefore drew up plans to reduce the line to the basic railway. Taking 'the back of an envelope' he calculated that costs could be reduced from the figure of £250,000 a year given to the TUCC to £84,000 by singling the line, providing automatic crossing loops and level-crossings, unstaffed stations and conductor guards. The revenue had been given as £120,000. Even if £30,000 were lost through lowering and simplifying fares, there would be an income of £90,000 against £80,000 movement *and* system costs.

The minister upheld the TUCC recommendation later in the year, in August 1966. Apart from the widespread opposition and political pressure, this was also because of the very isolation of the area which had contributed to loss of traffic. Distances and times on journeys meant complete dependence on road would result in real hardship. In 1984 three coaches left Ipswich daily, taking 2 hours 10 minutes, against 1 hour 30 minutes by stopping train. The earliest road service left at 12.30.

BR honoured its obligations and continued to provide an adequate service. The East Suffolk Travellers' Association, formed to oppose closure, co-operated to assist the marketing effort by distributing leaflets and sponsoring excursions. But the final moves to the basic railway did not come until 1983. These involved an investment of £1.6 million (£200,000 in 1966) in singling and improvement of track, radio control of trains from Saxmundham, automation of the still numerous hand-operated crossing gates, and the re-opening of Melton station.

Speculation as to how many other lines could have been reprieved, had there been a similar willingness elsewhere by BR to reduce costs and market services, is fruitless but irresistible. Oxford–Bletchley–Cambridge must almost certainly figure on any such list, which readers are left to complete from their own local knowledge.

But Fiennes must be allowed the last word in this chapter. Approached with a request to keep open Elmswell and Thurston on the Cambridge–Haughley line, he acceded, adding Kennett and Dullingham. By doing so, receipts of some £8,000 a year were retained at a net cost of £1,000, leaving £7,000 as a contribution to the operating and track costs of the service as a whole. In addition a £3,000 subsidy to replacement buses was avoided. Consent to close all four stations (which still remain open) had been given by the minister in response to BRB proposals. 'Of such is the crass folly of parts of the Beeching Plan.'

CHAPTER 6

Closed Main and Cross-country Lines

By 1870 there were 11,044 route miles of public railway open in Great Britain, according to Board of Trade returns. This was a similar-sized network to that of Barbara Castle's 'basic railway' of 1967. By 1870 the network of principal main lines had been completed, while the closure programme of 1950–67 brought the system back to a very similar network. Though by no means invariably, it was largely a case of 'last built – first closed'.

To analyse this network of main lines we can distinguish first those lines radial from London and from the major conurbations and those which are circumferential, and therefore cross-country. We can then distinguish between trunk lines, main lines and cross-country lines in roughly descending order of traffic volume.

This classification must to some extent be subjective, for there is no agreed level of traffic which distinguishes trunk from main and main from cross-country. Obviously, however, the West Coast main line and the ex-Midland line from Sheffield to Bristol via Birmingham are trunk lines, while that from Plymouth to Penzance is a main line and the Leicester–Peterborough one a cross-country line, in terms of traffic carried. There is no question too that the West Coast line is radial from London and the Leicester–Peterborough is cross-country. But while the Sheffield–Bristol route is cross-country as far as London is concerned, albeit a trunk line in terms of traffic volume, it could also be regarded as two radial lines from Birmingham.

Forgotten railways coming into the main and cross-country categories have broadly been closed for two reasons. First, they were built as competing lines, promoted by local interests and sanctioned by parliament in an age of railway monopoly as a transport mode to break the monopoly of one company in one area; they died when railway monopoly passed, when with its passing there was no longer any competition within the railway system. These we can call *duplicating* lines.

As we have seen (page 98) 'duplicating main lines' came into prominence after the publication of Beeching II. Sometimes there would be sufficient intermediate traffic to prevent a line being 'duplicating'. In this way all three lines from London to the West Country have survived. So too has the line along the Welsh Marches. A Cardiff–Hereford–Crewe service is still provided, although BR diverted all the through services via Birmingham, except for a few on peak summer Saturdays. On the other hand the ex-GC line from Manchester to Sheffield was regarded as a duplicating trans-Pennine line and therefore eliminated.

The second reason for closure is that the traffic or the strategic purpose for which the line was built has disappeared, or the traffic flow has been diverted to another route, and no satisfactory alternative traffic has been found. An excellent example is provided by the GN and LNW Joint line through rural Leicestershire. This ran from Welham Junction (Market Harborough) for 30 miles through Melton Mowbray to Harby & Stathern, where it forked to make various connections with the GN. The history of its inception is complex, but briefly the GN wished to reach Leicester (by a branch from Maresfield Junction) and to tap the iron-ore workings, while the LNW wished to tap the Nottinghamshire coalfield, so traffic flowed from Colwick to Willesden via Market Harborough and Northampton.

Then in 1923 came Grouping. As a result the LNER had access to Leicester through the GC, so the GN route lost strategic value, while the LMS had access to Nottingham coal via the Midland main line. Importation of iron ore replaced home-produced and production in Leicestershire ceased in the 1960s; local passenger and freight had disappeared; and prosperous Leicester went on holiday by car instead of by slow and devious Saturday specials from the barn of London Road station. So the Joint line over the years lost its functions, found no new ones and has become forgotten. Lines of this kind we can call *supplanted*.

As we have seen (page 58), the Hull & Barnsley was the first main line to lose its passenger service, which it did in 1932. The company had been promoted to build a 52 mile line from Cudworth on the Midland trunk line to Hull, principally as an alternative route for coal from the South Yorkshire pits to the port to break the North Eastern's monopoly in the Hull area. Opened in 1885, in addition to a local passenger service, expresses were put on between Cannon Street, the Hull terminus, and Barnsley. In 1923 Cannon Street was closed, a first-fruit of amalgamation, the trains being diverted to Paragon. But as early as 1932 the expresses together with all passenger services west of South Howden were withdrawn, only the suburban service from the latter into Paragon remaining, to be withdrawn in turn in 1955. This was an early example of the closure of a main line, which was also cross-country and duplicating.

The Great Central
The H&B was a main line. The 206 mile route of the GC from Manchester to Marylebone was a trunk line and, as such, its fate has, at least so far, been unique.

The GC had all the characteristics of a trunk line: express trains, not only

Under a forest of gantries and wires the 16.10 Manchester–Sheffield service passes the rebuilt Woodhead Station at the Western portal of the new tunnel. Regular passenger services ceased in 1970, four years after the photo was taken on 8 September 1966.

from end to end of the trunk line but through to places as far afield as Aberdeen and Penzance; heavy flows of mineral and long-distance freight; not to mention suburban services, rural stopping trains and pick-up freights. Its locomotives, especially in pre-Grouping days, enjoyed an excellent reputation, while some sections were the sites of technological innovation. Automatic electro-gas signalling had been installed prior to 1914 on part of the London Extension, while the first main-line electrification for both passenger and freight traffic in Great Britain was completed by BR between Manchester and Sheffield in 1954. It has been lovingly recorded from inception to closure, widely written about and even more widely photographed.

George Dow has produced the definitive history (*Great Central*, 3 volumes 1959–65, pub Ian Allan), while no student of the GC should be unaware of the numerous and high-quality photographs of the building of the London Extension which are in the possession of the Leicester Museum. R. Davies and M. J. Grant (Chapter 8 in the *Chilterns and Cotswolds* volume of the 'Forgotten Railways' series) have dealt with the section between Rugby and Aylesbury, while P. Howard Anderson (Chapter 4 in the *East Midlands* volume of the 'Forgotten Railways' series) has covered the Extension north of Rugby. These authors have described in some detail the past traffic, the associated landscape and the final run-down. The interested reader is referred to these books.

The inauguration of electric trains across the Pennines in 1954 required the construction of a new double-track tunnel under the Woodhead Pass. The next year a question was asked in parliament as to the possibility of converting the line south of Rugby into a road. The Minister of Transport replied that the BTC considered it to be 'an important route', carrying traffic which could not be diverted. At the time most students of railways would have agreed, and to many people – railwaymen, passengers and commentators alike – the events of the next fifteen years would have been quite unthinkable. Yet by 1981 not only had the Great Central ceased to exist as a trunk line, but much of its length south of Annesley had been torn up, while track and overhead equipment of the post-war trans-Pennine electrification lay unused and rusting.

The London Extension 'represents the ultimate development of railway construction, a fine mastery of technique and part of the final filling-in of the railway map. But . . . as a trunk route, was it necessary?' Thus wrote Davies and Grant. And they come to the conclusion, 'The answer must surely be no.' This may be true if the financial results experienced by the GC are taken into account. But on the other hand statements in railway histories penned subsequently to the run-down that after nationalisation the line had no long-term future do seem to benefit from hindsight. The question therefore remains: was death the result of natural causes or of murder?

The Manchester, Sheffield & Lincolnshire's line from Manchester to Sheffield was an early trans-Pennine one, opened in 1845. In subsequent years the coalfield south of Sheffield was penetrated and by 1892 the MS&L had joined up with the GN at Annesley, some 10 miles north of Nottingham. A disbelieving GN was told that was as far as the MS&L wished to go. Scepticism was confirmed when in 1893 the latter company obtained an Act for the London Extension to link with the Metropolitan in the wilds of North Bucks at Quainton Road. Four years later, in 1897, the change of name to Great Central underlined the new objective. The new Marylebone terminus was reached in 1899. In 1906 passenger services commenced on the alternative route from Grendon Underwood Junction, just north of Quainton Road, over the line owned jointly with the GW through Princes Risborough to Northolt Junction to rejoin the original line at Northolt Junction.

The Extension served no town of any importance which was not already on another trunk line, and it provided a longer route to all these places. True it was only ¾ mile further from Marylebone to Rugby than from Euston, but it was 19 miles longer to London Road, Manchester. Compared with the other routes to the North, passenger traffic was never heavy, and the five- and six-coach trains were light, especially compared with the lengthy caravans on the West and East Coast lines. But they were fast, punctual and comfortable and preferred by many regular travellers.

The importance of the Extension was greatly increased with the opening in 1900 of the 11 mile connection between the GC a mile south of Woodford & Hinton and the GW at Banbury. This provided the essential link in a NE–SW route of an importance forgotten today when all such trains run through Birmingham's New Street.

By 1900 there were nine services between Nottingham and London and this level was maintained until 1940. Most trains were routed through Aylesbury: the Princes Risborough route, born of a dispute with the Metropolitan, was never really developed after a rapprochement with the latter. The Woodford–Banbury link grew in importance with the inter-war increase in long-distance holiday traffic. In 1930 there were five southbound services through Banbury, conveying through coaches between a wide variety of origins and destinations, including Glasgow and Southampton Docks, Hull and Swansea and the longest through working ever, Aberdeen and Penzance.

As on other lines, the war years saw drastic cutbacks. *Bradshaw* of June 1946 shows three expresses from Marylebone to Manchester and one to Sheffield, supplemented by an overnight parcels/passenger train to Manchester and the 01.45 newspaper/passenger train to Nottingham. In addition four stopping trains loitered down north of Woodford. The Banbury link carried two through services, from Swindon to Sheffield and from Banbury to York.

But unlike other routes, this frequency (if such it could be called) was never greatly increased, except for the Banbury link. In August 1958 ten northbound trains used it on Saturdays. In 1947 the 07.35 Sheffield–Marylebone became the 'Master Cutler' and was accelerated. But in 1958, diesel-hauled and all-Pullman, it was diverted to King's Cross via Retford and the GN main line.

With the benefit of hindsight it might be considered that the long-term

prospects for passenger traffic, at least south of Woodford on the Extension, were not favourable after the creation of BR. It is clear that the passenger traffic was riding on the back of the freight traffic, but what was not then clear was the short life of that freight traffic.

But the coal, steel and fish, the mainstays of the line, were declining and the ex-Midland route via Birmingham, over which the remaining traffic could be diverted, was being provided with increased capacity. The NE–SW passenger traffic could also be diverted through Birmingham, and there were alternative routes for the other long-distance passenger (and passenger-rated) traffic. Suburban traffic to Aylesbury remained heavy, but northward lay the traffic desert of the south Midlands. In 1946 only five down trains called at Calvert on weekdays and as many at Charwelton. Of the Charwelton trains, two originated at Woodford, with no connections from the south, while the next train after the 11.07 was the 17.35.

In June 1959 drastic service reductions were announced and in 1960 the expresses from Marylebone ceased. In 1963 local passenger trains were withdrawn between Aylesbury and Rugby and most stations on the Extension closed. The Woodford–Banbury locals were also withdrawn, bringing to an end the sight of an A3 Pacific on a one-coach train calling at Eydon Road Halt. All that remained were three semi-fasts between Marylebone and Nottingham and the through services via Banbury.

The freight traffic continued for the time being. R. Leleux records that even in 1960 the marshalling yards at Woodford received 86 freight trains daily and despatched 90, though only 15 of the latter were for the London line. And, in 1962, D. Holmes, the last station-master at East Leake (north of Lough-borough), remembers that some 130 freight and passenger trains passed each 24 hours.

(*left*) The Great Central introduced the idea of modular stations. Its London Extension was characterised by island-platform stations with a standard range of buildings. This is Calvert. (*right*) Just before the rundown of the GC Line a train from Manchester leaves Woodford Halse for Marylebone on 29 August 1959. The spur to Byfield can be seen on the left.

However, through freight traffic south of Langwith Junction (Derbyshire) ceased soon after and the line between Calvert and Rugby, together with the Banbury link, closed altogether, leaving only a local service between Rugby and Nottingham, which lingered until 1969. North of Nottingham the service to Sheffield ceased in 1963, while the last through train between Bournemouth and York via Banbury ran in 1966.

The war-time curve from the Bletchley–Oxford line at Calvert and the line on to Aylesbury was retained. During the West Coast electrification and associated rebuilding of Euston, sleeping-car trains were diverted to Marylebone by this route, which is still used for specials and in emergencies. In 1984 Christmas-shopping excursions were run from Denham to Milton Keynes, calling at all stations to Princes Risborough and Aylesbury and even at Quainton Road and Winslow.

As for the Sheffield–Manchester section, electrically hauled expresses ceased in 1970 and the traffic transferred to ageing and uncomfortable DMUs over the speed-check ridden Hope Valley route of the Midland, listed for closure by the Beeching Plan. Local EMUs (25kV from 1984) still go out from Piccadilly as far as Hadfield, while DMUs used the line from Sheffield to Penistone en route for Huddersfield until 1983, when they were diverted via Barnsley and the Dodworth line, which had been closed for passengers for many years. Then even the freight traffic, which included 5 million tons of coal a year for Fiddler's Ferry power station, was diverted, and in 1981 the Woodhead line was closed altogether between Hadfield and Penistone. In 1982, a study was announced that would estimate the cost of converting the Woodhead Tunnel and its approaches into a road. One can only feel, in the light of the long-term oil crisis, that a cost/benefit study of re-opening the line would be more worth while.

The closure of the GC trunk line was basically due to its being a perfect example of the *bête noire* of the BTC/BRB – the duplicating line. The last trunk line to be built was the first to be closed, a good example of the 'last built – first closed' rule. It had lived by its freight traffic and with the latter's catastrophic decline and the ability to divert what remained, closure could follow and the line be allowed to sink without trace. Long-distance passenger traffic was limited and easy to divert, though Manchester–Sheffield passengers have had good cause to lament the electric smoothness of Woodhead. Of local traffic through the Nottinghamshire coalfield and the rural south Midlands there was virtually nothing left. Ironically, commuting development in the 1970s, which has filled the car-parks at Huntingdon, Wolverton and Northampton, and which might have filled Brackley and Woodford, came after closure. So there was no real fight, except for the Woodhead line and that long after the passengers had gone.

Nottingham (Victoria), sandwiched between two tunnels and with two large island platforms and numerous bays, has disappeared save for its clock tower, preserved in the Victoria Shopping Centre which submerged the site. But much still remains for the student of forgotten railways and to aid recall of the great days of the line. The road bed, with its heavy earthworks, still runs along the side of Longdendale, past the reservoirs and on up to the portal of the new Woodhead Tunnel, or strides through the rolling countryside of Northamptonshire, while its viaduct still traverses the lower parts of the city of Leicester.

The country stations on the Extension, many once busy with milk churns if not with passengers, were unique in their standardised island construction. Happily restored by the Main Line Steam Trust to their former condition, Rothley and Quorn, between Leicester and Loughborough, are typical. At Quorn the road crosses over the line. A door in the bridge parapet gives access to the stairs down to the booking-office on the platform. It is an entrance more associated with a seedy suburban station in a seedy part of town. From rail level the platform is seen to be adorned by a few low, red-brick erections that bear no relation to each other. Most conspicuous is the building set aside solely for the use of gentlemen. But the goods yard is spacious and the goods shed large.

At East Leake in 1962, we are told, Tilley lamps were lit on winter evenings, there being neither electricity nor gas. At Charwelton the platform is still there and from the overbridge at the north end, in the silence, it is easy in the mind's eye and ear to conjure up the sight and sound of a Robinson 2–8–0 with its long train of coal empties on their way from Woodford to Annesley rumbling through and giving a long whistle as it enters Catesby Tunnel.

But it is Woodford Halse that is the memorial of the Extension. Here, in the rural heart of Northamptonshire, was the vital junction with the Banbury line and the lesser junction with the Stratford-upon-Avon & Midland Junction. Where the line crossed a valley by a high embankment a station, goods yard and carriage sidings were provided at the south end and at the north a 35 acre marshalling yard and a locomotive depot. All these could be traced in 1984, though an industrial estate spreads across the marshalling yard as does birch and bramble across the station.

But in the remote countryside of the turn of the century there was no accommodation for the numerous staff needed. So on the eastern side of the line, between it and the tiny village of Woodford Halse, clustered round its church, 136 houses were erected, together with school and shops. And there it remains, a typical small railway town which has lost its railway. On the other side of the line the village of Hinton (Woodford Halse station was Woodford & Hinton until 1948) is more the kind of settlement one would expect in these parts.

A literary memorial is Sir John Betjeman's evocative poem 'Great Central'. This paints a splendid picture of the closing years. Sir John should be allowed a last word:

> And quite where Rugby Central is
> Does only Rugby know.
> We watched the empty platform wait
> And sadly saw it go!

The Midland & Great Northern

In contrast with the radial trunk line of the GC, the Midland & Great Northern was an east–west cross-country line straggling through East Anglia, mostly single track and always well in the rear of technical progress. It seemed to suffer no visible run-down and at a stroke 175 route miles were closed to passengers on 2 March 1959, when most of that mileage was closed to freight as well. Only the Melton Constable–Sheringham section continued to carry a passenger service, until 1964, while the few miles to Cromer have survived. Nothing like it had ever happened before. And it had taken place in the face of concerted local opposition.

The story of the M&GN's emergence was complex and convoluted and the reader is referred to the wealth of literature (especially D. I. Gordon's *Eastern Counties* volume of the 'Regional History of the Railways of Great Britain' series, and A. J. Wrottesley's *The Midland & Great Northern Joint Railway*). Sufficient to say it came about from piecemeal promotion by local companies of short interconnecting lines. Those companies west of Sutton Bridge amalgamated to become the Midland & Eastern and those to the east the Eastern & Midland. From the first the influence of both the GN and the Midland was strong and in 1893 the two local companies were taken over jointly by the major companies to become the M&GN. Until 1936 it was worked as an

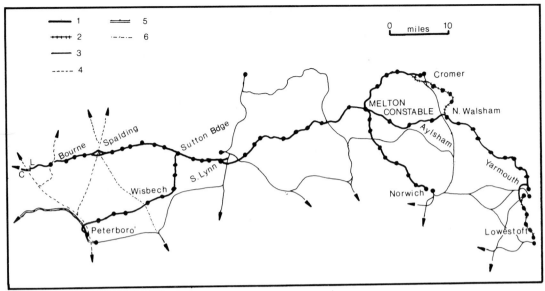

Fig. 8 The Midland & Great Northern.
1. Midland & Great Northern Joint. 2. Norfolk & Suffolk Joint. 3. Great Eastern. 4. Great Northern. 5. Midland. 6. Great Northern & Great Eastern Joint. C. Castle Bytham station. L. Little Bytham Junction.

independent line from headquarters at Melton Constable with its own loco-motives, most of which owed much to Derby practice, and coaches. In that year the LNER took over responsibility for operation.

The result of all this was a rather straggling system of 206 route miles, Y-shaped at the western end and trident-shaped at the eastern. The western arms made connection with the GN at Peterborough and with the Midland branch from Saxby (on their Leicester–Peterborough line) end-on at a place, in fact nowhere, called Little Bytham Junction. At the eastern end three lines fanned out from the system's Crewe, Melton Constable, the principal one to Yarmouth, the others to Norwich and to Cromer.

After 1923 the LMS and the LNER became the joint owners, but until 1936 there was little change. The local services were maintained by elderly loco-motives hauling short trains of miscellaneous obsolete bogie coaches and even more antique six-wheelers, lovingly recorded by the camera of Dr Ian C. Allen. But even then traffic between the small towns and numerous villages was sparse, as was the timetable. The only places of any size were Norwich and Yarmouth.

But it was also a main line. Before 1923 the GN ran from King's Cross to Cromer via Peterborough, while the 'Leicester' ran daily from Leicester to Yarmouth via Saxby from 1894 to the day of closure. Holiday traffic grew steadily. Even before 1914 there were Midland services from Birmingham and GN ones from the West Riding, while in conjunction with the GC there was one from Manchester. In 1939, on summer Saturdays, thirteen expresses passed through Sutton Bridge eastbound to the resorts and new holiday camps of the East Coast. Most of these were through trains or carried through portions from Manchester, Sheffield, Leicester, Nottingham, Derby, Gloucester, Birmingham and King's Cross. When it is remembered that they were often handed over at Little Bytham Junction or Peterborough late, that there was an equal number of westbound services, and that most of the route was single track, something of the operating nightmare is conveyed. This holiday traffic lasted until closure, though by then it was poised on the edge of a motorage decline.

Outward freight traffic was mainly agricultural and therefore also seasonal. But it passed in quantities which seem incredible these days. In the 1930s, at certain times of year, wayside stations such as Murrow (East), Long Sutton and Gedney each despatched a daily train loading up to sixty wagons. Even during the slack season six trains for potatoes were run.

R. S. Joby (*East Anglia*, Vol 7 of the 'Forgotten Railways' series) gives us illuminating glimpses of life on the M&GN. Particularly nostalgic is his vignette of the pick-up goods train, now of course a thing of the past:

> The great event of the day was the arrival of the pick-up goods train, often headed by a stolid Ivatt 0–6–0 maid-of-all-work, which on a summer Saturday would be hauling a Yarmouth special. The shunter performed miracles of dexterity with his clanging, unwieldy charges, perfectly co-ordinating manoeuvres with the footplate crew who interpreted his every gesture accurately amid hiss of steam and grinding of brake blocks. All too soon the performance would be over, the new wagons awaiting unloading, the train re-assembled and chugging slowly off, the guard's van accelerating with a convulsive lurch.

The 1958 pilgrimage the author made has been described in Chapter 1. The rare passenger trains seemed moderately well patronised and some freight traffic remained. But only at Melton Constable, where DMUs waited, forming

An M&GN train with its 'Derby' style loco enters Sutton Bridge Station. Contrast with the picture on page 11.

the connecting trains to Norwich and Cromer, was there any sign of modernisation. One suspected that costs of staffing the stations and numerous level-crossings, in those days before pay-trains and automatic barriers, and of maintaining bridges over rivers and drainage channels, especially those at Sutton Bridge and South Lynn, were becoming an insupportable burden as freight traffic declined.

So in the end closure came for essentially the same reasons as it came for the GC. Though on a smaller scale, there was a similar loss of the basic freight traffic, there was the ability to divert the through passenger traffic (in this case highly seasonal and likely to decline), and there was a sheer lack of local passenger traffic. Even so, immediately prior to closure, the 140 daily trains were carrying on average forty to fifty passengers.

Closure came in the face of strong local opposition, but we have seen that this counted less in the English rural areas than in the Highlands of Scotland. The procedures were quickly completed. Closure proposals were published in July 1958 and by October the East Anglia and East Midlands TUCCs had forwarded their reports to the CTCC. The minister speedily gave consent and closure came on 2 March 1959.

One of Noël Coward's characters remarked 'Very flat, Norfolk', and save for the short sections west of Bourne few earthworks were needed. In this highly farmed area long stretches of the right-of-way have been taken into the ploughed fields. But a number of lengths have become roads. These include the Lynn by-pass and Stalham–Potter Heigham, though the line west of Stalham can be traced to Melton Constable. Near Castle Bytham a short length is used to pass a minor road under the A1. A gas pipeline has been laid along the right-of-way between North Walsham and Mundesley. Cross Keys Bridge over the Nene at Sutton Bridge, with its swinging span, once shared between road and rail traffic, is now left with the former in sole possession. Many of the station buildings and crossing-keepers' houses survive.

But, like Woodford Halse for the GC, Melton Constable survives as the real memorial of the M&GN. It was the hub of the system, the junction of the lines from Yarmouth, Norwich and Cromer. At the island platform local and through passenger trains made connection with each other, or were made up or divided, while freight trains were re-marshalled in the surprisingly extensive yard. Here too were the workshops, closure of which lay behind the 1936 LNER takeover. Here in the midst of an isolated rural area was a considerable demand for skilled and unskilled labour. A small town was created, larger houses at the end of the terraces and detached ones for supervisory staff and a medical officer. R. S. Joby likens its Melton Street to 'a transplant from an East Midlands industrial town'. The town – schools, mission and all – survives, together with the buildings of the works, which have become the centre of an industrial estate.

The railway age brought the need to house workers in isolated spots. Not only were company estates added to existing settlements, but new ones were

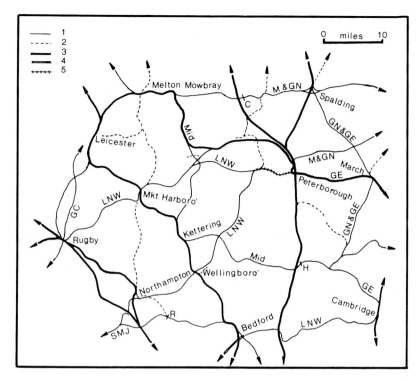

Fig. 9 Cross-Country Lines in the East Midlands and East Anglia.
1. Cross-country lines closed to passengers. 2. Other lines closed to passengers. 3. Main and cross-country lines open to passengers in 1984. 4. Cross-country line now carrying only local traffic. 5. Line re-opened by the Nene Valley Railway. C. Castle Bytham – junction between the Midland and the Midland & Great Northern. H. Huntingdon North – junction between the Midland and the GN & GE Joint. R. Ravenstone Wood – junction between the Midland and the Stratford-on-Avon & Midland Junction.

created. Some were large and well known, such as Crewe, Swindon and Eastleigh, but there were also numerous small ones: besides Woodford Halse and Melton Constable there were Hellifield, Tebay, Riccarton Junction and Carstairs, all isolated, one-employer communities in remote areas. We know little about them, in contrast with the mining communities, which they resembled in many ways.

Other Cross-country Lines

A glance at a map (such as Figure 9) will show the numerous cross-country lines in the south and east Midlands and East Anglia and how these lines have suffered extensive closures. These were never really competing lines. But they all lost their former functions and failed to gain new ones. They were all supplanted. Whether they could have been saved has not been satisfactorily settled. In their last years traffic potential was declining, but no consistent attempts were made to harness that potential. We have examined in some detail the cases of the Oxford–Cambridge line and the M&GN system. We now look at three more examples which form a group.

It is hard to imagine the east Midlands without the Midland south of Leicester and the GN south of Doncaster. But two of these lines were built by the LNW to penetrate a vast area then without railways. They were built to feed the West Coast line, and with the opening of the GN and the Midland they lost traffic destined either for London or the North.

From Blisworth on the main line a branch was opened down to Northampton, by-passed from the main line, and on down the Nene Valley to make end-on connection with the Eastern Counties at Peterborough. In 1850 a branch was opened from Rugby to Luffenham, where it joined the Midland's Syston & Peterborough, and in 1879 a link went in from Seaton to Wansford on the Blisworth line.

These routes served a rural area. Northampton, Wellingborough and Market Harborough were the only intermediate towns of any size. The Rugby & Peterborough had some pretensions as a through route. Some trains from Peterborough ran beyond Rugby to Birmingham and there were through coaches from Yarmouth. It could be regarded as being a route from the West Midlands to East Anglia in competition with the M&GN (though it could not compete for traffic from further north) and the Syston & Peterborough. It even had a night service, presumably mainly for mail but available for passengers, timed in 1953 to leave Rugby at 02.50 but with no balancing westbound train. In that year there was also one 'fast' train. This covered the 50¾ miles eastbound with two stops in 79 minutes. There were four other through trains to Peterborough which did the trip in times which varied from 100 to 105 minutes. Of these five trains, one had a through portion from Birmingham to Peterborough, another to Yarmouth and a third from Rugby to Yarmouth. Finally there were three departures from Rugby for Market Harborough. By no stretch of the imagination could it be called a good service or one aimed at attracting traffic.

As for the other line, Northampton Castle had become the western terminus. From here in 1953 there were only four regular weekday departures, five on Wednesdays and Fridays and six on Saturdays. The 12.20 took 99 minutes for the 43¾ miles. The service had deteriorated since 1946, when seven trains had left Northampton Mondays to Fridays. This at a time when most lines, even the Rugby and Peterborough, had shown some post-war improvement.

These were the sort of lines which, at least prior to 1968, would have been regarded as ripe for closure by the BRB. Like so many other cross-country lines there was never any thought of development, either of attracting traffic by a radically improved DMU service, or of significantly reducing costs by singling, simplifying signalling, and de-staffing stations. The only surprise is that they lasted so long, the Northampton line until 1964 and the Rugby line until 1966. They were both lost in the holocaust of those peak closure years, attracting as little attention in their death as in their life. There is a strange dearth of literature and little is known about them.

The author has a memory of Seaton, the junction of the original route from

Brampton Station (later Buckden) in 1985, 26 years after the last train from Kettering to Huntingdon called, seems ready to deal with the next train.

Rugby to the Midland at Luffenham, and the connection to the Blisworth line at Wansford, and the terminus of the short branch to Uppingham. One sun-drenched afternoon in 1964, together with a fellow rail fan he had arrived on a steam push-and-pull train which operated from Luffenham on Wednesdays only. It had deposited school-children at Morcott, the only intermediate station, and they were the sole passengers to descend at Seaton. They had 43 minutes to wait, time to savour to the full the timeless atmosphere of the primitive country junction, so much appreciated by connoisseurs of railways, and at that period so rapidly passing. No houses were visible, though the view across the meadow-floored Welland Valley was extensive. Only the steeple of Harringworth church could be seen through the arches of the mile-long Harringworth Viaduct that carries the Midland line to the far side of the wide valley. Seaton had the usual range of mean LNW single-storey buildings on the westbound platform and none on the eastbound. No cars came over the level-crossing and the silence was broken only by the grimy tank expensively simmering in the eastbound bay and the occasional passage of a heavy mineral train along the Midland line. But all too soon the semaphore signals came off for the coming of a three-car DMU to bear the two of them and the one other passenger away from that pleasant spot.

There was another unsung cross-country line in the region, dating from 1866, 27½ miles from Kettering to an end-on junction with the GN&GE Joint line from St Ives at Huntingdon East. The Midland worked it to 1879, when

131

they absorbed it, and also enjoyed running powers from Huntingdon on to Cambridge.

The line climbed at 1 in 59–70 away from the four-track Midland main line at Kettering Junction and wandered eastward over the ironstone-bearing upland to cross the Nene Valley, and the Northampton–Peterborough line which followed it, at Thrapston. The Oxford clay country beyond is only about 200ft high, but rolling topography, vast fields, long views and the contrast with the neighbouring Fens all give the impression of high land. Even in this motor age it is a curiously deserted countryside. The heavy grades – a mile at 1 in 80 up from Thrapston and another at 1 in 120 down to the Ouse at Brampton – also contributed to the impression of height. The line was always worked by light locomotives: Midland 2–4–0s and class 2 0–6–0s, and in BR days GE 0–6–0s and the first Standard class 2 Moguls.

It had very few pretensions as a through route. Until the early 1960s, when imported iron ore replaced the native product, the western end at Cranford and at Twywell was busy hauling out iron ore behind the 2–8–0s allowed up to the exchange sidings. In summer a double-headed train up to seventy wagons long, laden with fruit from the Cambridge area, would trundle westward into the sunset. During the war, too, it was busy taking bombs to the USAF airfields. But local passenger traffic was always exiguous. In 1939 there was a basic service of four short trains each way, reduced to two during the war and increased to three afterwards. In the immediate post-war years heavy, often double-headed, holiday trains would plod slowly from east Midland towns to Clacton. The journey, interminable, hot and overcrowded, was really no way to start a holiday. Local gossip had it that to miss a train was no real disaster: a hired taxi would catch it up at the next stop.

Norman Marlow, who doubled as a university lecturer and a part-time signalman at Kettering Junction, described the line as 'a little world on its own'. But in 1950 it would keep him busy in his box. At 17.30 'crawling down the bank' would come the ore train from Cranford, headed by a 2–8–0. Behind would be the pick-up goods from Godmanchester with five or so wagons. These trains had to be fed into the main line traffic to clear the branch for the 16.55 from Cambridge.

Most of the handsome station houses west of Huntingdon remain. Those at Thrapston, Raunds and Kimbolton were up to 2 miles from the only places of any consequence, hence the lack of passengers. The trains ceased in 1959. Twenty years later it was impossible to get a bus from Kettering to Huntingdon.

Short-term expediency and lack of forward planning in transport has now left but a single west–east rail link: it is of low quality, winding from Birmingham through Leicester to Peterborough and on to Ely and Norwich. Meanwhile our EEC membership has resulted in booming East Coast ports and endless streams of heavy lorries making life miserable in towns and villages or skirting them by costly by-passes. Could not some of the money have been spent on rail improvement, and what will happen when North Sea oil runs dry in twenty years? Investment in the Leicester–Peterborough route and retention of the integrity of the Oxford–Cambridge line could now have been paying off.

The Stratford-on-Avon & Midland Junction

Blisworth has already been mentioned as the original junction for the line to Peterborough. Its strategic importance has declined to vanishing point and the West Coast passenger is now hard put to spot its deserted site from his 100mph train. But until 1952 it was not only possible to travel up from Northampton in a steam push-and-pull train to the outside face of the up island platform with its short over-all roof, but then to cross to the small adjacent station, a two-road, single-platform terminus from which, eventually, a train would leave to reach, eventually, Stratford.

The Stratford-on-Avon & Midland Junction was an amalgamation of several struggling companies. Some of their mileage had even been closed temporarily and the brief career of one passenger service has already been referred to (page 33). The SMJ remained independent until absorbed into the new LMS in 1923.

At the small town of Towcester, always more important for being on Watling Street (A5), one line led eastward to Blisworth and another crossed the West Coast main line at Roade to join the Midland's branch to Northampton at Ravenstone Wood Junction. Westward from Towcester a little-used branch eventually reached Banbury. But the 'main line' went on to Woodford Junction, where there was a short spur to the GC at Woodford and thence through Byfield to Fenny Compton. Here the platforms lay alongside those of the GW and there was (and is) a World War II connection. From here the tracks ran below the grassy scarp of Edge Hill to Stratford, where there was an unpretentious station in a remote part of town and a war-time spur to the GW. Finally, Broom Junction on the Midland's Barnt Green–Redditch–Ashchurch loop was reached, 41 miles from Blisworth.

The tourist mecca of Stratford-on-Avon has always been neglected by the main lines, at least as far as scheduled services are concerned. The GW enforced a change for its London passengers at Leamington, and for LMS passengers there was a change at Blisworth, if you could find a train which stopped there, and a tedious journey westward. The shortest and quickest route, from Marylebone, was never properly exploited, though through coaches off one train were slipped at Woodford until 1936.

Whatever pretensions the promoters had about the line being part of a through west–east route it never worked out in practice for passengers, and Stratford was the only town of any importance. Passenger services were always extremely scarce. In 1939 the only through train, the 08.55 from Blisworth, reached Broom at 10.47. There were two more departures for Stratford, two for Banbury and one for Towcester. The Woodford spur was traversed by five round trips from Byfield and there were three trips from Stratford to Broom.

South Town, Stratford-on-Avon. The SMJ station looking east.

Loads were light. In the post-war years an ex-Midland class 3 or class 4 0–6–0 would be in charge of one or two coaches.

There has always been some through freight traffic, though never in the volume envisaged by the promoters. Bananas were conveyed from Avonmouth and in the post-war years iron ore went from Banbury to South Wales via the Fenny Compton and Stratford connections. Freight traffic continued for a time after closure to passengers. A brake-van trip from Towcester to Stratford was described in the *Railway Magazine* of April 1956. It took four hours and seven other freight trains were passed. Again, a combination of declining traffic and re-routing of the remainder led to total closure, except for the short section from Fenny Compton to Burton Dasset. Blisworth and Stratford have been razed and there are few remains.

The Port Road
A major Scottish cross-country line, known to railwaymen as the Port Road, ran westward from Dumfries for 73¾ miles to Stranraer harbour. Of importance as a link in the route from England to the North of Ireland, it was certainly a main line, though it cannot be said to have attained trunk status, and the local traffic was always light. The small market towns were widely scattered and the intervening countryside sparsely peopled. Dalbeattie, Castle Douglas and Newton Stewart had conveniently sited stations, but New Galloway and Gatehouse of Fleet lay 5 and 6 miles respectively from the stations which bore their names, while Kirkcudbright and Wigtown were on branches.

In 1859 Castle Douglas was reached from Dumfries on the Glasgow & South Western main line to Carlisle by a branch later taken over by the GSW. Portpatrick, south of Stranraer and 21 miles (by sea) from Donaghadee in County Down, was the original goal of the Portpatrick Railway, which opened its line from Castle Douglas in 1862. But the harbour at Portpatrick was dangerous, the government failed to improve it and the rail layout was ludicrously inconvenient. Ferry operations were transferred to Stranraer in 1874, though a local service lingered until 1950. The Portpatrick line was slovenly operated and its finances so poor that it was taken over in 1885 by a consortium of the LNWR, Midland, Caledonian and GSW, who worked it as the Portpatrick & Wigtownshire Joint line until they all passed to the LMS.

The Port Road and its highly individualistic branches never attracted photographers as did the West Highland, but have been fortunate in their literary recorder, David L. Smith, with his stylish pen and ready wit. The Port Road also figures prominently in two classic detective novels, Dorothy L. Sayers' *Five Red Herrings* and Freeman Wills Crofts' *Sir John Magill's Last Journey*.

It was the central section of the line which was the most interesting. From Castle Douglas it struck inland up the narrow valley of the Dee to New Galloway and then at 1 in 80 up into the wild moorland. Loch Skerrow passing-place was controlled from one of the loneliest signal-boxes in the country. It was never seen by passengers in the 'Port Road Paddy', the boat train, passing through in the small hours. In 1908 a goods train was marooned in the snow for three days, the crew living on the edible items of the freight.

From here was a vicious saw-tooth profile with the Big Fleet and Little Fleet Viaducts at the foot of steep inclines. D. L. Smith describes how in 1904 the first of four specials conveying Buffalo Bill's circus was brought to a stand on the 'Wee Fleet' by a plate-layer showing a red light in error. The big 0–8–0 stuck fast on the 1 in 76 up to Loch Skerrow and the train had to be divided and taken up in two parts. 'If Buffalo Bill could have seen the country in which he stuck (it was of course night) he might well have imagined himself back in the Black Hills of Dakota.'

Gatehouse of Fleet was the summit of the line. Dorothy Sayers paints the scene arriving at Gatehouse of Fleet station by road from the town, which in 1931 had a connecting bus:

> Over to the north-east, white in the morning, the graceful arches of the [Big] Fleet viaduct gleamed pallidly. And ahead, grim and frowning, stood the great wall of the Clints of Dromore, scarred and sheer and granite-grey.

The service in 1939 consisted of night boat trains from London and from Newcastle and a day train from London, supplemented by eight weekday trains from Dumfries to Castle Douglas, four continuing their leisurely way to Stranraer. Lord Peter Wimsey in 1931 had a theory as to this slow progress:

> Local trains are always late, it's one of the rules. It's done so that the guard and engine-driver can step out and admire the station-master's garden at every stop . . . The guard gets off at Kirkgunzeon . . . and measures the prize marrow and says . . . 'They've got one at Dalbeattie that beats ye by two inches.'

Until 1939 the Larne ferry was more for passengers and mail than for freight. But then a roll-on-roll-off service was inaugurated. War-time traffic grew enormously, not only military traffic to and from Northern Ireland, but

Long-forgotten branches proliferated from the Caledonian's main-line through Strathmore. A J37 0–6–0 approaches Brechin, terminus of the branch from Bridge of Dun.

imports from the port created at Cairnryan near Stranraer to relieve bomb-blasted Liverpool and Glasgow.

But though of strategic importance, it was not the sort of line to be viewed favourably by a government and BRB intent on immediate cost-savings at the expense of long-term planning. The Beeching Report envisaged closure of both lines to Stranraer. The Northern Ireland government pressed for the retention of one rail link, and local opposition to the closure of the Port Road was considerable, train crews offering to take reduced wages. But it was the line to Girvan which was reprieved, the whole Port Road being totally closed in 1965. The Euston–Stranraer boat trains were diverted via Mauchline and later via Kilmarnock and Ayr, putting Stranraer 165 miles from Dumfries, against 73¾ via Newton Stewart.

The viaducts at Glenluce and Big Water of Fleet survive and the course of the line can be traced through Cairn Edward Forest. But traffic on the Stranraer ferry has greatly expanded and Cairnryan has been revivified, in this case not long after the BRB, with unerring timing, removed the rail link. The BRB must surely be regretting its closure of the Port Road. By 1982 more through trains from Carlisle and beyond were reaching Stranraer via Kilmarnock than ever used the Port Road. But, as usually happens, run-down and closure of the railway was followed by a vast investment in the appalling A75.

A Miscellany

Space forbids an examination of all forgotten main and cross-country lines. Better a few obituaries than a mere death list . . . But mention should be made of the fate of the Caledonian's route to Aberdeen, which was part of the West Coast route from the South, as well as that from Glasgow, and which ran via Perth and Forfar. The rival North British route over the Forth and Tay Bridges joined it at Kinnaber Junction, north of Montrose. The Junction signal-box gained fame in the 1895 Race to Aberdeen, for whichever box to the south, Caley or NB, obtained 'line clear' for their contestant won the race for West or East Coast.

Kinnaber was 47 miles from Stanley, where the Highland line to Inverness diverged 6 miles north of Perth. The line traversed the fertile lowland of Strathmore, famed for its seed potatoes and its raspberry cultivation. There were eight branches, but Coupar Angus and Forfar were the only two towns directly served. In 1910 there were 153 daily services on the branches, but by 1955 all had been closed, together with ten stations on the main line. Only four

A busy scene at Torrington on 27 September 1958, though there do not appear to be many passengers around. Apart from holiday crowds, the mainstay of these lines was milk, meat and china clay.

On the Southern's 'Withered Arm'. In September 1959 the Padstow coaches of a West of England–Waterloo train leave Launceston in charge of a T9 4–4–0 No. 30715.

were left open. But the line then became a racing ground during the last years of steam, attracting fans from far and wide to photograph and to travel behind the Pacifics displaced from the East Coast line by dieselisation. Then in 1967 the Glasgow–Aberdeen expresses were diverted north of Perth to run via Dundee and the Stanley Junction–Kinnaber Junction section closed to passenger trains.

There was also the group of ex-Southern lines west of Exeter, rudely known among 'Southern Electric' men as their 'withered arm'. These included the undoubted one-time main line to Plymouth. At Coleford Junction outside Yeoford, it branched from the still-open line to Barnstaple to climb steadily to Okehampton, the first station of any importance, and on high up the slopes of Dartmoor. It ran past Meldon Quarry, now railhead of the freight-only line, and over the high and spindly Meldon Viaduct, to descend high above the deeply entrenched Tavy River through Tavistock, thence down the Tamar to Devonport and Plymouth.

It was a heavily graded line with long stretches at 1 in 75–77 and was never a real rival to the GW. In spite of the latter's 1 in 42 up to Hemerdon and the steep gable summit of Dainton, it was better laid out and 6½ miles shorter. The LSW tried some fast running, especially of Ocean Liner specials, which culminated in the Salisbury derailment of 1906. But by 1951 only the portions off the 09.00, 13.00, 15.00 and 18.00 from Waterloo and their equivalent up services had any pretence at being even semi-fast between Exeter and Plymouth.

138

At Meldon Junction a cross-country line, completed throughout only in 1899, wandered off to Launceston and on through North Cornwall for 73¼ miles to Padstow, that *ultima Thule* of the Southern, 260 miles in distance and light years in style from Waterloo. The line opened up a particularly remote area of poor farming and swelled the trickle of holidaymakers to that flood which eventually deserted it for their cars. Apart from Saturdays at the height of the summer, traffic was light. In 1950 the Atlantic Coast Express, calling at all fifteen intermediate stations between Launceston and Padstow, completed its journey 7hr 22min after leaving Waterloo. The names of some of those stations, Maddaford Moor Halt, Tower Hill and Port Isaac Road, indicate the amount of traffic to be expected and there were only four daily departures from Padstow for Launceston and beyond. 'West Country' Pacifics and N-class Moguls trundled two- and three-coach trains and the occasional short freight train. But some of the smartness and attitudes of the Southern reached out. A DMU driver at Okehampton, recounting to the author his experiences of firing Southern locomotives from Exmouth Junction shed, said, 'Ours was a proud line.'

We must also mention the GW line which ran for 52¾ miles from Ruabon, along the banks of the upper Dee through Llangollen, traversing the hills of Mid Wales and skirting Bala Lake, eventually to join the Cambrian Coast line at Barmouth Junction. This was closed in 1965. Also, in Wessex, there were the three north–south cross-country lines: the Didcot, Newbury & Southampton; the Midland & South Western Junction; and the Somerset & Dorset. Fortunately there is a wealth of literature on these three lost routes, for each had a colourful history, distinctive traffic and ran through countryside of great beauty. Unfortunately no part of the country was safe for secondary main and cross-country lines.

A Light Pacific brings in the normal short train to Morthoe Station at the summit of the climb out of Ilfracombe. Super power for branch working.

CHAPTER 7

Closed Urban Lines

We are apt to think of forgotten railways as a rural phenomenon. It is true that the greatest mileage of lost lines is in the country areas. It is also true that, at least in the major cities, suburban lines are still busy, there has been investment in electrification and in new stations, and in the last few years there have even been some lengths of line opened. But also there is naturally more interest in the lost rural lines. They ran through attractive scenery and tracing them on the ground is more pleasant and enjoyable than walking through decaying inner-city areas. They also tended to be lines of greater individuality, though those who knew the North Greenwich branch through London's Isle of Dogs or Edinburgh's Balerno branch might think otherwise.

But line closures are also an urban phenomenon; first the electric tram, then bus and car, have claimed their urban victims.

A glance at a map of the rail system in 1914 will show that the close network gets even more dense, not only around the larger cities, but also in the principal coalfields, which were then also the major industrial concentrations: the South Wales valleys, the north-west of England, the long strip from Nottingham northward to Leeds, the North East and the central lowlands of Scotland. Comparison with the 1980 map will still show the same intensification around the great cities, but elsewhere only west and south Yorkshire and the North West still stand out, though it might be argued that these areas are also essentially suburban as well as industrial. Figures 10 and 11 show in detail the differential rates of decline in central Scotland and in north-west England.

In this analysis of closed urban lines we will therefore look at three groups of forgotten railways: those in the great cities; those in smaller cities and towns that once supported suburban services; and those associated with the coalfields.

The Great Cities
We may distinguish between lines closed because of falling traffic on the one hand, and the closure of large terminal stations and their short approach lines for a variety of reasons on the other.

The London area has seen comparatively few closures. In relation to its total network it has suffered fewer closures than any other part of the country. The 1980 map shows no fundamental change from that of 1914. In the area defined by this author as Greater London (for Vol 3, *Greater London*, in the 'Regional History of the Railways of Great Britain' series) closures have been mainly in

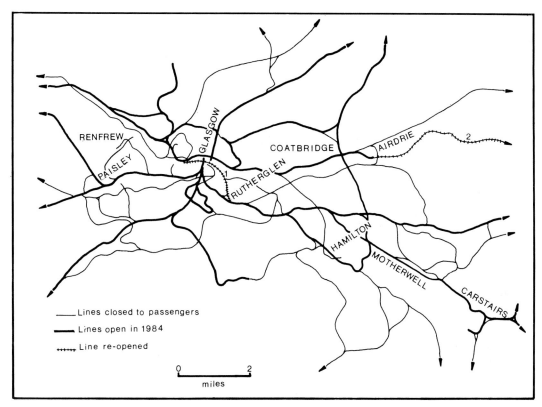

Fig. 10 Decline in Central Scotland. 1. Argyle Line via Central Low Level re-opened 1980. 2. Airdrie-Ratho via Bathgate scheduled to re-open in 1986.

the inner areas where distances were short and therefore more vulnerable first to tram and then to bus competition.

These lines include the Blackwall of 1840 (page 44). Nearby were two other short lines, branching from that to North Woolwich at Connaught Road and also traversing the once thriving dockland, now a waste. Containerised port activity has moved downstream to Tilbury, old industries have died and new ones have grown up elsewhere. One line ran along the back of the Royal Albert Dock out to the river itself at Gallions and was part of the Port of London's railway system. The other, owned by the Gas Light & Coke Co led across the marshes to a station at the entrance to their Beckton works. Over both branches a service, mainly for workmen but appearing in *Bradshaw*, was operated by the GE and later the LNE until bomb damage in 1940 provided a good excuse to bring the now little-used services to a permanent end.

The last war also saw the end of the once intensive service through the crowded East End from Dalston Junction to Poplar, though the line as far as Victoria Park was re-opened in 1979 on the initiative of the GLC for a Camden Road–North Woolwich diesel service. Further out, the London, Chatham & Dover's Greenwich Park branch was closed in 1917. The western end was re-opened for passenger traffic in 1935, when it and the new St John's flyover were

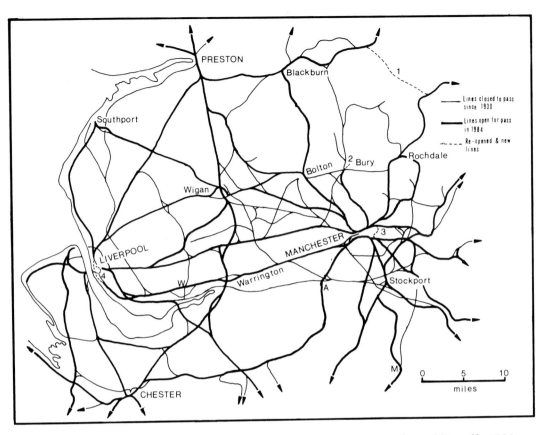

Fig. 11 Decline in North West England. 1. The Copy Pit Line re-opened to public traffic 1984. 2. Re-opened for through long-distance trains with the introduction of the 'European' in 1983. 3. New line to Bury Interchange (1980). 4. 'Loop & Link', opened 1977, to Hunt's Cross, re-opened 1983. A. Altrincham. M. Macclesfield. W. Widnes.

electrified. The eastern end has vanished beneath housing blocks and can be traced only with difficulty. The same company's 3¾ mile Crystal Palace branch, also from Nunhead, suffered temporary closure during both world wars, finally to succumb in 1954.

The line had a character of its own, unique for 'Southern Electric'. It climbed southward to the summit of the gravel-capped ridge on which Crystal Palace once stood. The intermediate stations were set discreetly on tree-lined streets to serve Victorian yellow-brick villas in large gardens amid parks and sports grounds. Even at the peaks the trains were never crowded. The terminus had four platforms beneath a vast high-vaulted roof. Except when a train arrived or left, it was so silent one could hear the water dripping down fern-encrusted walls. When last visited by the author, the site had become a quarry-like hole in the ground floored with 'prefab' houses. The closure of the line aroused little opposition: other stations with better services were easily accessible.

Over what was once rural Middlesex the inter-war tide of suburban building failed to save a number of short branches. The ex-GN branch to Edgware was closed in 1939 beyond Finchley Church End to allow electrification. But the 'juice' only reached Mill Hill East and the remainder never re-opened. The short Stanmore branch from Harrow also closed. After the opening of the Metropolitan's branch thither it was clearly redundant, though it lingered for many years. In the same way the branches to Uxbridge from Denham and from West Drayton were lost in the face of electric competition from the District and Piccadilly lines. West Drayton was also the junction for the Staines West branch, which had a number of unusual features. Intending passengers at Yeoveney Halt stopped the train by hand signal, while the terminus was converted from a mill manager's house.

One closure, early in date (1916) and short in length (½ mile), brought to an end a bewildering plethora of once thriving train services. This was the link between the City Widened Lines at Farringdon and the LCD at Ludgate Hill. In the 1880s some hundred southbound trains traversed it daily, originating at such places as New Barnet and Kentish Town and bound for Victoria, Addiscombe and Woolwich Arsenal. In West London there was a similar variety of services through Addison Road (now Olympia) – see page 36.

At the end of 1984 the principal London termini of 1923 were all in use, though two, having survived the Beeching era, were under threat of closure. Alongside the teeming ant-hill of Liverpool Street is the now nearly deserted Venetian barn, 1865 vintage, of Broad Street. This was once the hub of intensive North London Railway suburban services. Even as late as 1960 6,000 passengers arrived daily during the 07.00 to 10.00 peak period, which compared with 5,000 suburban passengers into Euston. But the Great Northern electrification of 1976 brought to an end the through trains to Finsbury Park and beyond over the Canonbury Spur. Broad Street's echoing wastes by December 1984 accommodated only the 20 minute Richmond service and a peak-period one to Watford.

The first closure proposal involved stopping the trains in a temporary terminus at Worship Street, over 500yd from the entrance to Liverpool Street (London Transport), for Broad Street has become embroiled in the plans to reconstruct its larger neighbour. The present short-term plan is to divert the Richmond trains from Dalston Junction over newly electrified lines to North Woolwich. Only the peak-period Watford trains will use Broad Street. The long-term solution is a new spur (the Graham Road Spur) to the Hackney Downs line and thence, after a tour of inner east London, to Liverpool Street. It might appear that a High Level platform would be more simple, but this has been rejected on 'aesthetic' grounds. But probably the real prize is to be able to give up the 2 mile, four-track viaduct in from Dalston Junction.

Marylebone is the newest and smallest terminus. Its pleasant, undistinguished façade is curiously provincial, more appropriate to a Hereford than to the Metropolis. Its concourse, at least off-peak, is one of the quietest spots in central London, especially since it has been shorn of long-distance functions (Chapter 6). By 1984 there were but two services remaining: the outer suburban ones to Aylesbury and to High Wycombe and beyond. It is considered that the former can be taken care of by a shuttle from the Metropolitan outer terminus at Amersham, with perhaps eventual electrification all the way, though whether London Transport 'Rapid Transit' type rolling stock is preferable even to worn out DMUs remains to be seen. The High Wycombe service can easily be diverted to Paddington, leaving only the 7 mile section from Northolt Junction to Neasden Junction to be completely abandoned, together with its four badly served and little-used stations. Closure notices were posted in 1984 at a time when many commuters were on holiday, so the limit for objections had to be extended. In addition the consequences of the 1962

Forgotten London services
(*above*) A train for Finsbury Park at the original Alexandra Palace. Opened in 1873 the line had been closed seven times by 1898. Final closure was on 5 July 1954, shortly after this picture was taken. (*below*) Swamped by the tide of suburbia flooding Middlesex, the GN's once rural Edgware branch remained unmodernised and suffered eventual extinction.

Transport Act have raised themselves. Local authorities took legal action against the London Regional Passengers' Committee, maintaining that its refusal to allow the BRB to be questioned at the inquiry was 'against natural justice'. The spirit of the 1960s was not yet dead. It might be considered unfortunate that judgement went against them.

In Birmingham an early victim of tram and bus was the short 2½ mile Harborne branch, which closed to passengers in 1930. It served a prosperous commuter zone, but the need to wait at the junction with the main line for a clear run into New Street unduly expanded journey times. The adjoining Black Country suffered more. All four lines into Dudley have gone, together with two circumferential lines: that of the Midland from Castle Bromwich to Wolverhampton via Sutton Park and that of the GW from Oxley to Bretell Lane via Wombourn, only built in 1925 but closed to passengers in 1932.

But the major closure has been that of the GW main line through Wolverhampton Low Level and Snow Hill (Birmingham). By 1968 both main-line and suburban services had been diverted to the rebuilt and electrified New Street and Wolverhampton High Level, and to the unrebuilt Moor Street. But until 1972 a local Snow Hill–Wolverhampton Low Level service was provided and the once proud Snow Hill suffered the final indignity of becoming the largest unstaffed halt in the world. Its site, now razed, is to become a shopping and office complex. At the time of writing work has begun on restoring the track from the south to a new Snow Hill, with a re-sited Moor Street on the 'new' line. The integrity of the right-of-way to the north is being retained.

Manchester lost two of its city-centre terminals on the same day, 5 May 1969: the Central station of the Cheshire Lines Committee and the LNW's Exchange. By a coincidence both had only 'temporary' frontages, Central because its permanent one, in front of the magnificent roof-arch, was never built, while that of the rather mean Exchange was destroyed in the last war. But the city also had two other terminals which became 'forgotten' with the opening of Victoria in 1844. Oldham Road, terminus of the Manchester & Leeds, remained clearly visible at the end of the original viaduct above the goods depot until demolished without ceremony or protest in the late 1960s. It is more doubtful if Liverpool Road, terminus of the 1825 Liverpool & Manchester, has ever been forgotten. Since 1844 it has survived in its original form and until recently in a state of increasing decay, doing duty as the offices of the goods depot until that was closed in 1975. Public interest was rekindled as a result of the 1980 L&M 150 celebrations, and this, perhaps the oldest surviving station, has been restored.

Manchester is characterised by the glaring contrast between the modernised lines radiating southward and the run-down northern lines, serving gaunt skeletons of once large and busy stations. But even these northern lines have survived to a remarkable extent. It is the peripheral and circumferential lines that have suffered most. These include both the Midland and the GC approaches to Central; the east–west route through Tiviot Dale (Stockport);

145

the route of the former Oldham Ashton & Guide Bridge between those places; and the Lancashire & Yorkshire line from Castleton (near Rochdale) through Bury to Bolton. Finally mention should be made of the complex of very early lines from Great Moor Station (Bolton) and also in the Atherton and Leigh areas of the declining coalfield.

In the same way Liverpool has also lost two historic passenger terminals: the Liverpool & Manchester's at Crown Street (1825); and the later (1864) Brunswick of the Cheshire Lines. As in so many similar cases, they both survived for many years as freight terminals, which have now been closed in their turn. More recently, in 1972 (see page 113) and 1977 respectively, Central and Exchange were closed, though their suburban services were diverted through the new underground 'Link' opened in 1977. Again it is the peripheral lines which have been eliminated. These include the CLC line from Hunt's Cross to Aintree and the parallel line of the LNW from Edge Hill to Alexandra Dock.

But the most forgotten Liverpool railway is the 6½ mile Liverpool Overhead, completed in 1896. A pioneer of electric traction, it also pioneered automatic colour-light signalling. Always an Independent, it suffered declining traffic through bus competition, wartime destruction in the area it served, and subsequent decline in port activities. It also failed to become a link in the outer suburban system. Even in 1955 it was still carrying 10 million passengers a year, but, as in so many other cases, it was the cost of capital renewal, in this case of the steel viaducts, that proved fatal. Closure came in 1956 and since then the long viaduct has completely disappeared and with it the memory of a once indispensable transport link, aptly dubbed 'the docker's umbrella'.

Apart from Townhead, the 1831 terminal of the Garnkirk & Glasgow, Glasgow has also lost two termini in recent years. Buchanan Street, which succeeded Townhead, was closed in 1966. It never really had a suburban service and the few main-line trains to Aberdeen, Inverness and Oban could easily be diverted to Queen Street. The much larger and busier St Enoch closed the same year when all trains were diverted to Central, which thus became one of BR's busiest stations, some 340 trains leaving the terminus and a further 210 the Low Level platforms during a normal weekday. St Enoch's buildings were on a grand Scottish scale, but Buchanan Street was little more than a wooden shack.

Glasgow also had two steam-worked lines under the city centre, which linked with a number of outer suburban branches. That of the North British, via Queen Street Low Level, was still just a going concern when electrification came in 1962. But the parallel Caledonian line through Central Low Level closed in 1964 and lay derelict and forgotten for many years until electrified and re-opened in 1980.

As for the PTE area in general, the picture is one of contrast: contrast between lines modernised with intensive electric and diesel services and numerous forgotten lines. The contrast was continued in 1982 when closure of

146

the Kilmacolm branch was finalised, and with it the GSW line to Paisley via Corkerhill, while at the same time the go-ahead was given for extending electrification from Paisley to Ayr.

The Smaller Cities

So far we have looked briefly at 'million-plus' conurbations. In cities of between 250,000 and 750,000 population the fate of suburban lines has varied widely. There is no clear theme – other than perhaps the consequences of geography. Edinburgh once had a complex suburban system which has virtually disappeared. The spacious terminus of the Caledonian, Princes Street, closed in 1965, all services being diverted to Haymarket and Waverley, just as conveniently located and offering commuters a wider choice. The suburban branches to Corstorphine, Barnton, Granton and Leith, in the last two cases both NB and Caledonian; the picturesque Balerno line, which closely followed the sinuous gorge of the Water of Leith, and which caused the survival of four-wheeled coaches until 1939; the South Side Suburban line, which ran a Waverley–Waverley service; and the Esk Valley group of branches to Glencorse, Polton, Penicuik and Dalkeith, have all gone. Only the North Berwick branch survives out on the Lothian coastal plain.

In contrast Newcastle upon Tyne had suburban services connecting the city with the commuter suburbs to the north and on the coast, which the North Eastern electrified in 1904, and which BR de-electrified in 1963 and 1967 and gradually ran down. But a better fate awaited: they were transferred to the Tyne & Wear PTE. The latter electrified and modernised them, connected them with a new underground section under the city centre and a new bridge across the Tyne, gave them bus–rail interchanges, and re-opened them as the country's first light-rail urban system, the Metro.

(*below*) Provincial suburban terminal. Barnton at the end of the short Caledonian branch from Princes St. (Edinburgh). Normally two-coach trains sufficed, but a peak period set is stored in the siding. Note the lavish layout and, even in the 1930s, the goods yard devoid of traffic. (*overleaf*) An early rapid-transit line. The Liverpool Overhead soon after opening in 1893. Closure took place in 1956 and the viaduct was demolished soon after.

The difference must be sought partly in geography. Edinburgh is very compact and has many high-class residential areas near the city centre, while slum clearance and overspill estates such as Saughton are remote from the existing rail system. Tyneside is more sprawling and chains of suburbs have grown up along the railways northwards from the city centre and out to the coast. But the difference is also to be attributed to differing political approaches. Tyneside has long been industrially depressed and consequently is more able to attract grants from central government. This is coupled with a greater willingness hitherto by Tyne & Wear Metropolitan County to invest in public transport.

There is a similar contrast between Bristol and Cardiff. Bristol is the larger, and since 1950 the city centre has enjoyed a greater growth. Though, in common with the rest of South Wales, Cardiff has experienced a considerable run-down of its rail system, for Cardiff it has been more in freight than passengers. Three lines from the Valleys still converge on the city, supplemented by purely suburban lines from Coryton, Penarth and Barry Island. In contrast, other than the main lines, only the branch to Severn Beach survives of the once extensive network in Bristol. A determined effort was made in the 1950s to improve and promote the system, but by 1962 this had failed and services were run down and lines closed.

Again the basic reason was geographical. Bristol has only one station for the central area, Temple Meads, which has always been peripheral, with modern growth having been towards Clifton and on the far side of the centre. In addition, until recently little was done to upgrade the 'down-town' bus service from Temple Meads. On the other hand, in Cardiff both Central and Queen Street are convenient for the city centre, while at the time of writing a new station is taking shape at Cathays, adjoining the government offices and educational establishments.

In other cities suburban services have also been forgotten. It is hard to imagine that Stoke-on-Trent station was the hub of an extensive and frequent system of suburban services. In 1904 between 16.30 and 18.00 eighteen local trains left Stoke compared with eight in 1982. Stoke station is nowhere near any central area of the Potteries. Hanley is the biggest, but lost its station. In 1904 the traffic would have been very short distance and almost literally station-to-station. It would therefore have been the more vulnerable to tram and bus competition. It was the LMS that began to run the services down immediately after Grouping. Only the three main lines remain, all the North Staffordshire branches have gone and the only way to re-create the Potteries Loop through Hanley and Burslem is to walk through the linear park now occupying the right-of-way and to use one's imagination. But it is no longer possible to go by train to Trentham Gardens, even in imagination.

Industrial Areas
Lines in the industrial areas, particularly the coalfields, outside large cities tend

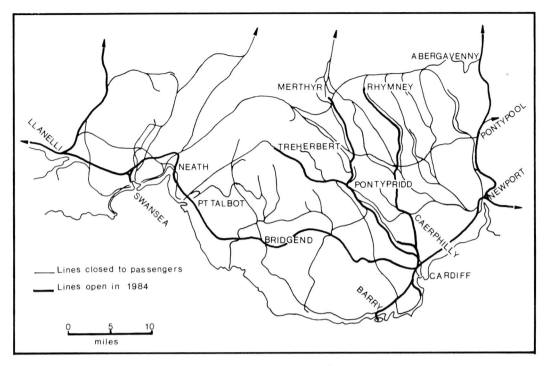

Fig. 12   The South Wales Valleys.

to be forgotten indeed. Possibly this was because they served unattractive areas and few travelled them either for pleasure or as exploring rail fans. They are therefore neglected by authors and photographers.

Perhaps it was South Wales where these forgotten lines and services were at one time most highly developed. The coalfield consisted of a high plateau, deeply scarred by a network of north–south valleys along which were the mines and urban villages. Each valley had at least one line which carried passengers as well as coal. Some had two or more as rival railways (there were five companies immediately prior to Grouping) strove to tap the mineral wealth. These services converged on the coastal towns: large ones such as Cardiff and Swansea and smaller ones like Neath and Port Talbot. In the 1930s seven lines carrying local passenger services fanned out from Newport alone. Now there are none. Besides the coastal ones, there were inland centres of services such as Merthyr, from which five routes originated in 1930, now reduced to the one to Cardiff. Even Dowlais had six stations.

Only two lines ran east–west across the grain of the country, and this resulted in heavy grades and conspicuous engineering works. To the north was the 'Heads of the Valleys' line of the LNW between Abergavenny Junction and Merthyr, which made connection with eight passenger-carrying lines leading southward. There was also the less well-known GW line from Pontypool Road via Aberdare to Neath. Its best-known feature was the great steel viaduct at Crumlin, where the line crossed the valley of the Ebbw.

A forgotten LNW outpost in South Wales, where even the LMS brought little change. Brynmawr. A train from Abergavenny arrives at the junction with the Blaenavon branch.

Closure started early, beginning with duplicating lines after the 1923 Grouping. More came in the 1930s as the coalfield began its long decline and bus competition became more fierce. The pace accelerated after 1950, and virtual extinction came in the 1960s, leaving only the lines from Cardiff up to Merthyr, Treherbert and Rhymney.

In the space available here it is impossible to trace the closure process affecting this complex area in any detail. Nor is it possible to evoke the atmosphere of the 'forgotten' lines which threaded the narrow valleys past rows of terrace houses and coal-mines with their attendant fans of sidings. The interested reader is referred to James Page's volume, *South Wales* in the 'Forgotten Railways' series.

The decline of services in South Wales has been matched by that in central Scotland between Glasgow and Edinburgh. The one-time network has been reduced to the main lines and to the Caledonian's secondary route between Glasgow and Edinburgh via Shotts. A similar decline to virtual extinction was experienced in the uplands south of Glasgow. Here the coalfield straggled westward from Lanark to the sea and gave rise to small isolated towns such as Muirkirk, Darvel and Dalmellington. Apart from the main north–south lines, the railways were mainly focussed on the two coal-exporting ports of Ardrossan and Ayr. Forgotten lines include that from Stonehouse to Kilmarnock, and that from Lanark to Cumnock and on to Holehouse, where it joined the forgotten Dalmellington–Ayr.

The passenger network once serving the Northumberland and Durham coalfield also drastically declined. Not only were the lines to the west of the East Coast main line, which climbed into the Pennines to reach Crook, Tow Law and Consett, all closed, but those eastward across the coastal plain also went. These included the one from Morpeth to Blyth and on to Monkseaton, and also the line which carried a rather primitive passenger service between South Shields (Westhoe Lane) and Marsden, originally run by the colliery companies and in its later years by the NCB.

152

The story is repeated in west and south Yorkshire, but to a lesser extent, for the coalfield area is at least in part still served by suburban and inter-urban trains fanning out from Leeds, Sheffield and Doncaster. But Barnsley now has trains only to Leeds, Sheffield and Penistone, against the six services, including that to Hull, listed in the 1930 *Bradshaw*. But the main casualty has been the once extensive GN network in west Yorkshire. A late-comer, it was for the most part forced out of the valleys and had to climb up to and over the hills by very steep gradients, which increased the difficulty and cost of operation. Thus at Ardsley the lines to Leeds and Bradford divided, the latter to struggle up to Morley Top and on to Batley by 2 miles at 1 in 43. It was all gruelling work for the firemen of the 0–6–2Ts usually found heading the three- and four-coach trains. The system duplicated other routes between all the main West Riding towns and it succumbed to buses and rationalisation, leaving only the Wakefield–Leeds–New Pudsey–Bradford line.

In Nottinghamshire all the services once connecting the coalfield with Nottingham, together with the numerous east–west services, have been forgotten. Three competing lines, Midland, GN and GC, interweaved their way southward from Kirkby in Ashfield, and all have been swept into oblivion. Sir John Betjeman provides an epitaph for the GC line in his poem 'Great Central', mentioned earlier:

> She waved to us from Hucknell South
>   As we hooted round a bend
> From a curtained front-room window did
>   The diesel driver's friend.

Mansfield, with a population of some 60,000, is without a station other than the distant Alfreton & Mansfield Parkway. Further north, in Derbyshire, the services centred on Langwith and Shirebrook have disappeared. These included

The North West has more than its fair share of forgotten electric lines. The Lancashire & Yorkshire used the Holcombe Brook branch from Bury for experiments, but the semi-rural line remained electrified until 1951, a year before closure. Where the American-style EMU is waiting there is now a suburban shopping precinct.

Nottingham (Victoria) on 18 August 1959. The view is of the southbound island platform of the 12-platform station (four through and eight bays). On the left is B1 4–6–0 61145 heading a York–Bournemouth train and on the right 61078 of the same class is ready to take out a stopping train for Grantham. The whole site is now occupied by the Victoria Centre.

the always rather sparse one on the Lancashire, Derbyshire & East Coast line. In spite of its name this started from Chesterfield (Market Place) and wandered eastward through the coalfield centres of Bolsover and Shirebrook. Beyond lay Edwinstowe, destination of miners and their families on day trips to the Dukeries and thus lavishly equipped with refreshment rooms and adjacent inns. At Tuxford the East Coast main line was crossed and a two-level interchange station of wooden simplicity provided for what must have been a nonexistent exchange traffic. After a traverse of deeply rural countryside, in complete contrast with the western part, it petered out at Pyewipe Junction, named after an isolated public house on the outskirts of Lincoln. This would be the scene of a rapid visit by train crews when delayed at the junction.

The theme, briefly touched on here, of forgotten services in urban areas and particularly in the coalfields deserves more detailed attention. Unfortunately sources are widely scattered and they have not attracted the detailed studies now appearing for rural branches. Particularly lacking is the statistical and anecdotal evidence without which it is difficult to re-create journeys up the Welsh valleys after an international match at Cardiff Arms Park, or rush hours on the steam-operated Glasgow Underground.

CHAPTER 8

Closed Rural Branch Lines

It is safe to say that every branch line was unique – unique at least as regards the countryside it traversed and the traffic it carried, while many were also unique in their equipment and operating methods. The list includes the Manifold Valley, narrow-gauge, its rolling stock 'colonial' in concept, its track hugging the beautiful and remote river, deep in the Peak District, its simple stations connected by narrow lanes winding steeply up to the stone-built hilltop villages they served. It also includes the Waveney Valley line in Suffolk, running through intensively farmed, gently rolling lowlands, carrying a heavy agricultural traffic and serving market towns as well as villages, its stations, signals and trains typical of its owner, the Great Eastern.

These pages have consistently underlined the fact that it is the rural branch lines, which once covered most of the country with a close network of railways, that have suffered most from the economies of the 1930s and from the massive closure programmes of 1950–70. So much so that the rural branch line is for practical purposes extinct, for even if occasional examples do remain, they have changed out of all recognition.

Travel over these few survivors provides only a partial and incomplete evocation of the past. The short dead-end branch of less than 10 miles is represented by fewer than a dozen examples, those to Braintree (Essex), St Ives (Cornwall) and North Berwick (Lothian) among them. Of the longer branches and loops there are perhaps rather more survivors, the Conway Valley to Blaenau Ffestiniog, Middlesbrough to Whitby, Nottingham to Grantham, and Oxted to Uckfield among them. On all these, while many of the station buildings may have survived, many are no longer staffed, passing loops and signals have been removed, goods yards closed and sidings torn up. The 'basic railway' has emerged, operated by DMUs, stations reduced in facilities to 'bus-stop' level, tickets sold on the train, distances between passing places often so great that only a reduced service can be provided, while freight and parcels have gone. The Windermere branch is now a 10 mile siding from Oxenholme into which a single DMU is locked for its tour of duty. One stage further has been authorised for the East Suffolk line (page 116): train control by radio between a central despatcher and the drivers, so that intermediate signal-boxes will disappear. A similar system on the Kyle line in the Scottish Highlands will mean that the passing loops can be de-staffed.

On the other hand the preserved lines (page 204) have had many of their

155

A typical Scottish junction, Maud on the GN of S and out of all proportion to the tiny village. Here the line from Aberdeen divided for Fraserburgh (left) and Peterhead (right).

stations lovingly restored to their pre-Grouping appearance, usually that of the 1900–14 period. From these a very good picture of the station of the past can be evoked. Rather less evocative are the trains, which tend on many lines to be modern and of quasi-main-line stock, even if they are steam hauled. But through no fault of the preservation societies, their lines lack two fundamental aspects of the traditional branch line: the traffic – passenger, parcels and freight – carried by them; and the junction with the main line. To re-create these we are dependent on literary sources and old photographs.

A Typical Rural Branch Line

Insofar as there ever could be a 'typical' branch line, it would always have joined up with another line. Though in its later years the Corringham (Essex) was 'isolated' in that it ran a passenger service which had no connection with another passenger line, in practice it was only narrow-gauge lines which had no physical connections. And even then, at Welshpool and Machynlleth the narrow-gauge lines had stations adjoining the main-line ones, while at Barnstaple the narrow-gauge Lynton trains left from a bay platform. In fact only the Campbeltown & Machrihanish line was literally isolated, though the standard-gauge Bideford, Westward Ho! & Appledore left from Bideford Quay, across the river from the LSW station.

The junction was thus of importance for the branch line and formed the usual starting point for visits. It might have been a major station. From the platforms of Crewe trains left for Northwich via Middlewich and Great Western ones for Wellington, while from Rugby trains left for Leamington. But in most cases the branches started at an ordinary wayside station on a main line, such as Burnmouth, Reston and Longniddry on the East Coast main line between Berwick and Edinburgh, or Pontrilas on the GW main line south of

Hereford. Sometimes the junction was itself on a branch. Titley (Hereford) was the junction for Presteign and for Eardisley, but itself was on the branch from Leominster to New Radnor.

The junction station would generally have its own local traffic, which if sufficient would mean survival, even if the branch was forgotten. Thus Whitchurch (Shropshire) survived the closure of the branch to Waverton and even the closure of the Cambrian line to Welshpool; Northallerton survived closure of the Wensleydale branch; and Yatton that of the Clevedon and Wells branches. But in many cases even the junction station has gone; Blisworth (on the West Coast main line), Essendine (on the East Coast main line) and Moat Lane (on the line to Aberystwyth) are but three examples from a lengthy list. Sometimes all the lines converging on the junction are forgotten. We have already paid some attention to Woodford Halse and Melton Constable (Chapter 6), but Brecon (Powys), Market Weighton (Yorks), St Ives (Cambs) and Dereham (Norfolk), with its four signal-boxes, are further examples. Occasionally the junction station was provided solely for interchange with the branch and thus was named after the branch terminus. Killin Junction (central Scotland), Bala Junction (Gwynedd) and Seaton Junction (Devon) are three such examples. These were naturals for closure with closure of the branch.

The train for Didcot waits in the up bay at Newbury on 2 September 1954.

At the junction

(*above*) A branch-line train for Northampton provides a connection at Bedford with a down semi-fast from St. Pancras. Even in 1938 the Midland 2–4–0 was sufficiently elderly to be regarded by the photographer as a 'scoop'. (*below*) Through coaches were once common. Adams 4–4–2T 30582 attaches a through coach from Lyme Regis to an Exeter–Waterloo at Axminster on 11 September 1959.

We can imagine a typical junction. The year is about 1930. The branch train of two or three elderly coaches headed by an equally elderly tank locomotive stands in the bay platform awaiting the arrival of the main-line train with a few local passengers already aboard. The main-line train, already signalled, appears in the distance – a large express locomotive and ten corridor coaches, including a restaurant-car – and draws to a stand. About twenty passengers change into the branch train, while the station staff transfer a few mail-bags and a number of parcels. The express pulls out and as soon as it has cleared the section the branch train pulls out with its thirty or so passengers, follows it down the main line for a few hundred yards, picks up the single-line token at the junction signal-box and diverges on to the branch. For the through passengers it is a very noticeably slower and rougher journey, for the coaches are old and track-maintenance standards lower.

The stations would usually be designed by the same architect, often in the vernacular style of the area and employing local building materials. On this particular branch they are in a style best described as 'Jacotudorbethan' and built of the local limestone. Each station has a passing loop and two platforms. The loop is fully signalled, but the signals provide for trains to keep always to the left, so the points have to be reset for each train, even if the trains are not passing one another. Points and signals are controlled from a large, well-built signal-box, manned throughout the hours of service, even though trains are scheduled to cross perhaps once. The platforms would often be adorned by gardens expertly cultivated by the staff in the long periods between trains.

Each station on our hypothetical branch would have two signalmen and two booking porters, one each on early and late duty. There would also be a station-master, who would carry out clerical duties. At the time our scene is set (about 1930) staffing would have been well down on previous levels. The accident report on the Abermule disaster of 1921 revealed that there was a staff of four on duty at the tiny roadside station, now closed: a stationmaster, a signalman, a porter and a lad who helped in the booking office. A photograph of the 1880s of the small Trawsfynydd station, on the GW Bala–Blaenau branch, shows eight uniformed staff on the platform as well as the train crew and some plate-layers.

The railway in the 1930s still played an intimate part in the life of the countryside through which it passed. Market days would bring increased traffic and extra trains would be run. Wednesdays were (and still are) market days at Hereford. The 1902 GW timetable shows a Wednesdays-only mixed train leaving Dorstone on the Golden Valley line at 07.55 with a connection for Hereford at Pontrilas. There was also a homeward-bound Wednesdays-only departure from Hereford at 17.20 for Hay and Brecon. In John Buchan's *The Thirty-Nine Steps* Richard Hannay, on the run from the police and a German spy ring, shares a compartment on the Glasgow & South Western with shepherds and their dogs. In the inter-war years increased wages and leisure would allow Saturday visits to cinemas and dances, and on many branch lines

159

an extra evening train would be run, no doubt smelling strongly of fish and chips. On Saturdays in 1930 it was possible to reach Dungeness on the 21.38 from Ashford.

Until the 1930s, when the Milk Marketing Board undertook collection from every producing farm, milk would be carted to wayside stations on lines such as the GC's London Extension south of Rugby, and the Ashbourne–Buxton line across the Peak District uplands, for early-morning trains, the churns expertly though noisily rolled along the platforms. The empties would be returned by afternoon services. Even when the milk went to factories for processing, many plants were rail-connected and tanks would be added to branch trains, as at Felin Fach on the Aberayron branch in west Wales, Hemyock on the Culm Valley branch in Devon, Bailey Gate on the Somerset & Dorset, and Mayfield on the Sussex 'Cuckoo Line'. Vans of watercress were attached to S&D trains at stations in the Stour Valley section south of Blandford. At Hawkhurst (Kent) at least one van-load of pot plants was regularly attached to the last up train of the day.

But apart from these special traffics, at most wayside stations the first train of the day would be met by the postman and general-store keeper for a mailbag and bundle of newspapers. Even in the 1950s the afternoon train from Hawes to Hellifield would bring medicines from the dispensary to Dent station, to be delivered to patients in the distant village by railway workers on their way home.

Freight traffic would also play its part. On our hypothetical branch each station would have a small goods yard with one or two sidings and equipped with a goods shed, small hand-operated crane and a livestock loading dock. Behind one of the passenger platforms would be a carriage loading dock, unused since the onset of the motor age.

Even in the 1930s goods traffic had fallen away, certainly in variety and often in quantity. The private siding to the local brickworks or quarry would have been out of use for many years. But several wagons would be standing in the sidings: private-owner's wagons of coal, with strange-sounding colliery names emblazoned on them or the names of local coal merchants (the merchant at Helmdon, Northants, owned a railway wagon); and box wagons with animal feed and fertilisers. The well-loaded 'pick-up' freight would call daily, and on it would be one or two 'road box' wagons for the sundries traffic (which would then have been called 'smalls') – cartons of groceries and tins of paint – to be unloaded at each station. But the goods would take empty wagons away, for it was the outwards traffic that had already been lost to road: the livestock, grain and vegetables and the products of small rural industries.

There were however examples of surviving outwards traffic, often from unexpected places. The autumn lamb sales at Kington (Herefordshire) meant special trains on the quiet line to Leominster and put this small station into the big league of livestock forwarding. Fuller's earth was despatched from Baynards on the Horsham & Guildford Direct, while flint shingle went from

(left) Passenger trains carried a great variety of traffic. At Drws-y-Nant bottled milk is loaded on the 09.27 Ruabon–Barmouth in August 1962. *(right)* At Bangor-on-Dee on 7 September 1962. The auto-train for Wrexham arrives.

Dungeness to the Potteries for glaze. Meat was loaded from Launceston on the Southern and fish from Peterhead and Fraserburgh in Aberdeenshire. Ten or more wagons were forwarded daily from Wallingford loaded with general goods.

As a typical example of goods traffic at an ordinary wayside station in the 1930s we may cite Welford & Kilworth (between Rugby and Market Harborough). Inwards traffic included cattle from Ireland and Devon, sheep from Hawick and Knighton, cattle-cake from the docks at Liverpool, Hull and London, domestic coal, farm machinery and fertilisers. Monday was 'rodeo day' when eight to ten wagons were loaded with cattle for Rugby, while after harvest grain was sent out in sacks. Income from 'parcels' traffic was swollen by the two to four milk tanks despatched daily from the milk factory.

The terminus of our branch is, as all too often happened, nearly 2 miles from the small town after which it is named. At Hawkhurst, Thaxted (Essex) and Lynton the termini were all very inconveniently sited and at Tollesbury (Essex), Laxfield (Suffolk), Red Wharf Bay (Anglesey) and Hulme End (Staffs) the lines really ended nowhere.

Often, too, the terminal layout would be on a very lavish scale. Frequently it would include a small engine shed, though this would in many cases have fallen out of use after 1930, when the branch loco would have been shedded at a nearby main-line depot. The branch timetable would now be organised from the junction end rather than the terminus. This would save the cost of staffing the out shed, but would increase empty running and light-engine working.

The Narrow Gauge

As has been said, every branch was unique. But it is possible to classify them in order to extract some themes. First we can distinguish the narrow gauge. Great Britain never had an extensive mileage and certainly lacked the complete systems of Switzerland, such as those of the Rhätische Bahn and the Montreux–Oberland Bernois/Gruyères, of the Belgian Vicinal, or even of Ireland. In the case of the latter, the County Donegal Railways (directed for many years by a joint committee of the GNR(I) and the Midland, later the LMS) was in every way a system with a number of branches, totalling 124½ route miles of owned and worked lines. The neighbouring Londonderry & Lough Swilly had 99½ route miles, which included the long 49¾ miles of the Letterkenny & Burtonport Extension, a straggling trunk line pushing through the bleak and lonely Donegal hills, and, because of the shocking roads, providing the only long-distance transport, even in the '30s. Elsewhere, the Ballymena lines, almost a system, totalled 48 route miles, and the Cavan & Leitrim 48½ miles, while the 16 mile Cork, Blackrock & Passage performed an essentially suburban function.

But though there was a bewildering variety of locomotives and rolling stock and such eccentricities as the Cork & Muskerry Light paralleling the tram line through the Cork suburbs, all the lines were of 3ft gauge. The only exception was the even more outlandish Lartigue monorail between Listowel and Ballybunion. In addition signalling systems, operating methods and station buildings were all essentially those of the broad gauge.

In contrast, the British narrow-gauge lines had a wide variety of gauges, from 15in to 3ft. They were also short, all under 25 miles and most under 10 miles, far too short to withstand transhipment costs. Operating methods were equally diverse. They were lines of great character and individuality, at least the equals in this respect of their Irish counterparts.

Scotland had but one line, the 7 miles of 2ft 3in gauge from the steamer quay at Campbeltown to the Atlantic-beaten sands of Machrihanish across the peninsula of the Mull of Kintyre. Built to aid the development of the small coalfield, it served as a tourist asset before closure in 1931. Incidentally, the nearest railway station was also on the narrow gauge, at Ballycastle in Northern Ireland.

In England there were seven public narrow-gauge lines, but by 1939 only two survived: the Romney, Hythe & Dymchurch, and the Ravenglass & Eskdale, both of 15in gauge. The 9 mile, 3ft gauge Southwold Railway connected the GE at Halesworth with the attractive Victorian resort of Southwold.

162

A line of great character, it has been lovingly recorded by R. S. Joby in his *East Anglia* volume of the 'Forgotten Railways' series:

> The sight which greeted main-line passengers at Halesworth in the years immediately before World War I was unique in East Anglia. A tiny blue locomotive, immaculate paintwork and burnished brass, stood bunker-first at the head of a mixed train of goods wagons, vans, and a couple of maroon coaches.

The Southwold closed as early as 1929, the Manifold Valley in 1934 and the Lynton & Barnstaple the following year. The passenger service on the Ashover (Derbyshire), a line completed as recently as 1925, lasted only eleven years.

Wales had by far the greatest narrow-gauge mileage. Lines were built primarily for slate and other mineral traffic, but they also carried workmen and other local people, and tourists in later years. In 1920 there were seven 'public' lines carrying passengers, and to these the Welsh Highland was shortly to be added. And what lines they were! The Welsh Highland (1ft 11½in) ran for 21¼ miles through the heart of Snowdonia, while the Corris (2ft 3in) climbed steeply up the narrow wooded and winding valley for 6½ miles from Machynlleth to Aberllefeni. By 1939 the moribund Festiniog was still operating, but would close on the outbreak of war; so were the country's only rack line, the Snowdon Mountain Tramway, the GW's Vale of Rheidol, now for tourists only, and the Talyllyn. On the grass-grown and rusted track of the latter Sir Haydn Jones kept a skeleton service going as a social necessity for the families living in Abergynolwyn.

These narrow-gauge lines were the most vulnerable to road competition. Passenger services were slow and uncomfortable: it took 100 minutes to travel the 19 miles from Barnstaple to Lynton, and one may still take the train from Llanfair Caereinion to Welshpool and imagine what it was like to use it weekly to reach Welshpool market. After 1920 the bus, however primitive, was quicker and more comfortable. For freight the need to tranship at break of gauge for the short onward journey was fatal. Mineral traffic could have been transferred easily at low cost, but the proper equipment was rarely provided. Only on the Manifold Valley were there four transporter wagons, used to bring standard-gauge milk vans down to Waterhouses from Butterton.

The tourists of the pre-war period were fewer in numbers and lacked the nostalgia for the narrow gauge felt by their successors of the 1970s as they crowded the trains of the preserved lines. Had the Lynton & Barnstaple and the Welsh Highland survived into the preservation era they would probably still be in operation. True it is possible to ride for a few hundred yards along the revived Welsh Highland, but it is a long way to the Aberglaslyn Pass, let alone Quellyn Lake. The disappearance of the Manifold Valley was particularly unfortunate, given the magnificent scenery and accessibility from the cities of the Midlands and the North. The shacks of the Hulme End terminus survive. The two locomotives were kept there and one of them was steamed to make the double round trip six days a week to Waterhouses. This leads to speculation on

163

what life was like for the crews and their families. Did they hanker after the glories of Stoke shed and the fleshpots of the Five Towns or were they keen fishermen? Where did their wives shop?

It is fortunate we can still travel on the Great Little Railways of Wales. Ironically there are now more of them than ever. But when one does so, one must remember they never used to be so impeccably smart and operated in such Bristol fashion – present conditions reflect the enthusiasm and pride of their volunteer workers. But these lines do keep alive the unique narrow gauge, and they traverse such wonderful countryside.

The Independents

The majority of the narrow-gauge lines were under independent ownership, that is not absorbed into the four 1923 Groups. But most of the surprising number of Independents were of standard gauge. One and all were eccentric and picturesque, differing from the branch lines of the large companies in their non-standard equipment, their rolling stock often second-hand, their rudimentary signalling, primitive stations and track often in the last stages of decay. On a journey over the Kent & East Sussex in 1939 the rails ahead were invisible beneath the grass, while the untrimmed hedges scraped the side of the one-coach train. Staffing levels were lower and demarcation lines less in evidence than with the major companies.

Perhaps it was the Bishop's Castle that summed up the eccentricities of them all. Bankrupt and in the hands of a receiver from opening in 1866 to final closure in 1935, its equipment and operating methods remained unchanged. With neither signals or telegraph, when the mixed train was despatched from Bishop's Castle, its whereabouts remained unknown until its return from Craven Arms. But it did a job and in 1877 the traders of the little town ran a barrel of beer on a trolley to where the bailiffs were blocking the track, enabling a train with freight to be run through while the beer was being consumed.

The line left the Shrewsbury & Hereford main line at Stretford Bridge Junction, ¾ mile north of Craven Arms, and ran up the beautiful wooded Onny Valley for 6½ miles to Lydham Heath, where a reversal was needed to reach the terminus, 2¼ miles beyond. There were intermediate stations, but no villages. The brick-built station at Plowden, headquarters of the line, survives intact, lonely and isolated in a Shropshire Eden.

In 1930 the mixed train made two round trips a day, with an extra trip on Mondays, Fridays and Saturdays. It would be hauled either by No 1, a 0–4–2T bought from the GW in 1905, or *Carlisle*, a 0–6–0 dating from 1868 and bought second-hand. The coach would have been an ex-LSW six-wheeler or a former Brecon & Merthyr or Hull & Barnsley four-wheeler, and behind it would roll three or four goods wagons. The line was staffed by a manager and six others.

There was one group of Independents which constituted a group by virtue of

164

the fact that they had imposed on them the direction and personality of Colonel Stephens from his Tonbridge office. Much ink has been spilt, including this author's, on their history, equipment and operation. But the definitive biography of Stephens has yet to be written. The colonel remains an irascible shadow, and still to be elucidated also is the motivation behind his collecting of light railways at a time when families such as the Crosland Taylors were staking their future on the motor bus. This author has dealt with the question more fully in his *South East* volume of the 'Forgotten Railways' series.

While the narrow gauge was mostly to be found in highland areas, the Stephens lines were in the lowlands, though they seemed to be equally rural. The Weston, Clevedon & Portishead linked three seaside towns and appeared to have had inter-urban potential, but certainly never fulfilled it. In 1930 there were only four daily departures from Portishead for Weston with two or three more from Clevedon. The East Kent was built primarily to develop the coalfield, but the latter never lived up to expectations. The Kent & East Sussex, the West Sussex and the Shropshire & Montgomeryshire were always very rural.

The Metropolitan Railway might not be thought of as belonging to this section of Independents. But we must not forget their line from Quainton Road to Verney Junction, later owned jointly with the LNE, and which was operated as an 'orthodox' branch, and above all the branch from Quainton Road to Brill, which was anything but orthodox. It was built privately in 1871 by the Duke of Buckingham and taken over first by the Oxford & Aylesbury Tramroad and then by the Metropolitan in 1899. At one time passengers rode behind an Aveling & Porter geared loco. But from 1899 to closure in 1935 the trains consisted of a 4–4–0T and a rigid eight-wheeled coach, both from the steam-worked Inner Circle. After 1933 the guard wore London Transport uniform, to open level-crossing gates among other duties.

The other Independents were in the main very short branch lines. They included the Easingwold, the North Sunderland and the Corringham. Both the Nidd Valley and the Derwent Valley lost their passenger services when so many branch lines closed, in the 1930s. But surprisingly the North Sunderland and the Corringham survived until after 1948.

Light Railways

A consistent thread through the development of the British railway network was parliamentary insistence that all lines, however important or insignificant, had to undergo the same costly procedures leading to authorisation. In addition the Board of Trade insisted on the same standards of equipment and operation, whatever the expected density of traffic. This imposed on branch lines a burden of capital debt and operating costs which eventually became intolerable. To ease the situation the 1896 Light Railways Act was passed. This simplified and thus reduced the cost of authorisation. It also permitted simplified operation, such as gateless and unattended level-crossings.

But the Act was aimed at a situation about to change irrevocably. By 1896 the rail net had reached its maximum. Few areas were unserved, while the remainder lacked the traffic potential to justify many new lines. It was no surprise that the lines opened under the Light Railways Act had limited traffic of a kind most vulnerable to road competition. That the last lines to be opened were among the first to be closed is only to be expected. So, by 1980 BR had no lines built under the Act which were open for passengers.

Several narrow-gauge and 'Independent' lines were legally Light Railways and a considerable mileage of electric street tramways was built under Light Railway Orders. But a large part of the Light Railway mileage consisted of 'orthodox' standard-gauge branches which came under the eventual control of the Groups. Though they were among the first to feel the impact of the 1930s round of economies, many survived into the nationalisation era. All were short. The Mid-Suffolk, 19 miles, was among the longest, but in many ways it was typical. It served an agricultural area without towns and ended 'in the middle of nowhere' some distance from the village of Laxfield. The extremely exiguous passenger traffic was accommodated in six-wheeled coaches until 1951. In 1930 they trundled up to Haughley three times a day.

Freight traffic on the Light Railways was provided for in mixed trains. The mixed train has always been unpopular: they were slow and long periods were spent at stations in shunting or, if there was no traffic, in just waiting. In Britain they were doubly unpopular, for the passenger coaches were the only vehicles with continuous brakes. They had therefore to be marshalled next to the engine, so the passengers were forced to take part in the shunting. Overseas they were at least left to meditate in peace.

A highly individual East Anglian Light Railway was the GE's Kelvedon & Tollesbury: 8½ miles from a Low Level terminus adjoining the main line at Kelvedon, over the intensively cultivated plain, to the shore at Tollesbury. The coaches were transferred from the Wisbech & Upwell Tramway in 1928. They were dwarfed by the little J67 0–6–0T working the branch and by the four-wheeled guard's van. In 1938 the author joined the 18.42 from Tollesbury, the last train. It was a sunny summer evening as the train meandered through the orchards. Behind the two tiny tramlike coaches trailed a couple of empty coal wagons, while a box wagon loaded with jam was picked up at Tiptree.

There were many other Light Railways, all deserving mention of their individual characteristics. The most northerly of them all was the 13½ mile coastal line running southward along the coastlands from Wick to Lybster in north-east Scotland, opened in 1899 and closed in 1944. It was distinguished by the Norse station names, Thrumster, Ulbster and Occumster, and by the amount of fish brought to the main line by the four daily trains (two of them 'mixed'). Then there was the 1904 Tanat Valley threading the beautiful green valley to end at the tiny mining village of Llangynog below the heights of the Berwyns. Local residents and the occasional fly fisherman were conveyed to and from Oswestry in trains of two four-wheeled GW coaches. The service, temporarily suspended in 1951 to save coal, was never resumed. And in complete contrast, pull-and-push units, powered by ex-SE&C 0–4–4Ts, crossed the low-lying Isle of Sheppey to reach the small bungaloid resort of Leysdown, on the mud of the Thames Estuary and the terminus of the Sheppey Light Railway. The list can be extended almost indefinitely.

Roadside Railways

Though common enough on the Continent, the passenger-carrying roadside railway, as opposed to the electric tramway, was unusual in this country. The dividing line between the two is fine, but apart from the Portsmouth & Horndean, the Llandudno & Colwyn Bay and perhaps the Burton & Ashby there were few examples of the electric tramway in rural areas.

All the British examples were eccentric in the extreme. The 2½ mile Wantage Tramway connecting the market town under the Berkshire Downs with Wantage Road station on the GW main line along the Vale of White Horse between Didcot and Swindon has already been described (pages 48–9). The GE opened in 1883 a 5½ mile roadside line from its station at Wisbech through fruit- and vegetable-growing Fen country to Upwell. The trains were hauled by steam locomotives with boilers and motion totally enclosed, replaced in the final years by diesel locos, their wheels also enclosed. Carriage of passengers ceased in 1928, as we have seen, the coaches going to the Tollesbury line. Freight traffic continued until 1966, trains of forty wagons or more trundling along the road to Wisbech. In Wales the 2ft 4½in Glyn Valley line ran up the Ceiriog Valley for 6½ miles, for the most part along the roadside. At Glynceiriog, the terminus, connections to the slate quarries fanned out along the streets. Passengers were carried until 1933 and, judging by photographs, loads were sometimes heavy. Scotland's contribution was the Fraserburgh & St Combs Light Railway.

Branches to the Seaside

So far we have been looking at the less orthodox branch lines. However they were always in the minority, though attracting more than their share of affection and interest. To study the orthodox majority of lines it is better to consider them by function, as they shared a basic similarity of equipment and operation. First, then, branches to the seaside.

An important social phenomenon which developed during the nineteenth century was the vast expansion in day trips to and holidays at the seaside. Not all the resorts were large; not all were Brightons and Blackpools or even Worthings and Fileys. There were numbers of small resorts all round the coast of Britain, resorts such as Bude, Sidmouth, Mablethorpe and Gullane. Not all were successful, and there were plenty of complete failures: Littlestone and Allhallows (both in Kent), Ravenscar (N. Yorks) and Westward Ho! to name but a few. But if any resort was to have any chance at all it had to have rail access, a station on an existing line or, if the main line ran inland, the provision of a branch.

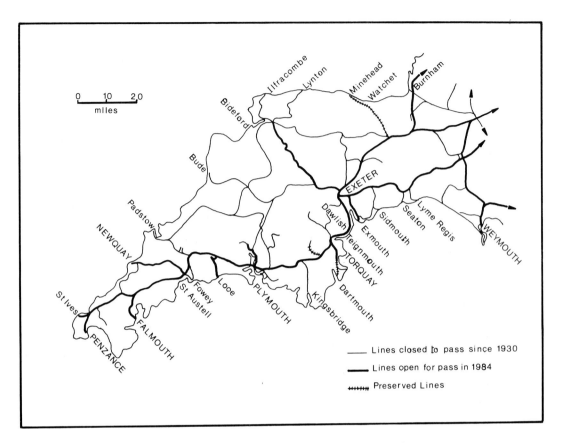

Fig. 13 Coastal branches in South West England.

Thus all round the coast, except on stretches where there was already a coastal main line, such as between Prestatyn and Bangor or Dovey Junction and Pwllheli, branches were built to pre-existing resorts such as Lyme Regis or to creations of land speculators such as Hayling Island and Withernsea.

It is interesting to note that these branches showed a remarkable tendency to survive. Prior to 1948 it was really only the more eccentric that were lost, among them the Southwold, Lynton & Barnstaple, the Lee-on-the-Solent, the West Sussex and the Gullane branch of the North British. Even by 1962, though the closure list had swollen, that of the survivors was still remarkably long. But among the 1948–62 closures were the whole of the Isle of Wight system except the Ryde–Shanklin section, the North Norfolk appendage of the Midland & Great Northern, the northern part of the Mablethorpe Loop in Lincolnshire and the coast line between Scarborough, Whitby and Saltburn.

But the Beeching Report saw no future role for the railway in the seaside traffic. Its seasonal peaks and the consequent need for the retention of additional rolling stock were anathema to the new thinking. Closures came apace, concentrated in the short period 1964–7, frequently in the face of bitter opposition. With hindsight it is hard to see that the closures inflicted any lasting harm on the small resorts, now turning to holiday flats and caravans reached by car. More serious was the way of thinking engendered in the railway authorities which saw no scope for positive approaches and aggressive marketing. In 1963 it was never envisaged there would ever be a reaction against the car. The park-and-ride shuttle service introduced in 1978 between Lelant Saltings and St Ives (Cornwall) and the successful promotion of the Cambrian Coast service would have been inconceivable.

The LSW main line from Salisbury to Exeter provides a good example of this policy. In the three years 1965–7 the three branches to Lyme Regis, Seaton and Sidmouth were closed. In addition, except for the Exeter–Barnstaple section, the whole of the Southern's 'withered arm', which served a number of small resorts in North Devon and Cornwall, also disappeared. On the East Coast there was equal slaughter; Aldeburgh, Hunstanton, Sutton on Sea, Hornsea and Withernsea all lost their services at about the same time.

A classic example of the new economic thinking and its consequences was the Hayling Island branch from the electrified main line at Havant. Until closure in 1963, on peak Saturdays a half-hourly service of four-coach trains operated full and standing, while operating costs were covered through the year. But the Langstone Viaduct would only support non-standard 'Terrier' 0–6–0Ts. Even to maintain the viaduct required £400,000. On straight accounting there was no alternative to closure. But the parallel road viaduct received interest-free grants from the Ministry of Transport for its maintenance.

Inland Market Towns

The market town is a basic component of rural areas. It is here that the produce of the district is sold and then shipped away, and here that the country-dwellers buy necessities brought in from outside. No such town in the nineteenth century could afford to be without a railway. As with the seaside towns, some of these towns were fortunate in lying on or near a main line. But the others were forced to encourage the promotion of branch lines linking them with the railway system. If they failed their decline was certain. Odiham (Hants), which never had a railway, declined relative to its neighbours, Basingstoke and Farnham.

The GW main line was laid out by Brunel as a trunk line catering for through traffic. Westward from Reading for 70 miles to Bath, the only towns served directly were Swindon and Chippenham. But the countryside was fertile and densely populated by rural standards, so there were a number of market towns within a few miles of the line. Short branches were therefore built to Wallingford, Faringdon, Highworth, Malmesbury and Calne, together with the Tramway to Wantage. Again, the Oxford branch, in response to the pleas of the citizens, was planned to pass through Abingdon. But opposition from a landowner forced an easterly route and later a branch was provided from Radley to Abingdon.

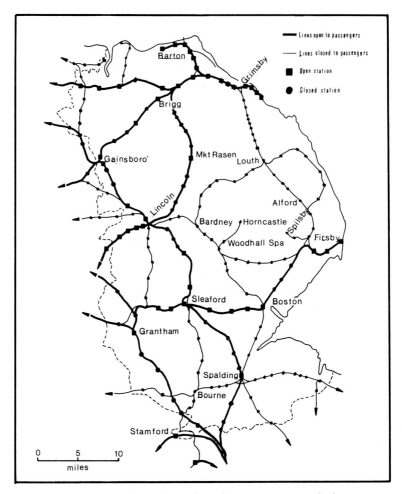

Fig. 14   Rural branches and market towns in Lincolnshire.

It was the changing pattern of access to these towns which led to the closure of their branch lines. As far as passengers were concerned, from dependence on rail communication the towns moved first to buses and then to private cars. In many cases, as with all the GW examples just given, their accessibility in the motor age was increased by their lying at main road junctions, even if they were remote from main-line railways and thus inconveniently served by rail. All the branch lines from the GW main line we have listed have been closed to passengers.

Regional Contrasts
In the Highlands of Scotland railways were always very thin on the ground. Paradoxically, in terms of lines closed as a proportion of the system at its greatest extent, this area, with the exception of south-east England, has suffered least. True the Beeching Report envisaged no lines north of Inverness, but these were in large measure saved by the vociferous Highland lobby.

170

But the areas bordering the Highlands have suffered heavily. All lines branching from the Aberdeen–Inverness main line have been lost since 1963. Further south, in Strathmore the numerous branches from the main line had already declined to extinction by the time it too closed (page 137). The southern uplands of Scotland lacked the political lobby the Highlands have. If we extend the area slightly and include the English side of the border north of the Newcastle & Carlisle line, this large region is now served only by four main lines: the East and West Coast main ones; that of the G&SW via Dumfries; and the Girvan–Stranraer. But even on these the intermediate stations have been closed. Between Alnmouth and Dunbar on the East Coast main line only Chathill and Berwick remain open; between Carlisle and Carstairs on the West Coast main line only Lockerbie, Annan, Dumfries and Kirkconnell on the G&SW line south of Kilmarnock (though Auchinleck was re-opened on a new site in 1984); and Barrhill on the Stranraer line. Only these stations remain to serve the whole of southern Scotland and the Borders.

In England as a whole the massacre of the rural branch line has been almost complete. The eastern part of Yorkshire and the southern part of Lincolnshire once had a close rail net. This has been eliminated except for some main lines such as York–Scarborough and Scarborough–Hull or the line from Grantham to Skegness. But Barnetby in north Lincolnshire, with its three-way junction controlled by a vast array of semaphore signals, standing isolated in the Wolds, remains as a working museum of times past. In contrast the North West has suffered less.

The broad swathe of country we can term the south Midlands has already been referred to a number of times. It lies east of the Oxford–Leamington line

On the North British section of the Tweedmouth–St. Boswells line. The one-coach steam train with its three-man crew operating infrequently on well-maintained track through beautiful but deserted country all betray the loss-making character of the line.

A J39 0–6–0 on a Carlisle train drifts into Canonbie on the NBR's Langholm branch.

and west of that between Cambridge and King's Lynn. This area has been particularly badly hit in relation to its density of rural population and numerous towns. But then too have East Anglia, Wessex, the West Country and the Welsh Marches. In the whole County of Gloucester six stations remain open to passengers and in neighbouring Herefordshire (the pre-1974 county) only three.

In contrast southern England has been less affected. Though a high proportion of non-electrified lines, such as the Buntingford branch in Essex and the secondary lines in the Weald of Sussex, have been closed, by 1982 the majority of even the rural lines had been electrified and the Southern's electric system has survived virtually intact.

Finally, Wales has lost almost all its lines, let alone the rural ones. Virtually all that remains is the main lines along the north and south coast to Holyhead and Fishguard respectively, the Shrewsbury–Aberystwyth with its Cambrian Coast branch to Pwllheli and the Cardiff suburban lines. Only the Central Wales from Craven Arms to Llanelli remains as a memorial to rural lines. In this context, the growing list of 'Great Little Railways of Wales' takes on a new importance.

CHAPTER 9

Last Rites and Occasions: A Footnote

Early closures attracted little attention when they actually took place. But in later years ceremonies accompanying the last workings emerged and in the end assumed almost ritualistic forms. At the height of the Beeching era between 1963 and 1967, when the Southern's 'withered arm' west of Okehampton together with numerous ex-GW lines were having sections lopped off with numbing frequency, a roving band of over a hundred mourners – 'rent-a-wake' almost – provided closure rites supported by a variable number of local residents.

In pre-war days last trains carried in many cases no more, and probably sometimes less, than their normal passenger complements, while few photographs were taken. Final closure of the Basingstoke & Alton Light, re-opened under public pressure in 1924 after war-time closure and track lifting, aroused virtually no opposition and little interest. On 12 September 1932 the last train, the 19.30 Alton–Basingstoke, was formed of a single bogie composite coach and a four-wheeled brake, and carried one solitary passenger. Again, it was reported that in the following year the last train from Lee-on-the-Solent, terminus of the short branch from Fort Brockhurst, had a complement of six men and one dog. In 1937 the Aberdeen suburban service was withdrawn. The last 'Subbie' left at 22.50 on 3 April. There were no ceremonies and the *Press & Journal* reported 'even less interest than expected'.

But a glaring contrast was provided by the final day of the Lynton & Barnstaple, 29 September 1935. The last train provided a round trip from Barnstaple and was formed of two locomotives and six coaches into which some 300 passengers jammed themselves, 50 persons per narrow-gauge bogie coach. The weather had turned wet and this probably kept the crowd down, obviating the need for a second train. David Thomas comments that the atmosphere and many of the details set the pattern which was to become all too familiar. In some senses it was a joyous occasion for the many who had long given up train travel. But nostalgia was also rife, tears were shed, and anger was expressed at the arbitrary decision of the Southern, taken without regard to local sensitivities or real needs. The unique character of the line, its association with holidays enjoyed in the past, and the last day being a September Sunday must have all conspired to increase interest.

R. S. Joby (in the *East Anglia* volume of the 'Forgotten Railways' series) tells us that the closing of the Southwold on 11 April 1929 also attracted much attention:

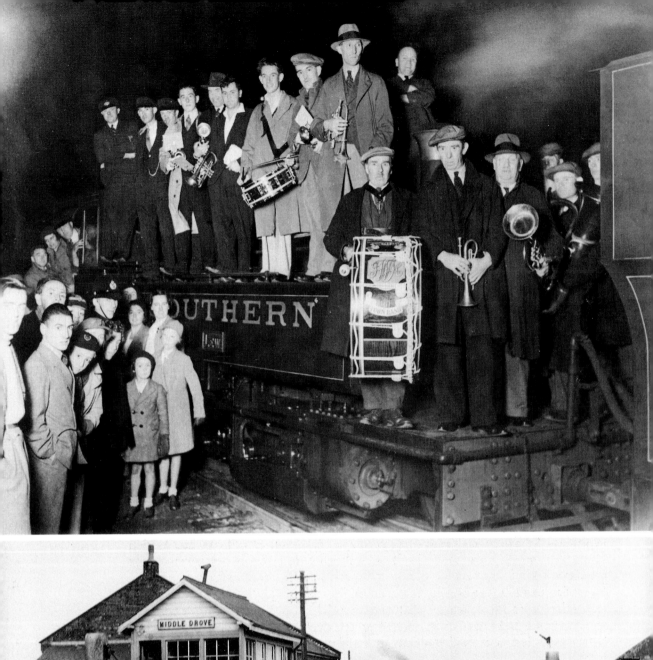

The finale of the Southwold Railway was given 'the works' by the media of the day, newsreel, press and journals, with hundreds of people to see the last train which was grossly overcrowded in consequence.

Even in the years immediately after the War the closure of the East Kent Light aroused little interest and a single coach sufficed up to the end. Edwin Course travelled on the 10.55 from Queenborough to Leysdown on the last day of the Sheppey Light in 1950. Admitted it was not the last train, but he counted ten passengers. On 8 September 1951 the last 'Bunk', the 19.25 Malmesbury–Swindon, left with twenty people aboard. The only official representative was Alderman Jones, who had ridden in the inaugural train. The *Swindon Advertiser* remarked, 'Into Little Somerford and the mighty main line – not a soul to welcome us. Brinkworth was the next stop. Here was great excitement – two ladies and two boys.'

But during the 1950s things changed. In the last few weeks traffic would visibly build up, and a week or so before the final day the hitherto lightly used trains filled up with rail fans and others. The last day would see traffic perhaps never experienced since opening day. On the last day of the Deeside line in 1966, Ballater experienced its busiest day for many years. Unheard-of queues formed for tickets for the 12.30, which left for Aberdeen with an all-time record load. On the last day at Wallingford the booking-office queue extended across the forecourt almost to the main road.

In steam days the usual train formation, a single 'auto' car, a pull-and-push set, or two or three coaches, would be replaced for the final journeys by a full-length train, and in diesel days the single-set train would have one or two more sets added. A five-coach set, normally used for school trains, was pressed into service for a series of last journeys as the Padstow–Bodmin General–Bodmin Road line was dismembered piece by piece in 1967. The last train from Hayling Island, on 4 November 1963, was made up to six jammed-full coaches. With a 'Terrier' 0–6–0T fore and aft, it was the heaviest load ever to cross the Langstone Viaduct, the repair costs of which were the reason for closure. The last trip from Weymouth to Portland on Saturday 1 March 1952 was strengthened to six coaches, headed by two 02 class 0–4–4Ts; while the very last Somerset & Dorset train blasted up to Masbury summit at a speed never before equalled, ten coaches behind two West Country Pacifics, electric headlamps ablaze.

Not that the last train was invariably packed. In contrast with scenes earlier in the day, the last Deeside trains, the 20.35 from Aberdeen and from Ballater, carried 70 and 35 passengers respectively. But packed was what they often

(opposite) *(above)* The closing of the narrow gauge Lynton & Barnstaple in 1935 was one of the first such occasions to attract the crowds and closure ceremonies which became so familiar in later years. *(below)* Last-day operations in East Anglia. A DMU sets off across the Fens from Middle Drove for Magdalen Rd. The line from March was closed to passengers in 1951.

were. In 1961 the final trip to Upton upon Severn left Ashchurch at 17.10 with 150 people crammed into the two coaches and an overspill on the tender and footplate of the class 3 0–6–0, No 43754. Yet more passengers boarded at Tewkesbury and Ripple.

But last trains almost invariably left amid a cheering crowd, a barrage of detonators and a fusillade of camera flashes. The locomotive or the front of the DMU would usually be adorned with wreaths and, after 1963, an effigy of Dr Beeching would be ceremonially burned. The final trip from St Margaret's to Buntingford on Saturday 14 November 1964 was typical. We owe the account to P. Page (in his *Buntingford Branch*, Oxford Publishing Company). The three-car DMU left at 21.45 filled with locals and enthusiasts, and detonators exploded at Widford, where the passengers booed a bus on a parallel road. Large crowds watched the train leave Hadham and Standon, and at Braughing and Westmill yet more passengers were taken up. Arrival at Buntingford was delayed as the communication cord was pulled on the approach. A mass of would-be passengers and of spectators filled the platform and the train was soon full and standing. With a fanfare on the two-tone horn the return trip began. The train left amid exploding detonators and the strains of 'Auld lang syne' and 'Wish me luck as you wave me goodbye'. At Standon the crowd gave three cheers as the train receded into the night. The communication cord was again pulled outside Hadham, the subsequent delay being taken light-heartedly by crew as well as passengers. Though not booked to stop, the train paused at Widford to set down a party of villagers and, as it pulled into St Margaret's, surprisingly only 20 minutes late, the noise of the detonators could be heard in Ware. At Wallingford, 'The customary detonators were placed on the track and the station resounded with cheering and laughter.' On the last trip from Bishop's Stortford to Braintree the communication cord was pulled outside Dunmow and a hunting horn provided an accompaniment for the passengers as they fought to board at that station.

Closure would often be associated with a special train organised by the Locomotive Club of Great Britain or a similar body, and records reveal their passage sometimes to have been more eventful than the runs by scheduled services. Closure of the Somerset & Dorset brought a plethora of audience participation. On the last weekend 2,000 people were conveyed by the chartered specials, which were pursued from vantage point to vantage point by streams of cars. At Prestleigh (south of Shepton Mallet) the fields were black with figures rushing to record on tape and film two immaculate green Pacifics fighting their long train up the 1 in 50. On the last day of the Dart Valley in 1958, grease was laid on the curve outside Ashburton to stall a restaurant car special and so allow the cameras a better chance.

A restaurant-car special was also chartered during the last week of the Kingsbridge branch in September 1963. The steam-hauled four-coach train left Brent at 18.55 and a stop for dinner was made at Gara Bridge. Kingsbridge should have been reached at 20.20, with the return to be made ten minutes

(*above*) An enthusiasts' special *en route* for Tenterden pauses at Northiam in 1960. (*below left*) Late arrival. Amid the North Wales hills a railtour reaches Bethesda on 20 October 1963. The branch from Bangor closed to regular passenger services in 1951. (*right*) A view rapidly disappearing from even open lines as manual boxes are superseded. East Winch Station on the last day of working between King's Lynn and Dereham, 7 December 1968.

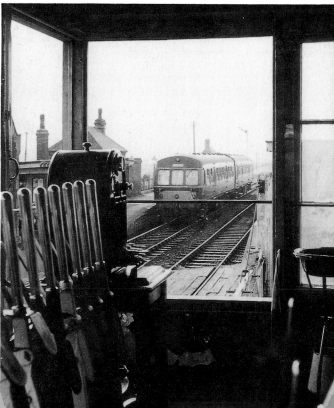

Special last train in Mid-Leicestershire. A stop at East Norton on 18 May 1957 on the line from Market Harborough to Tilton.

later. But the original drink allocation was running out (the train had started from Plymouth) and a stop was made at Avonwick to purchase two cases of whisky from a nearby pub. There had also been a sweep, the winner of which was to pull the communication cord. In spite of official disapproval, this duly happened at Topsham level-crossing, one of the passengers detraining with a full glass for the keeper. A motorist, surprised to see a steam train, got out of his car, leaving the engine running, to find out more. He was invited aboard for a noggin and the train duly proceeded. It returned three hours later, pausing to put down the motorist. The divisional passenger manager, who had come with the train, spent the time at Kingsbridge on the 'phone placating Control, the police and the general public. Constant whistling from the engine had brought complaints from lineside farmers on behalf of their frightened cattle. It is said that Plymouth was eventually reached at 00.40.

All in all closure rites were enacted in an oddly cheerful and good-humoured atmosphere. When the last train left Wallingford 'The station resounded with cheering and laughter.' The *Wallingford Herald* added that there was 'an atmosphere of happy excitement more in keeping with a royal visit than the death of a railway'. The historians of the line, P. Karau and C. Turner, thought this 'a curious reaction peculiar to such occasions'. Perhaps this underlies the fact that for most people attachment to the line was only sentimental and no extensive hardship or even inconvenience was expected. An occasional gesture

178

was made. One of the farewell specials on the S&D was brought to a halt at Binegar and in the floodlight of camera flashes Ernie Cross, a railwayman who had led the fight against closure, handed to the organisers a prepared statement on the 'vicious attitude' of the Western Region.

There was also occasional delay and even damage, but this was the result of high spirits. There seems to have been only one occasion when the situation became ugly. It has been described by John Thomas in the *Scotland* volume of the 'Forgotten Railways' series. The weekend of 3 January 1969 was the last for the Waverley Route, and Saturday 4 January was a day of sullen protest. The departure of the 09.30 for Carlisle from Waverley was delayed by a bomb scare, as was an excursion for Whitley Bay when it got to Millerhill. At Hawick a coffin, inscribed 'Waverley Line, Born 1849, Killed 1969,' was paraded beneath the noses of the passengers, who were jeered as the excursion pulled out.

The last train of all, the 'Night Midland' sleeper, left Waverley at 21.55 the next day. At Hawick the coffin reappeared and was placed in the brake-van addressed to the Minister of Transport. There was a rumour of trouble to come and a light engine was despatched ahead. It was midnight before the train left. It climbed through the night to Riccarton, but on the descent it was brought to a halt when the communication cord was pulled in a toilet. The guard wisely pursued the matter no further. But at Newcastleton there was no choice but to come to a stop behind the pilot. A bad-tempered crowd had assembled on the level-crossing beyond. Conspicuous among them was the minister of the kirk,

(*left*) The last train prepares to leave Much Wenlock for Wellington at 19.15 on 21 July 1962.
(*right*) The desolation of six years. The same scene in 1969.

who in the end was arrested. For over an hour the well-filled train stood while the argument continued. Eventually David Steel MP, who was aboard, arranged with the crowd to let the train through provided the minister was released. Eventually the light engine was re-started and the Night Midland went on to Carlisle without further incident, but many hours late.

At first it may seem surprising that such direct action was so rare. For it is unquestionable that the demonstrations which delayed the opening of London's Westway led to the passing of the 1973 Land Compensation Act, which authorised much improved terms for householders suffering environmental deterioration from urban motorways. If this could be achieved through public protest, why could not such measures halt a closure? The most probable answer is that it is easier to prevent something from being started than to force something to continue. In the case of the Waverley Route, whatever might have happened the night before, the next 21.55 Night Midland simply did not leave Edinburgh. However strong the measures the Borderers were prepared to take, they could not make it run.

David Thomas, then a journalist, attended a number of West Country closures in his professional capacity and has generously provided many of the details of this chapter. The stories of some of these occasions conclude it.

The Princetown branch, closed on 3 March 1956, was the first important West Country line to suffer this fate. The last train, of six coaches headed by

(*right*) Fortunately not really the last. The last BR passenger train for Shrewsbury at Bridgnorth on 7 September 1963. The station is once again busy as the northern terminus of the Severn Valley Railway. (*left*) The forgotten end of the Severn Valley. On 19 August 1963 the 14.31 train for Bridgnorth and Kidderminster pulls out of Coalport.

two locomotives, climbed through a thick fog whirling in a strong cold wind. Normally the train would have been stabled overnight at Princetown, where the loco depot was still open. But on this last trip it was worked back to Plymouth. Permission was given for the numerous enthusiasts to return on it, so that they were not stranded. But they had to remain on the freezing platform while the engines ran round separately and the train shunted to the goods shed to offload the Sunday milk supply.

But Authority did not invariably enter into the spirit of the occasion. As on the Princetown branch, the last train of the day on the 8¾ mile Helston branch was kept there overnight. But on the final day of working, 3 November 1962, it was re-scheduled to return empty to Penzance. David Thomas suggested to the Plymouth district manager that passengers might be permitted to return with it. The manager's reply was that this would not be possible as the train would remain overnight at Helston. On being told there was information to the contrary he inquired as to who knew most about his railway – he or David Thomas.

In due course, on arrival at Helston the guard confirmed that the train was indeed returning to Penzance. It was obvious what the crowd had in mind, causing the station-master to take fright and retire homeward. There being no other officials on hand, it was the guard who had to bear the brunt of the justifiable public wrath. He was moved to make to David Thomas, acting as spokesman, a statement he had cause to regret: 'It is advertised as empty and if you travel on it, it won't be empty, will it?' This appeared on the front page of the Monday's newspaper and the guard was teased about it for months.

So the empty train drew out with 300 empty seats, leaving 300 enthusiasts to find their way back somehow to civilisation. Fortunately the private-enterprise refreshment room had been granted a late licence, so they could set out fortified to beg lifts or to walk.

In contrast BR set out to maximise revenue from the last train from Tiverton. This normally returned to Exeter via Tiverton Junction, but on the last night it provided a final scheduled run back down the Exe Valley. Its departure was so delayed, until a few minutes before midnight, that an enthusiast pulled the cord

A special last train on the Tetbury branch at Rodmarton Halt, 5 April 1964.

to ensure that the train did not leave until the next day, which it did with hardly a seat to spare.

It was Nature that had the final say in the last rites attending the closure of the long 34¾ mile branch from Plymouth to Launceston through Tavistock and Lydford. In its final years traffic had declined so much that the infrequent trains were down to a single 'auto' trailer (page 26). But these were replaced on the last day, Saturday 29 December 1962, by four-coach trains. But steam was used to the end.

The last trains were scheduled to leave Launceston at 20.35 and Plymouth at 20.40. At Tavistock, where they would cross, the planned ceremonies included enthusiasts dressed as undertakers' mutes and a bugler to sound the last post. But at midday snow started to fall and by early evening it was being whipped by a 70mph gale. The 17.40 from Launceston reached Marsh Mills at 19.50, only 30 minutes late. But it was unable to gain the main line at Tavistock Junction, ¼ mile beyond, until 22.05. Meanwhile the 18.20 for Launceston had eventually pulled out of North Road station at 19.32. After waiting for the train from Launceston to clear the branch, it reached Marsh Mills at 22.14. In spite of brakes freezing on the 1 in 60 grade and more frozen points, the 4 miles on to Bickleigh took only a further hour, by far the highest speed so far.

At Bickleigh the 19.10 from Tavistock had been waiting for 3¼ hours, and in fact proved to have finally stuck. The northbound train plodded on into the screaming blizzard. Passengers alighted at each stop to make their hazardous way to their homes. By the time the train struggled into Clearbrook Halt, 9 miles from Plymouth, it was five hours late. Until Horrabridge the crew were still insisting they would not only make Launceston, but would return thence as the official last train. But at that station the passengers were informed the train would not be returning, the last trains in both directions having been cancelled.

In fact it got no further than Tavistock South, for the signal wires beyond had been brought down, and with no communication with Lydford no staff or ticket could be issued. The twenty-five local passengers for stations beyond spent the night in the first two coaches, heated by the 2–6–2T and fed by the station-master and signalman, who remained on duty all night. Next day they were taken to the church hall and eventually taken on home by road. Fifteen enthusiasts went to the North station, but the Southern's line was also blocked. They eventually returned to Plymouth on a train which got through to the North station from Plymouth.

At Bickleigh the locomotive ran out of water, so the three passengers retired to the signal-box. On Sunday a relief engine came out from Plymouth and twenty hours after its arrival, the train resumed its journey. The passengers were joined by four walkers enjoying the unexpected bonus of a Sunday train, and on the day after closure. So the 19.10 from Tavistock steamed into North Road with the distinction of being the last passenger service on the line.

Natural disaster at least once precipitated closure. John Thomas related (in *The Callander & Oban Railway*, David & Charles), how it was planned to

183

divert the Glasgow–Oban trains up the West Highland to Crianlarich (Upper), rejoining the ex-Caledonian route by the spur, thus allowing closure of the 40 miles between Dunblane and Crianlarich (Lower) on 1 November 1965. But on 27 September a landslip in Glenogle between Balquidder and Killin Junction blocked the line completely. Until Saturday 2 October, at the scheduled times of departure for Oban, two trains would leave Buchanan Street: a DMU for Callander and a locomotive-hauled train for Oban, which ran via Sighthill and the West Highland. A bus was provided between Callander and Crianlarich. On Monday 4 October the Oban trains left from Queen Street, DMUs leaving Buchanan Street for Callander and the connecting bus. Then, finally, on official closure day, the bus ran the whole way from Dunblane.

We end this chapter with a service which went out with a whimper of official muddle rather than a ceremonial bang, and which perhaps sums up the confusion of the time. It was announced that closure of the Uckfield–Lewes section would take place on 6 January 1967. But there were difficulties in licensing the replacement buses, so a shuttle service was arranged, as the new timetable had been designed on the assumption that the trains from London would turn back at Uckfield. The engineers then took a hand by insisting that the Ouse Viaduct at Lewes should be closed on 23 February as it was becoming too dangerous. So buses were hired to replace the shuttle service. But tickets were not issued on the buses, Isfield and Barcombe Mills booking offices being kept open for this purpose. The station at Barcombe Mills stood at the end of a long approach road, which the buses were unable to negotiate. The procedure for anyone sufficiently foolish to join the bus was to walk up to the station to buy their ticket. They would then be conveyed back to the bus-stop in a taxi hired by BR for this one-way trip. The farce was brought to an end when the official replacement bus service started on 6 May. The author's task would be much more arduous if bureaucracy provided him with no such opportunities for merriment!

PART III

THE FORGOTTEN RAILWAY
IN THE LANDSCAPE

On the Festiniog. In 1938 there were still four daily trains each way when 'Merddyn Emrys' was photographed traversing deteriorating track near Carnedd Tunnel.

CHAPTER 10

The Physical Remains

The technology of the railway is such that it must have a continuous and separate 'right-of-way' on which the 'permanent way', the track, is laid. The latter – rails, sleepers and to a lesser extent the ballast – can easily be recovered for its scrap value, so the track rarely survives on a forgotten railway. But the right-of-way, though it may, for one reason or another, be taken over for other uses, tends to survive over long distances and so becomes the most obvious of the many physical remains of the forgotten railway.

Gradients and curvature of the right-of-way must be limited, particularly on main lines, but to a lesser extent even on unimportant branch lines. Therefore the relationship between the right-of-way and the landscape is an intimate one and involves considerable earthworks and associated engineering features. The more broken the landscape and the greater the requirement for high speeds and increased train weights, the longer and higher are the embankments, and the longer and deeper the cuttings. Thus in hilly country the physical remains will be more obvious, and more difficult – and therefore costly – to eliminate. Also, the remains of main lines such as the GC London Extension and the Hull & Barnsley have survived to a considerable extent.

Engineering Features and Their Survival
The engineering features associated with a railway will include numerous bridges. Most of these will be small, to allow roads to pass over or under the line or to allow the line to cross a small stream. But in hilly and broken country they may become much larger and there will be impressive viaducts across deep valleys or wide rivers. Examples were the numerous bridges between Keswick and Troutbeck (Cumbria) where the line crossed and re-crossed the River Greta, the great Conisbrough Viaduct on the Dearne Valley line (S. Yorks) which still stands, and the Caledonian's cantilever structure across Loch Etive at Connel Ferry on the Ballachulish branch. There will also be the occasional tunnel.

The survival of these structures will depend on a number of factors. Road overbridges tend to have the highest survival rate, for normally they cross sections of line which are in cuttings, and unless the road needs widening, or unless there are sharp curves on the approaches to the bridge, it is regarded as being too costly to fill in the cutting. However on the A604 at Cranford (Northants), the bridge over the Kettering–Huntingdon line has been removed and the former S-bend eliminated. But on the other hand many road over-

Last remains of the Lancashire, Derbyshire & East Coast Viaduct finally demolished in 1984 to make way for the Inner Relief Road along the line of the Great Central's Chesterfield Loop.

bridges survive across the wide cuttings on the GC London Extension. Where a road crosses over a line where the latter is on a level with the land, there is more likelihood of the bridge being eliminated, though humpbacked bridges survive on minor public or on private roads. Between Gamlingay and Old North Road on the LNW Bletchley–Cambridge line humpbacked bridges span the former right-of-way, which has now disappeared under crops. The bridge carrying the A299 Thanet Way over the trackbed of the Canterbury & Whitstable also survives with its approach embankments. Built in the 1930s, it is wide enough for a second track that never would have been provided.

Where the road passes under a line, bridges are much more likely to disappear. If the bridge is of steel-girder construction, as most were, it will be recovered for scrap. If it is of brick or stone it will be removed if the road is widened or the approaches to the bridge are improved. It will also be demolished if deemed unsafe due to lack of maintenance. Examples are too numerous to mention, but the observant student of forgotten railways can soon spot the brick or stone pier on one or both sides of the road, or the cut-back ends of the embankment. Bridges over streams are more likely to survive, but will seldom be encountered unless the searcher is walking the right-of-way. In 1976 walking the Horsham & Guildford Direct line north of Baynards had been made more difficult by the collapse of two bridges over the infant Wey.

187

Whether in town or country, tunnels are the most difficult engineering feature to convert to new uses. (*left*) On the Crystal Palace High Level Branch. (*right*) Cressbrook Tunnel in Monsal Dale.

Of the larger bridges and viaducts, survival again depends on the material of which the structure was built. The spectacular steel-lattice viaducts, including the Crumlin Viaduct on the Pontypool–Neath line, that on the Barry Railway at Taff's Well, and the Belah Viaduct on the Stainmore line, have all been demolished for their scrap value. But the stone viaduct by which the Ingleton branch approaches the junction with the West Coast main line at Low Gill can still be seen from trains on the latter as they traverse the Lune Gorge. But where they have got in the way, some stone and brick viaducts have been demolished, sometimes spectacularly blown up, such as the one at Chorley (Lancs) on the Blackburn branch, sacrificed to the M61.

It is difficult either to eliminate tunnels or put them to alternative uses. Their survival rate is thus very high and their bricked-up portals can normally easily be seen. Although most of the Crystal Palace High Level branch has disappeared, the portals of the Upper Sydenham tunnel are still visible.

The right-of-way of a railway is comparatively narrow. A single track of standard gauge does not need one of more than 12ft wide if the line is on the level, though of course it will be wider if on an embankment or in a cutting with sloping sides. But at stations it broadens out to accommodate the sidings and buildings. A considerable area was needed if the station was built to deal with a

188

heavy passenger and freight traffic, especially if there was also a locomotive depot and a marshalling yard. At Woodford Halse the sites of all these can be identified.

Station Sites

The stations, unless they were located immediately alongside or under a public road (as were those on the GC London Extension), would have to be connected to the public road by a private road. Often there was separate access to the goods yard. The sites of stations can frequently be identified by these approach roads.

Stations normally dealt with passenger and freight traffic, but sometimes, especially in urban areas, they dealt only with passengers. More rarely they dealt only with goods. At one time public sidings were also quite common. On the West Coast main line the site of Loughton Siding has been submerged under the new Milton Keynes station, but that of Langford, south of Biggleswade, can easily be identified from East Coast trains. On the Hawkhurst branch (Kent) public sidings were provided at Churn Lane and Pattenden.

In addition there would have been an even larger number of private sidings, though many of them would have been taken out even before the line was closed. If the plant served, whether factory, warehouse, quarry or brickworks, was alongside the line a simple siding was usually provided. In other cases a length of private line would have been built from a simple exchange layout and these can often be traced.

Occasionally marshalling yards and even locomotive sheds were provided at remarkably remote locations. On the closed Midland line across the High Peak, Rowsley (4¼ miles north of Matlock) was a wayside station, with a small goods yard on the site of the original terminus of the 11½ mile line of the Manchester, Buxton, Matlock & Midland Junction. But it also had an extensive marshalling yard and an engine shed. Sometimes passing loops were provided on single lines to break up long sections between stations. One such was Loch Skerrow on the 'Port Road' to Stranraer, between New Galloway and Gatehouse of Fleet stations, where the line traversed the lonely moorland below the Cairnsmore of Fleet.

Fencing

With the exception of the few roadside lines, rights-of-way were continuously fenced. Materials varied greatly, including hedges, iron railings, and wire fences supported by wood, iron or concrete posts. Fences tend to survive most changes which affect forgotten railways and can be used in tracing them. In 1976 the author found a short length of iron railing as the only reminder of Goudhurst station on the Hawkhurst branch, the whole site having been built over.

Particularly in rural areas, the right-of-way of the forgotten railway can frequently be traced, even if there are no revealing earthworks. For the practised eye there are the narrowly parallel lines of overgrown hedges running rather more straight or in rather more sweeping curves than bridleways or lanes. Straightening of the A483, which crossed the Cambrian line on the level at Pool Quay, north of Welshpool, led to demolition of the station and obliteration of the site. But the severed right-of-way can be traced as it converges on the road by means of the line of parallel hedgerows.

If the right-of-way is not used officially or unofficially as a footpath, bridleway or farm track it quickly becomes overgrown with tall grass, brambles and woody vegetation. In 1971, when the Manchester, South Junction & Altrincham electric line was converted from 1,500 volts dc to 25kV ac the short approach line to the car sheds, themselves on the site of Bowdon station, was closed and the sheds were demolished. Ten years later, the site, in the middle of Altrincham, was a healthy young deciduous woodland, the trees all being self-sown. If one walks the right-of-way of the former branch from Huntingdon towards St Ives, passage is easy at first, but when an official footpath parallels it the growth of vegetation is such that the right-of-way is impassable.

Most railway companies were free with gates, not only at level-crossings over public roads, but at 'accommodation' crossings where private roads and farm tracks crossed the line, as well as at entrances to stations and goods yards and even across rail tracks at the boundary between those of the railway company and the private firm. Many of these survive and they are often pointers to the forgotten line. Stiles were also provided where footpaths cross the line and again these often survive.

The less obvious furniture along the line included huts to store tools and to provide shelter for plate-layers. These were built of old sleepers, brick and, in more recent times, of concrete. Many still remain. Mileposts, gradient posts and notices would normally escape the attention of those reclaiming the track, but more and more they have become objectives for souvenir-hunters. Railway administrations have always lavishly provided cast-iron, and later enamelled, notices exhorting drivers to whistle or to stop and pin down brakes, and the public to 'Stop, look and listen' and, above all, to refrain from trespass. At least within living memory trespassers at Orpington (Kent) were still being threatened with transportation, while potential trespassers were apparently regarded by the Festiniog management as being monoglot Welsh speakers.

Station Buildings

Except on Light Railways and other cheaply built lines, stations were usually substantial affairs. They usually incorporated a dwelling and for this reason many have survived. But even the wooden structures of the South Eastern, which only housed offices, have been converted to dwellings on closed lines such as the Elham Valley (page 209). Their chance of survival may be linked to their architectural merit. It is not the place here to comment at length on station architecture. Sufficient to say that some companies, the LSW, the LCD and GN among them, provided rather mean and featureless station buildings. But others were of considerable architectural merit. Those of the North Staffordshire were of good quality Elizabethan style and the stone buildings of the NE and its constituent companies were usually of a good vernacular style. J. W. Livock designed some excellent stations for the London & Birmingham and its subsidiaries. One survives at Wansford (Rugby & Peterborough), built of local Barnack stone and in the tradition of the 'Stone Belt'. Unfortunately it is not in the possession of the preserved Nene Valley Railway. Station buildings imposed a characteristic stamp on a line.

Survival may also be linked to the location of the station. Many are in very pleasant rural surroundings and therefore in greater demand for country dwellings.

While small independent companies often provided very simple stations, such as the wood-framed, corrugated-iron huts of the 'Colonel Stephens' lines, the even more simple 'halt' almost invariably belonged to the present century. Sometimes, especially on the Southern (Chestfield & Swalecliff is an example) these were quite substantial affairs, but the GE was apt to provide little more than a name-board and a strip of cinder by the lineside. Even where the station buildings have disappeared completely from a forgotten station, the grass-grown platform with its brick, concrete or wooden edging frequently survives.

Other features at stations included goods sheds, which frequently remain when much else has been demolished, particularly as there are so many alternative uses to which they can be put. Signal-boxes were sometimes substantial affairs. Most have gone, though their foundations can be traced. But a few

Wolferton for Sandringham in 1977. *Sic transit gloria mundi.*

remain. That at Hartington on the LNW line from Buxton to Ashbourne now does duty as an office for the warden of the Tissington Trail along the right-of-way.

Another important feature was the staff accommodation, a row of cottages or a single dwelling provided at stations, intermediate signal-boxes and at level-crossings. Again the survival rate is high and the row of cottages often survives even where the station has been completely demolished. Cottages in the characteristic style of the particular company still mark the site of many a forgotten level-crossing. A Queen Anne style cottage just beyond the Ouse Bridge at Huntingdon and almost under the elevated A14 is all that can be traced of the GN&GE line in the vicinity of Godmanchester station.

Lines and Landscapes

On a small scale, as we have just seen, it is often surprising how many features of a forgotten and apparently vanished railway have actually survived and also what can be traced by those who know what they are looking for. After the author had been told by a local resident where the site of the West Sussex terminus at Selsey was to be found, he was able to recognise pieces of fencing outlining the site. He was also able to trace the location of Brambledown Halt on the Sheppey Light by the property boundaries of houses built after closure of the line.

On the larger scale, one may be tracing and looking at lines which for considerable distances are so well preserved that they seem to lack only track and trains to bring them back to life. In-between there is much variation between lines which have largely survived and those which have virtually disappeared.

The remains of the GC's London Extension have been commented on frequently in these pages. They provide an excellent example of the forgotten railway in the landscape. Engineered on a grand scale, northward from Calvert Spur the formation strides uninterrupted across the rolling uplands to Rugby and on to Leicester. The fact that it was built after neighbouring trunk lines had taken up the easier routes meant that earthworks were heavy. There is a great contrast with other abandoned lines in the area – the LNW from Weedon to Leamington and the Stratford-upon-Avon & Midland Junction from Blisworth to Stratford.

On the GC, deep cuttings with high road overbridges alternate with high embankments; there are brick viaducts at Helmdon and Woodford as the line undulates on a generally rising grade of 1 in 176 up to Catesby Tunnel. North of the site of Rugby Central station, though the formation has been built over, the steel viaduct still crosses the West Coast main line and beyond that again a high embankment and bridges take the formation across the Avon Valley.

In high country, the Port Road from Dumfries to Stranraer winds round the hill block of the Cairnsmore of Fleet, crossing the Big and Little Waters of Fleet by the grey stone viaducts (pages 135–6). Across the moors of the Brecon Beacons and down their steep northern face the lines from Neath and Merthyr to Brecon can easily be traced. So can long lengths of the GW's Princetown branch ascending to high Dartmoor.

Lines along the coast or shores of estuaries have a particular attraction and the formation of forgotten railways can be traced in several such locations. These include most of the 33¾ mile Ballachulish branch, the formation of which skirts the shore of Loch Linnhe and Loch Leven in the West Highlands. The line from Wadebridge to Padstow, as it were the last dying gasp of the Southern, in fact died very pleasantly indeed along the shore of the Camel estuary, while Sandsend station on the line from Whitby to Saltburn was almost on the seashore. The Penrith, Keswick & Cockermouth line included a

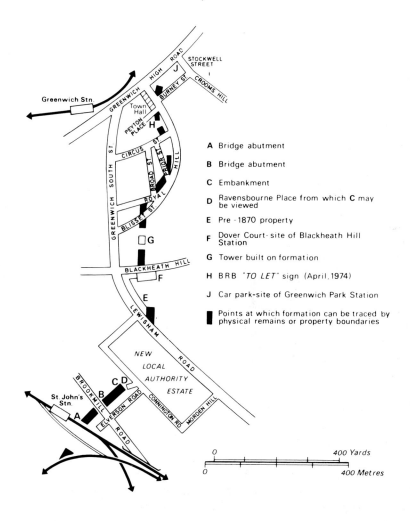

A Bridge abutment

B Bridge abutment

C Embankment

D Ravensbourne Place from which C may be viewed

E Pre-1870 property

F Dover Court - site of Blackheath Hill Station

G Tower built on formation

H BRB "TO LET" sign (April, 1974)

J Car park - site of Greenwich Park Station

■ Points at which formation can be traced by physical remains or property boundaries

Fig. 15 The Greenwich Park Branch. As surveyed in 1974, fifty-seven years after closure. An example of the forgotten railway in the urban landscape.

193

delightful stretch along the shore of Bassenthwaite Lake, but unfortunately the formation has been taken in to the widened A66.

All this is in complete contrast with lines in lowland areas. In the Fenlands of East Anglia the branch from Holme on the East Coast main line to Ramsey has for the most part been taken back into the fields from which it came and all traces of the formation have been lost. A similar fate has overtaken most of the formation of the St Ives–Ely line of the Great Eastern.

The formation of lines in urban areas also provides a challenge to those tracing forgotten lines in urban areas. Here land values are extremely high and closed lines have been absorbed into the urban landscape as those just mentioned have been absorbed into the rural. Thus blocks of flats have obliterated the LSW line from Studland Road Junction (Hammersmith) to Olympia. Figure 15 shows better than mere description what has happened to another London branch, that to Greenwich Park. On the other hand, the right-of-way of the former Midland line still cuts through the South Manchester suburbs from Chorlton to Cheadle Heath, an unofficial footpath and a reception area for old bicycles, pram frames and mattresses.

Date of Closure and Survival

Because earth-moving machinery is now so much more efficient, the cost of eradicating the forgotten line from the landscape is that much lower. The paradox thus emerges that, as a rule, the lines closed at an earlier date are more easily traced than those closed much later.

We can take two examples from southern England. In 1974 the author found a row of bungalows perched on top of an embankment, part of the formation of the line from Hythe to Sandgate, closed in 1931. The front doors were approached by steep steps and the gardens sloped equally steeply from the back doors. In contrast the site of Hythe station, closed in 1951, was being obliterated by bulldozers levelling the land for housing.

Again, north of Lewes the original line of the Lewes & Uckfield Railway, closed in 1863, can be easily traced from the site of Uckfield Junction on the electric line to Keymer Junction, even the keeper's house at each of the two former level-crossings being in good order. But the 1863 deviation, closed in 1969, has been destroyed in building the new ring road.

CHAPTER 11

Alternative Uses

The land occupied by forgotten railways represents a formidable total. There are some 8,500 miles which once had passenger services, and most of that mileage has been completely closed. The right-of-way of a single-track line on the same level as the surrounding countryside is about 20ft wide between fences and that of a double-track line about 30ft. This will consume a minimum of 2½ acres of land per mile in the former case and 3¾ acres in the latter. The width of the right-of-way will increase with height of embankments and depth of cuttings, especially if the 'batter' or slope of the earthwork sides is gentle, as it will be when the line is through clay or some other unstable geological formation. In addition, every few miles there are the sites of the stations, which may be several acres if the goods yards were spacious or if there were marshalling yards and motive-power depots. It is therefore possible to conceive of the land available as being in the form of a string of beads, widely spaced on a thread of varying width.

In Great Britain as a whole the population is dense and land for any purpose is in short supply and consequently high-priced. The thousands of miles of old railways thus represent a major financial resource and a valuable national asset.

The Process of Release
After closure and subsequent reclamation of the track, the land of a disused line is transferred to the Estates Department of the BRB. Permission to sell the formation must be obtained from the Secretary of State for Transport. In the past this consent appears to have been given too readily, thus hindering later consideration of re-opening or other major re-use. But the BRB was under pressure to sell as quickly as possible from a number of directions. In the first place transfer to the Estates Department included residual responsibilities such as maintaining the fences. The BRB thus had an incentive to sell, in order to rid itself of the maintenance costs and other obligations. There was also pressure from neighbouring landowners, not only from those who wanted to purchase, but from those who did not want to see the land becoming derelict. Finally there was the BRB's need to increase its cash flow for short-term purposes. Some felt that the BRB should be relieved of its financial responsibilities, so that the pressure for unplanned and uncoordinated quick sales would be reduced.

The land for sale had first to be offered to the appropriate local authorities. Many made good use of this privileged position, but many more allowed a unique opportunity to be lost. The formations between stations were then offered to adjoining landowners and thus broken up into small parcels. The station sites were rightly put up for general sale as they would thus get higher prices than if they were sold for agricultural uses. With planning controls over non-conforming uses, for the most part these sites have been put to good use, though no attention was given to ensuring rights-of-way through or round them.

Prof Appleton, in his report to the Countryside Commission (1970), strongly criticised this procedure as failing to ensure that the land was put to the best use in the public interest. This brought forth from the Department of the Environment changes in the procedure to allow local planning authorities more time to consider and arrange for alternative uses. But unfortunately the horses had frequently bolted before the wide-open stable door was half closed.

Alternative Uses – A Classification

If we are to consider the various alternative uses to which the land can be put, we must first of all distinguish between those uses which require a continuous, uninterrupted right-of-way and those which do not. Secondly we must distinguish between those uses which require a comparatively large parcel of land and those which do not. Finally, we can distinguish between those uses which merely require the land and those which make use of the buildings and other fixed equipment.

Uses requiring a continuous right-of-way

Turning first to those uses which, like the original railway, need a continuous right-of-way, the first point to be made here is that the integrity of the right-of-way must be preserved when the line is closed if these alternative uses are ever to employ the route. If the right-of-way is severed by the sale of small parcels or complete station sites, or the demolition of bridges, it becomes useless. The second point is that this range of uses are all connected with transport and communications, even if the purpose is in connection with leisure activities.

The most controversial use to which forgotten railways can be put is their conversion into public roads. It is true that since the last war there have been advocates of converting even working railways into roads: there has been no lack of theoreticians anxious to forward the policy, initiated by the late Brigadier Lloyd, founder of the Railway Conversion League. There are however two drawbacks to converting lines to roads.

The first stems from technology. A guided system, such as a railway, needs a much narrower track than the non-guided road system. A rural road built to Department of Transport standards requires a right-of-way 42ft wide, of which 18ft is carriageway and the rest verges. An urban road, with a footpath on either side, is 34ft wide. A main road with dual carriageways requires a width of 47ft 9in for the surface and median strip. These figures must be set against the 20ft for a single-track railway and 30ft for a double.

The second drawback is that the route of the former railway is not necessarily the preferred one. The railway may in fact have been closed because of declining traffic along the route and not because of loss of traffic to road.

On the other hand, even if the old railway line is too narrow for the new road, at least the land provides a good beginning for the compulsory acquisition of land for the new or realigned road. One of the earliest conversions, dating from 1953, was a 1½ mile stretch of the Manifold Valley line between Ecton and Wettonmill, which provides a valley-floor road. It includes the tunnel south of the site of Butterton station, so narrow that two cars cannot pass in it. The right-of-way had been dedicated by the LMS to the county council as a long-distance footpath, so a moral breach of faith has been involved. In this connection it is worth remembering that it was the desire of Kent County Council to incorporate the formation of the Westerham branch in a motorway scheme which lay behind its opposition to a consortium formed to take over the line from BR and to continue operating it. Local authorities are not always on the side of those seeking to retain a line.

A number of trunk roads have made use of long stretches of forgotten railways. This has resulted in the remains of the line being obliterated even further and so becoming even more of a forgotten line. An early example was the A465 'Heads of the Valleys' road in Gwent between Brynmawr and Merthyr, which took over long sections of the LNW Abergavenny & Merthyr line. Further west the GW Pontypool Road–Neath line has been used beyond Hirwaun. The realigned and improved A40/A449 from Monmouth to Newport has also made use of the GW line between Monmouth, Raglan and Usk, while more recently the A470 Cardiff–Merthyr road has used the Quakers Yard–Merthyr line formerly owned jointly by the GW and the Rhymney. Elsewhere the A34 Oxford–Southampton road has incorporated the right-of-way of the Didcot, Newbury & Southampton Railway for a by-pass round Whitchurch and on across the chalk Downs to Sutton Scotney. As a final example the new M62 has been aligned along the Hull & Barnsley formation in the area of Sandholm, west of Hull.

In urban areas short stretches of former railway have been taken over. These include the GN's Suburban line in Nottingham. There are other examples at Birkenhead, where the former Seacombe branch has become an approach to the second Mersey road tunnel, while the site of Belgrave Road station (Leicester) has been incorporated into an inner ring road.

The remoteness of a railway station in relation to the town centre was often a cause for complaint. This was due to the builders skirting the built-up area of the town and thus saving on land acquisition and construction costs. This means abandoned lines are sometimes suitable for conversion to by-passes. The example of Whitchurch (Hants) has already been mentioned. Another is at Market Drayton (Shropshire), where a new by-pass utilises part of the GW line from Wellington to Nantwich. The King's Lynn by-pass similarly makes use of the M&GN line, while that round Bury St Edmunds uses the right-of-way of

the old Bury–Sudbury line, and the Great Dunmow by-pass the former Bishop's Stortford–Braintree line. In a more urban context, the H&B line has been used for a by-pass round Willerby, a suburb of Hull.

At Brampton (Cambs) the realigned A1 crossed over the Midland branch from Kettering to Huntingdon (East). The new bridge has been used unaltered by the northbound slip road to the A141. Similarly, further north, a minor road from South Witham to Castle Bytham has been diverted under the dual carriageway by the bridge built to take the main road over the old Midland branch from Saxby to the M&GN at Castle Bytham.

Occasionally a line has been taken over for a private road reserved for heavy lorries. The port of Par (Cornwall) is the nearest to the china-clay workings in the St Austell area, but it dries out at low tide. Accordingly the English Clays company leased from BR the deep-water port of Fowey and as part of the scheme converted the 4 miles of disused line from Par into a road for heavy lorries, which could reach the port independently of the already overcrowded roads. The ¾ mile Pinnick Tunnel can only accommodate a single line of traffic, so is controlled by traffic lights. Rail access remains from Lostwithiel. The trackbed of the upper part of the Wrexham, Mold & Connah's Quay branch to Brymbo has been converted for lorries to reach the Gatewen railhead on the GW Brymbo branch from open-cast coal workings.

The Monsal Trail

(*left*) A Manchester–St. Pancras express crosses Monsal Dale Viaduct as it threads the Peak District. (*above*) The line after closure has been converted to a long-distance footpath. A view of Miller's Dale. The nearer viaduct is used by the trail.

Miller's Dale station building is used as a Ranger Centre.

There are a number of other examples of conversion to private roads. In Northumberland the Forestry Commission has taken over 27 miles of former line, notably the NB's Border Counties line where it traversed Kielder Forest north-west of Bellingham. Between the A5 and Broughton Astley station, 4½ miles of the Leicester–Rugby line of the Midland have been converted into a road used for testing tyres.

But by far the most common use is for farm access roads. By their nature these are in short stretches, but in total they add up to a significant, though unrecorded mileage. To take but one example, the site of Moreton Pinkney station on the SMJ was in 1982 used for stacking bales of straw brought in from the surrounding fields along the former railway line. And on the old Cambridge–Mildenhall branch bridges have been taken over as farm tracks across fenland drainage ditches.

Footpaths and bridleways
The second major use of rights-of-way is for footpaths, bridleways and cycle tracks, where the activities of walking, riding and cycling can be pursued free from interference from motor traffic. There are a number of excellent examples of this alternative use. In Derbyshire the Tissington Trail has been created, utilising the LNW line from Ashbourne to Buxton from the outskirts of Ashbourne as far as Parsley Hay, where it joins the High Peak Trail along the right-of-way of the historic and unique Cromford & High Peak. Access is

200

provided at the station sites, such as Tissington itself, where there are car-parks, picnic areas and toilets. At Hartington the station buildings are used as a tourist information centre and the signal-box as a warden's office, while the engine houses on the C&HP at Middleton Top and Sheep Pasture Top have been restored.

Cheshire County Council have made a very good job of incorporating the CLC's Winsford Branch into its Sandstone Trail along the ridge of hills diversi-fying the Cheshire Plain. On this, Whitegate station has been preserved as a residence for the warden and the small goods yard has been converted into an attractive picnic site and a car-park. In the north-west of England part of the Rawtenstall–Bacup line has become a nature trail and the New Mills (Central)–Hayfield branch has been turned into a walkway through a linear park. In South Wales the Dare Valley Country Park uses abandoned lines of the former GW and Taff Vale companies.

The nature of the countryside through which the abandoned line passes has some importance. Most of the 'trails' which have been successfully established have been through countryside with some scenic pretensions, even if not of outstanding interest and beauty. When the GW line from Wellington to Nantwich was closed, it was the intention of Shropshire County Council to convert it to a footpath. But south of Market Drayton it traverses the feature-less Weald Moors and for this reason the scheme fell through.

But even where a route has no scenic merit there is a strong case for lines to be used as footpaths and cycleways. This is for two reasons. First, the right-of-way can be used to link existing paths and thus improve their 'network' aspect. Second, such use can improve access for local residents. At Milton Keynes the New Town Corporation has converted 2¾ miles of the Newport Pagnell branch into a cycle/pedestrian way up to the outskirts of Newport. Inspection of old lines will soon reveal the extent to which they are informally (and illegally) used as footpaths. This indicates a demand which the local authority should consider seriously.

The use of forgotten railways in urban areas as walkways and linear parks should not be overlooked. The pioneering work of the City of Stoke-on-Trent is of particular importance. Lengths of the Potteries Loop line have been con-verted into such a facility at Burslem. This is part of the overall programme of reclaiming derelict land and has contributed in no small measure to the improvement of the environment. Although suburban, rather than urban, another good example is the conversion of the GW and LNW Joint line between Hooton and West Kirby into the Wirral Way, the core of the Wirral Country Park. This was initiated by Cheshire County Council, though it is now in Merseyside. Incidentally, Hadlow Road station has been restored to its appearance in the early 1900s.

Some of these leisure routes are lengthy. In North Yorkshire there is a 16½ mile track along the Scarborough–Whitby line between the outskirts of Scarborough and Hawsker. Sixteen miles of the GW Wye Valley line south of

Monmouth have also been taken over. West Sussex County Council has taken over the LBSC branches from Christ's Hospital to Shoreham (or rather Beeding cement works) and to Guildford (Peasmarsh Junction) as a bridleway between Steyning and Baynards Tunnel. Christ's Hospital station, on the Mid-Sussex line, is still open, so diversionary paths have been provided round this and the few other obstacles. Although some of the station sites have been disposed of, West Grinstead was retained to provide the expected facilities for parking and picnics.

When the author looked at the line in 1975 he found a considerable contrast between the sections south and north of Baynards Tunnel, at the boundary between West Sussex and Surrey. The northern part had been taken over by Waverley District Council. But unlike West Sussex that authority had made no attempt either to provide facilities or to ensure the continuity of the right-of-way. Users were advised that they did so 'at their own risk', though there was no objection to walkers using the line, if they could get along it (two bridges had collapsed) (page 187). Since then the path has been much improved.

A survey carried out in 1981 for the Department of Transport by John Grimshaw and Associates revealed a total mileage of paths open of 678 in England and 29 in Wales. This however was only about 8 per cent of the total length of closed lines. The survey points to the fact that in most cases nothing is done to the surface after the removal of the track. Pedestrians and cyclists benefit from smooth all-weather paths. There is no evidence of conflict between walkers and cyclists on paths 6½ft wide, but horses must be separated as they will damage the main path. The survey gives as an example the 5 mile asphalt path between Bitton and Bath along the Midland line from Mangotsfield which runs up the Avon Valley. This was commissioned in 1980 and in the next year was carrying over 3,000 cycle trips per week. The cost was estimated at £9,600 per mile.

Study of utilisation of forgotten lines for these purposes soon reveals the differing policies of the local authorities. Some – Cheshire, North Yorkshire and West Sussex among them – have done a lot in this respect. Others – such as Kent, Dorset and most Welsh counties – have shown little or no interest. It is a matter of great regret that the opportunity was not grasped of treating the whole network of forgotten railways on a national basis in order to develop policies for exploiting their potential as recreational routes or as pedestrian/cycle ways in urban areas. Instead a national asset was squandered for very short-term financial advantage. The integrity of the rights-of-way was destroyed by the sale of land to finance short-term deficits of the BRB. The money gained was not even earmarked for capital improvements to the remaining routes, and could have been offset by a relatively small, once-for-all government grant. The contrast with the canals, which by the 1960s had lost all their commercial traffic, is unfortunate. The 1966 White Paper on Transport recognised their potential as 'cruiseways' and the position was regularised in the 1968 Transport Act.

On the Ffestiniog. By 1938 Ffestiniog trains had ceased to call at the station in Blaenau it shared with the GW. Not until 1983 did they return, this time to the new interchange built virtually on the old site.

'Linda' (from the Penrhyn Railway) storms into the re-opened Minffordd Station.

Use as railways

The use of closed lines for the purpose for which they were built – as railways! – has developed to an extent quite unforeseen in 1962. The preservation movement started with the taking over of the almost derelict, but still working, independent narrow-gauge Talyllyn and the very recently closed 'Bluebell' line (Sussex), which had gained a lot of publicity over the protracted battle against closure which had forced BR to re-open for a while. As the movement spread and proposals multiplied, it was widely felt that the pool of volunteer labour, on which preserved lines depend, would soon be exhausted. But the fear, so far at least, has apparently been groundless.

By 1981 there were nineteen stretches of standard-gauge line of 1 mile and over, totalling some 125 route miles, operated by preservation societies and companies. There are also a number of narrow-gauge lines, but definition of 'preserved' is more difficult. They do however include a number of historic Welsh lines which can be classified as 'public': the Ffestiniog, Talyllyn, and Welshpool & Llanfair.

We can distinguish a number of ways in which forgotten lines have come to be used in this way:

1. The taking over of lines in working order, eg the Bluebell and the Talyllyn.
2. The restoration of a derelict line, even where the original track has been removed. This is a much more common case and includes the Mid-Hants, North York Moors and Ffestiniog.
3. The laying of narrow-gauge tracks on rights-of-way of old standard-gauge lines, eg the Bala Lake Railway on the GW Barmouth branch, and the section of the Brecon & Merthyr line from Torpantau to Pant, which has been leased from the purchasers, the Forestry Commission, for a 2ft gauge tourist line.
4. While it is not strictly within our terms of reference, the taking over of industrial lines for passenger services, eg the narrow-gauge Sittingbourne & Kemsley and the Leighton Buzzard, and the standard-gauge Foxfield line near Stoke-on-Trent.

For the most part the lines have been financed by the preservers, who in one way or another have raised the money to lease or purchase the line. For some time the potential of these lines as a tourist asset was not recognised by the authorities. The Lakeside & Haverthwaite found that at first their plans were opposed by the Lake District National Park planning board, while at the time of writing, the Peak Park planning board have rejected an application to re-open the ex-Midland line northward from Matlock.

On the other hand, an enlightened local authority, Peterborough District Council, purchased the abandoned line between Orton Mere and Wansford from BR and leased it to the Nene Valley Railway. They saw a preserved steam line as an adjunct to their Nene Park leisure area. The Northamptonshire County Council have declared themselves to be anxious for a preservation

Freight over forgotten lines. Fowey (Cornwall) was reached by two passenger lines. The one from Par has become a private road for clay lorries. But the one along the estuary carries clay for shipment. In 1984 a long train from St. Blazey reaches Lostwithiel, where the locos will run round to take it down the branch to the pier at Carne Point.

society to take over the Northampton & Harborough line and have promised assistance to any group so doing. Cumbria County Council have bought the right-of-way of the Alston branch and leased it to the South Tynedale Railway, a 2ft gauge line extending southward from Haltwhistle. The potential of preserved lines is becoming more widely accepted.

We must also remember that a few stretches of line either closed completely or hitherto open for freight have been re-opened to passengers by BR. The abandoned line through Glasgow Central Low Level, relaid and electrified, has already been mentioned (page 146). In 1977 Inter-City trains began using the Leamington–Kenilworth–Coventry link in order to serve the new International station. This line had lost its passenger service in 1965, but had remained open for freight. The North London line between Dalston and Poplar had been closed to passengers in 1944, but in 1979 passenger trains began to use it regularly between Dalston Western Junction and Victoria Park Junction when the western terminus of the North Woolwich service was moved out to

Camden Road. At the time of writing work was proceeding on preparing to restore passenger services between Newbridge Junction and Bathgate.

In addition, part of the Yate–Thornbury branch from the Midland main line to Bristol has been restored to serve a quarry at Tytherington; a part of the CLC Glazebrook – St Helens branch has been re-used to provide rail access to the Haydock petroleum distribution centre; and a section of the abandoned Saltburn–Whitby line has been reinstated to serve a new phosphate mine at Boulby. It is probable that in the long term there must be more of this as North Sea oil declines and the comparative cost of road transport increases.

Other linear uses
There are various other uses to which an old railway can be put. They can be used as rights-of-way for transmission lines, as was done along the SE line from Ramsgate Town to Margate sands. The old Woodhead Tunnel has also been used for this purpose. A gas condensate pipeline from the Bacton North Sea gas terminal makes use of the old line between North Walsham and Mundesley (Norfolk). Part of the Bedford–Cambridge line in the area of Lord's Bridge station is used for a radio telescope.

Non-linear uses
The main non-linear use has been for agriculture. Small parcels of the old line are incorporated into the fields and cultivated. When the line is on the same level as the land, this provides few problems, once the ballast and fences have been removed. If this is not the case, it is often considered worth while to level

Knockando was on the Speyside branch of the GN of S, closed to passengers in 1965. A 1979 view of the station, restored as a visitor centre for the local distilleries, reached by a path along the right-of-way.

Clare Station on the Great Eastern's Stour Valley Line closed in 1967. It is used as a residence for the Warden of a Country Park.

embankments and cuttings, as has been done south of Uckfield on the abandoned line to Lewes, and south of Ternhill on the Wellington–Market Drayton line.

More and more old lines are disappearing in this way. The drawback is that the continuity of the rights-of-way is severed and linear uses of long stretches may be prevented if a small section has been sold off.

Cuttings provide good opportunities for waste disposal, as tipping sites are always in short supply and in this way the land is reclaimed at low cost. Examples include a site at Steyning (Sussex) on the old Shoreham–Christ's Hospital line and another south of Somersham (Cambs) on the former GN&GE Joint line between St Ives and March.

Station sites provide a wider opportunity. With care, too, they can be put to alternative uses without destroying the linear integrity of the right-of-way. They are being used in increasing numbers for small housing developments. Some have already been mentioned in passing. Newick & Chailey (Sussex), Cold Norton (Essex) and Cleator Moor (Cumbria) are other examples. The site of Plodder Lane (Bolton) locomotive depot has also been used in this way.

The station site at Holcombe Brook (Greater Manchester) has become a shopping precinct, this suburban area north of Bury having grown considerably since the closure of the branch which saw some of the earliest experiments in electrification by the L&Y. In town centres, Ebbw Vale (High Level) and Chesterfield (Market Place) have become multi-storey car-parks, while, as already mentioned, Nottingham (Victoria) became a large shopping centre. At seaside resorts the sites have become car-parks, funfairs and caravan sites, as at Leysdown (Kent) and Hunstanton (Norfolk).

Many station sites have been taken over for industrial purposes. In some cases coal merchants have continued to use the old goods yards. Other sites have been taken over as county council depots, as at Raglan (Gwent). Hawkhurst (Kent) was taken over by a wood-turning firm, while at Hay (Powys) the site is occupied by a firm of builders' merchants, a timber merchant and a farmers' co-operative. Sometimes the sites have become industrial estates as at Norwich (City) and at Ross-on-Wye. Some small rural sites have been used to put up buildings to extend farmyards. This has been done at Kimbolton (Cambs) and Culworth (Northants). The list of conversions can be extended indefinitely, but perhaps the final indignity was suffered by North Walsham Town (Norfolk) – it became a sewage unit.

New uses for urban stations. The façade of Bath Green Park has been sensitively preserved, together with the trainshed, which now serves as a car park for the supermarket seen in the left background. The restoration was by Sainsbury's in association with Stonechester Ltd. and the City of Bath.

Utilisation of buildings

The value of station buildings is twofold. As we have seen, they often include a dwelling and are of a good architectural standard. A large number of station buildings have thus survived, a number of them to become listed buildings. To catalogue them would be tedious, but within a few miles of where this is being written, Brampton, Grafham and Bluntisham have all been well converted. Mention should also be made of the excellent conversion of Nannerch (Clwyd), which unfortunately was later demolished on the altar of road improvements, and of Welshampton (Shrops) which narrowly avoided this fate. At Rotherfield (Sussex) the platform canopy has been filled in to create a large sun lounge, while the space between the platforms has been used as a swimming pool. At Lyminge (Kent), the goods yard having been taken over as a roads depot by the county council, the station became a dwelling and office (page 190).

Station buildings have also been turned to a wide variety of other uses. Nottingham's London Road (High Level) became a showroom and store for a firm of office-furniture suppliers; Llansantffraed (Powys) a restaurant; Llanybyther (Dyfed) a rugby-club headquarters; and Hartfield (Sussex) a play school. Yarmouth South Town, a listed building, was taken over by an oil-rig supply firm as offices, their materials being stored in the old goods yards. Other uses have been even more unusual. In Blaenau Ffestiniog the old Festiniog station serves as a public convenience. Walsingham (Norfolk) became a Russian Orthodox monastery, embellished with a gilt dome, while Glapwell (Derbyshire) became a gospel mission.

Utilisation of city-centre buildings has often had a less happy history. For sixteen years after closure, the gaunt decaying train shed of Manchester Central did duty as a car-park, while endless wrangles went on over its ultimate use. Only in 1984 did conversion to an exhibition centre begin. The fate of Bath Green Park (formerly Queen's Square) provides a happy contrast: the classical façade fronts a supermarket, the train shed being preserved as a car-park.

Many level-crossing houses have become dwellings, while former railway cottages continue in this role. Goods sheds have become factories, workshops and stores, while to complete our list of conversions to sacred purposes, the shed at Caton (Lancs) became a Roman Catholic church. A number of signal-boxes have survived, to be used as greenhouses if for nothing else.

Finally, to sum up this brief introduction to alternative uses, in 1973 the following uses were recorded for station buildings and sites along the former Midland & LNW Joint line between Nuneaton and Moira. From south to north they were: Stoke Golding, a scrapyard; Market Bosworth, a garage; Shackerstone, the headquarters of the Midland Railway Society; and Measham, a motor showroom.

As has been emphasised, lost opportunities on the macro-scale provide the melancholy theme for this chapter, even if balanced by opportunities seized on a small scale. But the short-sighted large-scale approach was consistent with the myopia of official bodies towards the closure programme generally.

CHAPTER 12

Nature and Forgotten Railways

Old Africa hands are wont to refer to 'MBA', approximately translated as 'Miles of blooming Africa', as a comment on the monotony of the scenery: a few basic elements are repeated over and over again for hundreds of miles before any real change comes over the landscape. In contrast, the comparatively small island of Britain has been richly endowed with an extraordinary variety of landscapes. This is the result of an equal variety in the environmental elements of geology, physiography, soil, climate, vegetation and the work of man in modifying the natural environment.

Since, as we have seen, there is an intimate relationship between railway lines and the land through which they run, and since forgotten railways are to be found in every part of the country, so there is an almost infinite variety in the old railways just as there is in the landscape. Comments on this have been made throughout the book, but it is appropriate to give a few random illustrations at this point.

Railways and scenery – 1: In the Lake District. A train leaves Keswick for Penrith on 12 February 1972.

Railways and Terrain

The most obvious association between railways and the physical features of the landscape is to be found in mountains and moorlands, for here the terrain closely dictated the route taken. It would involve heavy gradients, up which at long intervals steam trains pounded at full throttle, the column of white exhaust blown by the wind along the mountain slopes, the sound of the hard-pressed engine echoing across the valley. From the train the views were magnificent, while from across the moors the train looked less an intruder into the solitude than a necessary adjunct to the landscape.

One such line was the alternative route of the Highland Railway pushing north from Aviemore. The newer and more direct one, still in use, reaches Inverness over Slochd summit. The other, now forgotten, continued down the Spey Valley through Boat of Garten to Grantown, with the high Cairngorms, their lower slopes forested, away to the east. Happily the section between Aviemore and Boat of Garten has been re-opened as a preserved line.

The route now has to leave the deep valley. From Gantown 5½ miles, mostly at 1 in 80, brought the labouring train up to the 1,052ft summit on the lonely Dava Moor. Shortly after began the long descent, a great deal of it at 1 in 70–75 down the side of the Findhorn Valley right down to sea-level, to Forres and to join the Aberdeen–Inverness line. With only five down trains in 1958, and lacking the glamour of the Slochd route, it was a route truly 'forgotten' in the literature.

The run from Callander to Crianlarich (page 183) was much better known. It involved penetrating the mountainous area between Ben More and Ben Vorlich. At first there were considerable stretches of level track along Loch Lubnaig, but after the Balquhidder stop, where connection could occasionally be made with the line along Loch Earn to Crieff and Gleneagles, the grade steepened to 1 in 60. Rising rapidly above the Crieff line, Glenoglehead passing place was reached. This was a real gable summit and the line immediately turned down at 1 in 70 through the narrow rocky Glen Ogle to Killin Junction. Here the line turned westward down the glacial trough of Glen Dochart. A line certainly not forgotten, but vividly remembered by all who made even one trip.

In southern Scotland, the Waverley Route and the 'Port Road' to Stranraer have received due attention in these pages. But the branch line that straggled across the moors from Lanark to reach its ultimate goal, Ayr, has been almost totally neglected. Not even John Thomas says much about it, in his volumes of the 'Forgotten Railways' and 'Regional History of the Railways of Great Britain' series. The Caledonian reached the one-time coal-and-iron boom town of Muirkirk, now derelict and isolated amid the bleak moors. It penetrated into the moorland area by the valley of the Douglas Water. The Caledonian met end-on the Glasgow & South Western coming up from Auchinleck, but through working only began with the LMS.

In mid Wales the GW branch from Bala Junction to the slate Eldorado of Blaenau Ffestiniog climbed up into and threaded the gloomy passes among the

Railways and scenery – 2: In the Welsh Marches. Near Blaisdon the 13.40 train from Hereford to Gloucester threads forested hills on 18 April 1964.

Arenig mountains. Some miles of the right-of-way are now drowned beneath Llyn Celyn reservoir. It then shared the narrow Cwm Prysor with the A4212 to reach Trawsfynydd and turn north past the site of the atomic power station. Rails are still *in situ* thence through the old town of Ffestiniog and on high up the mountainside to a terminus where now BR and the Ffestiniog share the new Blaenau station.

At the exchange platform of Bala Junction (which did not even appear in the timetables) connection was made with the 53 mile line from Ruabon to Barmouth Junction (now, bereft of junction function, named Morfa Mawddach). It traversed the mountainous interior by following the valley of the Upper Dee through Llangollen and Corwen. The valley is always deep and above Llangollen narrow and gorge-like. Beyond Bala the line closely follows the shore of Bala Lake before ascending briefly to the summit in a glacial trough. Thence it descends for 10 miles at 1 in 50–65 down the steep-sided and narrow valley to Dolgellau and along the now broad one to join the Cambrian at Barmouth Junction.

From Llandderfel, the next station east of Bala Junction, the more energetic could climb out of the Dee Valley and walk over the Berwyn mountains to drop down to Llangynog, the terminus of the lovely branch which came up the valley from the Cambrian main line at Llynclys.

Further south was the Manchester & Milford, which in spite of the pretensions of its title carried a smattering of local passengers between Aberystwyth and Carmarthen. From Aberystwyth it climbed up the valley of the Ystwyth, less spectacular and less well known than the adjoining Rheidol valley. Beyond, the wild upland was traversed. Strata Florida station was in the village of Pontrhydfendigaid and a long way from the abbey it was called after. Perhaps it was an easier name to ask for when booking a ticket. The only other place was the tiny market town of Tregaron.

A contrast was provided by the LNW line which ran southward from Buxton through the High Peak to Ashbourne. The line is a high-level one with long views across the rolling uplands. But it wound over a limestone plateau, a land of short-grass fields enclosed by grey and white stone walls. Fortunately it is now part of the Tissington Trail, and the unique countryside can be enjoyed by walkers free from motor-car intrusion.

A number of lines were associated with the coast or with hugging the shores of estuaries or lakes. One of the most spectacular of the coastal lines ran northward from Scarborough through Whitby and on to Saltburn, a distance of 45½ miles. Here the coastline is one of high cliffs separated by bays, backed by steep hills. The author prefers to imagine a trip made in a train of four non-corridor coaches headed by an ex-NE 4–6–2T of class A8, which was associated with the line for so long. From Cloughton on the northern edge of Scarborough the line climbed up Stainton Dale, which, like Newton Dale to the west (now traversed by the North York Moors Railway), is a glacial overflow channel. Beyond Staintondale station the climb steepened to 1 in 41. At the top the train emerged on the very cliff-top at Ravenscar. The level stretch only extended the length of the station and the line dropped at 1 in 39 down to Fyling Hall. It then rounded Robin Hood's Bay, high above the red-roofed town clinging to the steep slopes. Then came a climb at 1 in 43 and a similar drop to Hawsker. The Esk was crossed above Whitby on a high twelve-arched viaduct. Soon after Whitby (West Cliff) the line regained the coast, descending to Sandsend, where the station was almost on the very foreshore. This entailed a fearsome climb back to the cliff-tops at Kettleness, to round Runswick Bay and thence on above Staithes to Boulby, where the line from Saltburn now ends.

Equally spectacular scenically, though not from the operational viewpoint, was the 27¾ mile Ballachulish branch of the Caledonian. The junction with the Oban line was at Connel Ferry. After crossing the bridge built on the same principle as the Forth Bridge the line ran for many miles along the shores of Loch Creran and of Loch Linnhe itself to turn up Loch Leven to the Ballachulish terminus. The line ran flatly along the shore at a low level, but the

A train for Swanage traverses the gap in the Chalk ridge in the Isle of Purbeck with Corfe Castle in the background.

views across the wide sea-loch to the hills and mountains of Ardgour were unforgettable.

Further north along the Great Glen was the spectacular, but long-forgotten branch of the NB to Fort Augustus, which has already been mentioned (pages 39–54). For almost the whole of its length it ran along a ledge excavated high above Loch Lochy and Loch Oich. In the West Country, running through more subdued but no less beautiful scenery, the Southern's line beyond Wadebridge reached its ultimate terminus at Padstow (page 193) along the low sandy shores of the Camel Estuary, crossing backwaters by two viaducts. The small station and goods yard at Padstow was itself on the very shore, adjacent to the fishing harbour.

In contrast, lowland lines might run through what at first glance might be thought of as dull and featureless country. A line through the fen country of East Anglia can be taken as an example. It was built by a local company, the Ely & St Ives, later becoming part of the GE. It was of course almost level and

lacking in earthworks. But it was by no means straight as it crossed the black fenlands. The stations were remote, for they served villages located on low clay islands rising from the peaty levels. The low ridges, surmounted by church towers, lent perspective and some variety to the view, enclosing space which seems almost limitless below the high arch of the sky.

The rolling scarplands of southern England may not be very high – under 600ft for the most part – but they contain an infinite variety of scenery, fertile and intimate rather than wild and rugged, but ensuring interest in rail journeys, because of the necessary heavy grades and earthworks.

To select an example, there was the 11½ mile Hawkhurst branch. This left the main line to Dover via Tonbridge at Paddock Wood. The line turned south and climbed steeply into the Kentish High Weald through seemingly endless orchards and hop gardens. The first part of the climb was at 1 in 66 to Horsmonden, the H class 0–4–4T at the head of the two-coach pull-and-push blasting its slow way through the apple orchards. Beyond, the line ran up the valley of the Teise to climb round the base of the hill on which Goudhurst stands, as proudly as any Italian hill town, to reach Cranbrook. Climbing continued at 1 in 85 to the short Badger's Oak Tunnel, the summit of the line. From there there was a short downhill stretch at 1 in 85 to the hilltop terminus, by no means at Hawkhurst. It was a line of great beauty and character and is dealt with more fully in the *South East England* volume of the 'Forgotten Railways' series.

Obviously such a brief survey, so briefly embarked on to link forgotten railways with the country through which they passed, could be extended indefinitely. Readers are therefore invited to add their own favourites to the list for themselves.

Railways and Geology

Because the physiography, just described, often depends on the geology, the relationship between a railway and the geology of the country through which it runs is also close. The rocks and their structure are exposed in the cuttings, and a walk along a forgotten railway enables one to learn much about the geology. One author described the Midland & South Western Junction as 'the finest geology primer I know' – a proposition we will take a closer look at.

Cheltenham lies above the plain of the Severn, being located on the Lias terrace below the Oolitic Limestone escarpment of the Cotswolds. The high (600–800ft) plateau of the latter was gained over the GW's Kingham line, climbing steeply through Charlton Kings to Andoversford Junction. Here the MSWJ line struck south across the rolling limestone uplands, characterised by stone-walled fields, the stone houses and barns roofed with thick slabs of limestone (Stonesfield Slate). It gradually descended through Chedworth to Foss Cross and reached Cirencester perched on the low Marlstone Scarp. The line then crossed the Oxford Clay lowland. In the area of South Cerney the numerous flooded gravel-pits mark the terraces of the Upper Thames, crossed at Cricklade.

The line passed between the low hills of the Corallian Limestone to reach Swindon in the Vale of White Horse, formed on the Gault Clay and Lower Chalk. Just to the south the trains used to pause at Chiseldon, a place with a geological name, for it means 'a gravel-filled valley'. It lies below the chalk scarp. A steep climb would bring the train on to the wide rolling plateau of the Marlborough Downs, almost treeless with enormous fields. At Marlborough town the valley of the Kennet was crossed. At Savernake, where the Berks & Hants main line and the parallel Kennet & Avon Canal were crossed, these lines of communication make use of the anticlinal valley of the Vale of Pewsey, on the floor of which rocks older than the chalk are brought to the surface. Southward lay another area of chalk plateau, traversed by the line all the way to Red Post Junction, where the route of the LSW main line was reached for the short run into Andover Junction and the end of the line.

Local Habitats

Within the relatively short distance of 68½ miles (as the MSWJ ran) there is

216

thus a very wide variety in the underlying geology. Stemming from this is an equally wide variety in the physiography – in the soil and in the vegetation. This is repeated on many another old railway line over an equivalent distance. Since the old railway provides a corridor, albeit a narrow one, it displays a wide variety of habitats for flora and fauna.

This variety is also increased by the existence of earthworks along the line. For example, a cutting provides variations in the local climate and environment and therefore in habitats. In 1962 the line from Hooton to West Kirby was closed. At Neston there was a cutting through the Bunter Pebble Beds of the Wirral Peninsula. About 25 ft deep, it has been cleared of the rubbish at first allowed to accumulate and left as a natural habitat. A sewage pipe has been laid along it, but the concrete casing has been allowed to be colonised by the same range of mosses found on the cutting sides.

The cutting runs east and west across land which slopes northward. Water therefore drains into the cutting along the south wall. The latter is therefore damp and the north one dry, while cool and damp air is trapped in the bottom of the cutting. Within this habitat 115 plant species have been identified, but of these only 25 are common to both sides. There is thus a different 'association' of plants on each side. In addition there is a stratification of plant species from the bottom of the sides upwards.

Railways have always been associated with the spread of plants, seeds being kept in motion and distributed over long distances by air displacement from the constant passage of the trains. The classic example is that of the Oxford Ragwort. A native of volcanic ash habitats in southern Italy, it was introduced into the Oxford University Botanical Gardens. By the early eighteenth century it had spread outside and reached Port Meadow. With the coming of railways to Oxford it began to spread along the linesides, where there was good opportunity for the seeds, scattered by the draughts of passing trains, to take root in the ballast, ash and clinker. There are also examples of exotic plants taking root alongside sidings whither they were brought in the packaging of goods.

Although in steam days there was a certain modification of vegetation resulting from lineside fires, there was normally less disturbance to the flora along the right-of-way than in adjacent fields. The Brighton line between Three Bridges and Haywards Heath is well known for its displays of primroses and of bluebells, while nearby of course is the preserved 'Bluebell Line'. Even when it was still open the Uppingham branch was regarded as a nature reserve, especially in its later years when, because of economy measures, the lineside was seldom cleared. A writer describing a journey on the Bishop's Castle said, 'You could reach out from the carriage windows and pick hazel nuts, wild roses and honeysuckle.'

But after closure the right-of-way makes an even better nature reserve, and the importance of the forgotten railway in this role is increasing. This is for a number of reasons. In the first place the right-of-way is no longer in regular use, except perhaps by walkers and more occasionally by horse-riders. This means that the road-bed is normally interfered with only by the treading of people and horses. The boundary hedges tend to be left uncut, or trimmed back at rare intervals. The sides of the cuttings and embankments, which at least in clay country slope gently, are also left uncut and undisturbed.

This allows the vegetation to develop undisturbed towards the natural 'climax' association (the final stage reached by a plant community, at which it is in equilibrium with its environment) to be expected in the particular habitat. This association will depend on such factors as geology, soil, slope, aspect and drainage. With the increasing trend towards grubbing hedges to provide larger fields for more complex machinery, and the mechanical cutting instead of more labour-intensive layering of the remaining ones, there is a constant loss of the habitats for wild plants, animals and birds along hedgerows and associated ditches. In addition the farming of recent years has led to greater areas coming under the plough and selective weed-killing eliminating wild-plant species, especially in grasslands. Woodland management also tends to the monoculture of conifers and the reduction of herb-layer species.

Thus the line of a forgotten railway, such as that from Huntingdon to Kettering, provides one of the few areas of sheltering woodland, ditches, embankments and cuttings in an open landscape than can best be described as prairie-like. Even in the western counties, where stock farming and therefore hedgerows are more common, abandoned lines, such as that of the Cambrian from Whitchurch to Oswestry, provides valuable extra shelter. This was stressed in a report by Lindsey County Council (see page 220), a local authority with a good record in the utilisation of forgotten railways.

Flora

When a line is first closed the ballast will repel life. Sometimes it may be removed, but normally, because the line has been run down before closure, it is too dirty to bother with. It will be first colonised by creeping plants coming in from the sides and forming a matted tangle of runners. These are followed by low-growing plants such as purple Creeping Thistle, yellow Groundsel and white Chickweed. In turn they are followed by medium-sized plants, up to 2ft, including Toadflax, Mullein and giant Thistles. Finally woody species invade: Hazel, Willow, Holly, Alder and Blackthorn. The thorns of the last named may eventually completely block the line, forcing walkers to make a detour.

The variety and number of species growing along the trackbed will be affected by the type of ballast, and whether it is limestone, granite, gravel, cinders, and so on. The line through the High Peak from Ashbourne to Hindlow was taken over by the Peak Park planning board and developed as the Tissington Trail (page 200). To reduce the visual impact of the white scar formed by the right-of-way and to improve the surface for walking, 4in of soil were laid down and seeded with grass. But subsequently horses cut up the grass and the trail was resurfaced with dark-coloured waste ballast. The trail now provides a wide variety of habitats and 5 acres are maintained as nature reserves by the Derbyshire Naturalist Trust.

Damp cuttings will not only encourage a greater number of species, but the woody growth may develop into a dense impenetrable tangle up to 20ft high. Embankments and more gently sloping cutting sides provide a very favourable habitat. Primroses and cowslips, eliminated from more and more cultivated meadows, are typical refuges. A survey of a section of embankment at Beighton (S. Yorks) revealed thirty-seven plant species in the 50 × 10yd area.

The Botany Department of Aberdeen University made a special study in 1973 of the former Deeside line. Two areas were selected for survey. The first was one of 2½ acres between Cults and Culter. Here 150 plant species were recorded, a surprisingly high number for a semi-suburban area with a reasonably high population density. They do however include 'escapes' from gardens such as Solomon's-seal, Buddleia and Toadflax. On the damp walls of station buildings numerous ferns were found, including species rare in lowland areas. Woody species were also common: Sycamore, Ash, Beech, Cherry, Wych Elm, Birch and Willow, with Dog Rose, Gorse, Broom and Snowberry in the more open spaces.

Savernake High Level in early Grouping days, with a Swindon bound train on the former M&SWJ Line. The now-closed GW station was 250 yards down the road. Even in those days the station was getting overgrown.

At the other site investigated by the Aberdeen researchers, at the western end, the land is higher and more isolated, while the climate was more severe, colder and wetter. The old railway, however, with better drainage and improved conditions, encouraged an even greater range of species. There were two distinct habitats: where the line passed through birch scrub and coniferous plantations; and where it passed through farmland and as a result 'took on the character of a herb-rich meadow'.

Within the two sectors species totalled 249, including 29 grasses, sedges and rushes, 30 mosses and liverworts, and 11 ferns. The list of domestic plants is quite mouthwatering: strawberries, raspberries, gooseberries and potatoes.

In the surroundings of Burghclere station on the erstwhile DN&S there is a mix of wild species and 'escapes' from the platform and station-house gardens, for which the station was once well known and a prizewinner. Along the platform are the bushes once given over to the art of topiary, while White Stonecrop covers the platform edges and Everlasting Sweetpea grows everywhere. Domestic escapes also include Marguerite, Golden Rod, Lupin, Cherry, Laurel, Guelder-rose and Conifer. Wild species include Vetch, Bird's-foot Trefoil and Wild Marjoram. Dog Rose and Field Rose and sloe (Blackthorn) spread along the tops of the cutting, while the limestone ballast attracts Black Mullein.

Fauna

The protective habitats provided by the vegetative growth which has taken over so many stretches of forgotten railway attract the fauna. The areas surveyed along the Deeside line sheltered ten species of butterflies and twenty-eight of birds. Butterflies are everywhere attracted to old railways, the mix of species depending on the particular plant association. Bird life depends on the type of cover and the available food supply. Forgotten railways provide adequate cover and nesting sites. They also provide food from the insect life as well as seeds and berries. Adjacent fields are additional sources of food. All this encourages smaller birds such as tits and many medium-sized species, some of which are distinctly rare: thrushes, magpies, jays and woodpeckers. Larger birds, too, are attracted: game birds seeking shelter in the shooting season and numerous hawks encouraged by the supply of prey.

Mammals are also attracted, by the availability of shelter and the unbroken chains of food supply. Thus on the one hand mice, voles and rabbits are encouraged and on the other weasels and foxes. Badger setts too are on the increase.

Nature Reserves

Forgotten railways thus act as nature reserves, whether or not they are formally designated as such. In 1970 Lindsey County Council published a report underlining the importance of old railways as providers of almost undisturbed environments for wild life. They cited as examples the right-of-way of the

Woodhall Junction–Horncastle line, which traverses heath and coniferous woodland, and the neighbouring one from Woodhall Junction to Bellwater Junction which passes through and connects flooded gravel-pits, themselves acting as reserves. The Louth–Firsby line also traverses grassland, scrub and mixed woodland.

Where they have not been eliminated, most surviving stretches of old railways are almost completely undisturbed. But as we have seen (Chapter 11) a number of rights-of-way have been taken over by local authorities and much will depend on the management strategy adopted. In Lincolnshire the whole of the Horncastle branch has been taken over to form the 7 mile Spa Trail, but though the gravel-pits referred to have been designated Sites of Special Scientific Interest, nothing has been done about the connecting railway line. Aberdeen Botany Department recommended action to enhance the value of the Deeside line as a walkway. This included selective weeding, and cutting back to open up attractive views and to allow plants to survive. Some species could usefully be planted for their looks and to encourage butterflies and birds. Some of this has been implemented following the conversion to a footpath of the first 8 miles to Culter and the last 4 from Cambus O'May to Ballater (covering the two surveyed areas described).

Associated with several of these footpath conversions has been their development as nature reserves and nature trails. The Wirral Country Park (page 201) has been established along 12 miles of the Hooton–West Kirby line. This includes Neston cutting, which has been developed as a nature trail and has some half-million visitors a year. Thurstaston station has been taken over as an exhibition centre, with displays of the local geology, soils, flora and fauna and a model of the siltation of the Dee Estuary. A nature trail has been established by Bedfordshire County Council at Stevington on the edge of the Ouse Valley, along the former Midland line from Oakley Junction to Northampton. In Avon there is the Lyncombe Vale Nature Trail in the secluded area outside Bath between Devonshire and Combe Down Tunnels on the old S&D line. Outside Edinburgh, along the gorge of the Water of Leith between Slateford and Juniper Green, the line of the Caledonian's Balerno branch has also been taken over. A nature reserve has been set up along the old line at Willoughby (Lincs) and a private one along 1½ miles of the former railway between Upton on Severn and Malvern Wells.

In Urban Areas
Special measures are needed for the rehabilitation of old lines in urban areas. If left undisturbed they are capable of developing plant 'successions' (developments in a plant community, towards a state of equilibrium with its environment). The Bowdon carriage sidings at Altrincham were abandoned in 1971 with the conversion of the line from 1.5kV dc to 25kV ac. By 1984, immediately prior to conversion to a car-park, it had become an area of silver birch scrub up to 8ft high. But this is rare. More often the rights-of-way in

urban areas have become dumping grounds for litter and rubbish of all kinds, fences are broken down and they become unsightly waste areas. In addition there is a lack of vegetation on bordering sites to act as a source for colonisation of the old line.

Under these circumstances the urban forgotten railway provides an adverse environment, so indigenous plants are less likely to survive. Careful planning is therefore necessary. The London Borough of Haringey has taken over portions of the former GN 'Northern Heights' line, deserted after conversion beyond East Finchley for London Transport trains and the withdrawal of the Alexandra Palace service. These have been planted with species which are attractive but hardy, with a good chance of survival. Near Muswell Hill station site a cutting has been extensively planted with bushes of Gorse, Rose, Bamboo, and Cherry Laurel and trees such as Silver Birch, Norway Maple, Alder and Hawthorn.

But there is a problem. The plants just listed are common to parks and though obviously much better than dereliction, the setting is formal and public-park like. For this reason another scheme, this time jointly with the Borough of Islington, was prepared for a 2 mile stretch of the Highgate–Finsbury Park section: a less formal layout with more chance for natural regeneration. At Brinnington (Stockport) the long-abandoned spur along the Thame from Reddish Junction to Tiviot Dale there is more open space bordering the right-of-way and hedges are proposed, mainly of Hawthorn, Wild Rose, Elder and Holly.

Walking Forgotten Railways

The forgotten railway thus provides a formal or informal nature reserve. This, together with the views of the surrounding countryside and freedom from motor traffic, can all be enjoyed by walking along the old lines. Some aspects of the conversion of former railways to footpaths have already been dealt with in the previous chapter (page 200). It was noted however that only about 8 per cent of the closed lines have been formally taken over by local authorities as public footpaths.

Some examples were given of these conversions. To them may be added some Scottish examples of significant length. One such is the 25 miles between St Andrews and Leven of the largely coastal North British line through the East Neuk of Fife. A similar length of the Caledonian's Oban line, closed east of Crianlarich, has been taken over between Dunblane and Lochearnhead through Callender. To date the Speyside Walkway covers the 16 miles of the Great North of Scotland line between Dufftown and Craigellachie and on to Ballindalloch. As a final example there is the 10 mile length of the 'Port Road' eastward from Gatehouse-of-Fleet through Cairn Edward Forest.

County Durham has purchased a total of 70 miles of track, including 17½ miles in the area of Consett and 18½ miles around Durham City. As mentioned earlier, the spectacular Scarborough–Whitby line has been taken over for 16½ miles between Scarborough and Hawsker. Avon has created a 10 mile Cheddar Valley Walk between Yatton and Cheddar, while Devon has acquired the Princetown branch. Unfortunately there are no such examples from Wales.

The position is of course constantly changing and the picture is not invariably one of advance. The 8 mile Cuckoo Walk was established on the right-of-way of the Cuckoo Line between Heathfield (Sussex) and Polegate. In 1982 it was reported that Wealden District Council were seeking to sell off the land as they were no longer able to afford the upkeep. Happily so far this has been rare. Even though all this effort does represent a small proportion of the possibilities, it is surprising how many of the outstanding stretches of line mentioned throughout the book have also appeared in this brief list.

For the rest there is an unrecorded mileage of 'informal' paths. Though in private hands, including of course those of the British Railways Board, access is unofficially permitted. Thus well-worn paths can often be seen along the right-of-way, pointing to the extent of the use. But of course there is also a large mileage to which there is no access.

But there are ample opportunities for exploring old lines. The countryside's beauties can be enjoyed without intrusion from the otherwise all-pervasive motor vehicle. The natural vegetation and wild life can be studied at close quarters. And not least, the spirit of the railway when in operation can be re-created.

CHAPTER 13

The Future

In these pages the story of railway closures has been outlined, together with the ways in which some 8,500 route miles of line which once carried passenger trains have become 'forgotten railways'. Some account has also been given of the changes (or, far too often, the resistance to change) in traffic carried and operating methods, as well as of the external factors – economic, social and political – which led to those changes. We have also seen something of the extent to which the features of the closed lines have survived and how old lines can be recognised and traced on the ground. Finally, the alternative uses to which the old lines can be put are examined, especially their use as footpaths.

It must be emphasised that the purpose of the book is to provide an introduction to the question of closed lines – in no way is it a complete survey. Readers should not be disappointed if the forgotten railway in which they are particularly interested has received no mention, in spite of its unique features and special importance. All lines have their own particular interest, but all cannot receive attention here. Readers wishing to pursue the story of a particular line are referred to the appropriate regional volume in the 'Forgotten Railways' series.

The question of closed railway lines is of concern to numerous groups and individuals, who approach it from a number of different directions, though these are by no means exclusive. First, there are those, interested in local history in general and in railway history in particular, who are anxious to study the reasons for the promotion and building of the line; the reciprocal relationship between the line and the area through which it passed; the job the line did while in operation; the nature of the traffic and the methods of operation; and the way in which the line died.

There are also those interested in industrial archaeology, who are concerned with the artifacts of the line: its engineering features, station buildings and so on. They are particularly interested in tracing the line on the ground. There are also those who are especially interested in the landscape through which the line passed and the relationship between line and landscape. Finally, there are the enthusiasts, fascinated by the locomotives, rolling stock and signalling of the past.

But it is not only a question of looking backwards. There are also the public bodies and private individuals concerned with the ways in which the old lines can be put to new uses and with the best policies to achieve this end. Not the least of these groups are the preservation societies. So far they have put back

Then and now at Denbigh

(*above*) In April 1962 a train from Chester arrives at a station which then had a considerable freight traffic as well. (*below*) In 1985 the yards had given way to a supermarket and associated car park.

into or kept in service nearly 200 route miles of line so that we can all enjoy journeys, often through superb scenery, and experience what the pre-1960 railway looked like and how it worked.

Nor is the story of the closures without significance for the future. We have seen time and time again the long-term harm resulting from short-term expediency, and from the lack of consistent policies. In this way a national asset has been frittered away twice over. In the first place there has been a lack of formulated overall objectives in transport and of policies to achieve these. Of course the rail network of 1950 was over-extended and some contraction was inevitable. But it is equally true that many miles of closed line would still be in service if the commercial policies and the operating standards and methods ruling in 1980 had been developed twenty years earlier. And in the second place, in the subsequent utilisation of the network of closed lines there has been the same lack of overall policy, the same sacrifice of the long term in pursuit of the short term.

It is of equal concern that many of the negative attitudes that led to the events described in these pages are still prevalent. In many ways nothing has been learnt. Thus the attitude still persists that regards the road infrastructure as a social service and at the same time insists that the rail infrastructure should 'pay its way' in the narrowest of senses.

As far as urban areas are concerned, the view that the rail system should be put on the same basis as the road system was given legislative support in the 1968 Transport Act, though in the mid 1980s the government was seeking to dismantle this legislation. The 1970s saw the more enlightened view beginning to spread to the inter-urban and even the rural scene. But at the time of writing the survival of negative attitudes and the nature of the struggle to come are indicated by the narrow terms of reference underlining the Serpell Report of 1982. Those who do not wish to see further portions of the rail system becoming forgotten must continue to ponder the lessons of the 1960s, and persevere with the application of political pressure.

The question is not academic. Nor will it go away. Short-term over-production of motor fuel only defers for a short time the coming home to roost of our lack of a national transport policy. As these words are being penned there is news that one of the largest North Sea oilfields, the Forties, is past the peak of production. Another twenty years will see the decline of North Sea oil and increasing dependence on our electric railways – if we still have them. But perhaps by then the Motorways to Railways Conversion League will have become a power in the land!

The Settle & Carlisle: A Case Study?
In the mid 1980s much remains unchanged, but there has also been some change during the period since 1967 (which we took to be the end of the Beeching era). The curious case of the Settle & Carlisle line shows clearly both aspects. Most historians of course would agree that this 72 mile main line

should never have been built. It was born of the LNW hatred of the Midland. The latter had acquired the 'Little' North Western as a northern outlet from the industrial West Riding of Yorkshire. But the obstructive attitude of the LNW at Ingleton, where the Midland made an end-on junction, forced the latter to construct an independent access to Carlisle and the Scottish lines across the High Pennines, which was opened in 1876. As a feat of engineering it was prodigious, for in spite of traversing some of the highest and most rugged country in England, gradients were kept down to 1 in 100. It remains a monument to Victorian enterprise and engineering, and passes through spectacular scenery. The 'Long Drag' has a secure place in railway history and in the hearts of a vast following of enthusiasts as well as in the literature and in thousands of photographs, including those of Bishop Eric Treacy, who made the line his own.

Passenger traffic was never heavy and was built around four services: one day and one night between St Pancras and Glasgow (via the G&SW); and the same between St Pancras and Edinburgh (via the Waverley) respectively. The 1938 working timetable showed only six down expresses passing Ais Gill Summit daily, together with four locals and a curious unbalanced working described as empty stock, but which picked up loaded cattle wagons where required. But freight traffic was heavy, at least until 1970, and there were a lot of trains and assisting locomotives about on the night of Christmas Eve 1910, the night of the Hawes Junction accident. The line survived the Beeching holocaust save for the withdrawal of the local service in 1971 and the closing of all the intermediate stations save Settle and Appleby. Even after electrification of the West Coast main line, freight trains of unbraked wagons were routed this way.

But in the later 1970s the measures which have become so familiar in these pages were applied. More and more traffic, passenger and freight, was diverted away from the line. By 1983 there were but two passenger trains daily each way between Leeds and Carlisle only, together with an unbalanced early morning departure from Settle to Leeds, and there were no through trains at all in the columns of the freight working timetable. At the same time, other than switching out a few signal-boxes, nothing was done to reduce costs, many boxes remaining open to control the double track.

But the potential of the line attracted the attention of others when BR had little interest in its development. In 1975 the Yorkshire Dales National Park Committee hired trains on summer weekends from Leeds to re-opened stations between Settle and Appleby. So successful was the venture that in later years stations between Appleby and Carlisle were also re-opened and trains were hired to enable local people to shop in Leeds. In 1984 on certain weekends there were up to two stopping trains each way between Leeds and Carlisle together with a round trip between Preston and Carlisle. The service was marketed as 'Dalesrail', but it was ignored by BR, there being no mention of it in their timetables. On the other hand BR did use the line for steam-hauled excursions.

Threatened main line
(*above*) A 1967 view of Ribblehead Viaduct with a northbound pick-up freight crossing. BR appear unable or unwilling to finance repairs to the structure.
(*left*) A steam special in charge of the preserved A4 Pacific 'Sir Nigel Gresley' leaves Blea Moor Tunnel on 27 August 1967. The train is about to traverse Dent Dale, one of the more spectacular stretches on the Settle & Carlisle.

Then came the inevitable closure threats, based chiefly on the deteriorating state of Ribblehead Viaduct and on the prohibitive (and constantly varying) estimates of the restoration cost. In December 1983 closure notices were published.

By now there was increasing public awareness that the line is a national asset. First, it will provide a valuable alternative route when, as is inevitable, long-distance traffic returns to rail with the slackening off of North Sea oil production. Second, it provides access to a holiday area which is growing in popularity, but which cannot support great increases in motor traffic without damage to the very environment which provides the attraction for visitors. Finally, in its own right, the line provides matchless scenic travel.

BR, as we have seen in other cases, took insufficient care in preparing its case. For example, it overlooked a fact that could be verified from a glance at any Ordnance Survey map — that for 2½ miles between Ais Gill Summit and Garsdale station the line runs through North Yorkshire. Because of this a further Area TUCC was involved, so closure notices had to be re-advertised and the period of objections extended.

On the other hand, the protestors had learned a lot. A Joint Action Committee was soon set up and in November 1984 this was registered as a limited-liability company. Its organisation has been excellent. Among other measures, forms on which objections could be registered were distributed on every train. On one very well-filled train on which the author travelled, several hundred completed forms must have been collected for forwarding to the TUCC.

The local authorities concerned also set up a steering committee. The latter commissioned a report published under the title 'The Settle & Carlisle Railway'. The consultants estimated that the cost for track and signalling over twenty years would be £21.1 million, including £2.1 million to keep the Ribbleshead Viaduct operational (BR had estimated £4.5 million for this latter). Costs would include those of reduction to single track, with well-located passing loops. A cost/benefit analysis, similar to that applied to road improvements, indicated that huge social benefits would be lost by closure, even if operating losses would be unlikely to be reduced below £105,000 per year. But even at that level the loss per mile would compare very favourably with many other lines kept open under the Public Service Obligation (page 106).

The steering committee of local authorities summed up thus their policy:

> ... the line meets important social needs and is coming into its own as an important national tourist and recreational attraction. We remain fully committed to the retention of the Settle & Carlisle Railway.

Objections from public bodies, interest groups and private individuals reached 21,000. During 1984 there was also an upsurge of passenger traffic as a result of the publicity. It was later revealed that this was on a sufficient scale to earn a surplus on the direct operating costs.

The end of the line for the Somerset & Dorset. On 5 March 1966, the last day, a local train heads away from Wellow for Templecombe.

In October 1984 BR announced that there would be no closure for at least five years. Meanwhile they undertook to market vigorously the line's potential. By January posters had appeared advertising trips to savour the winter beauties of the line at very reasonable fares. Whether, apart from singling over Ribblehead Viaduct, other serious attempts to reduce costs will be made remains to be seen. But to some extent at least things have changed. In the Beeching era BR rarely showed any willingness to react to public opinion.

But for all concerned with railways in particular, with transport in general and with the well-being of the environment, the position is alarming. If the public and BR have learned something, the government has learned nothing. On the narrow terms imposed on the nation in 1962 and which, amid reptilian tears successive administrations have promised much and done little to remedy, the BR closure proposal was a correct one. The line needs investment, for the most part revenue does not meet operating costs, and it would appear to be difficult to prove widespread *hardship* in the strict legal sense. The charge BR has to answer is that it deliberately made no effort to reduce costs and that there was little effort to develop the line's potential for tourism, that is, to seek a new function to replace the ones that have died.

The real indictment is against the various governments of the past thirty years which, with the honourable exception of Mrs Castle's period in office, have consistently failed to look at transport as a whole and in the long term. So BR is forced to apply a narrow profit-and-loss approach, while investment in roads is justified by social cost/benefit analysis. BR estimates £7 million for rehabilitation of the Settle & Carlisle (among the many figures put forward). A large sum perhaps, but only equivalent to perhaps 3 miles of motorway, and a fraction of what will be spent, after cost/benefit justification, on road improvements in the area once the line is closed. It is therefore to be hoped that a special grant can be arranged on the grounds of preservation of the environment, development of the area's potential, and the retention of a national heritage. Perhaps commonsense may be assisted to break through with a realisation that closure of the line was one of the major issues in the 1982 Penrith by-election which the government all but lost.

A Last Memory

But a return to the past for a last memory . . . One day, in September 1957, the 09.05 stopping train set out for Bath from the S&D platform at Templecombe. Behind a BR standard class 5 4-6-0, the set of four ex-Southern coaches descended the curve from the 1930s 'Odeonesque' station to join the line from Bournemouth in front of the busy locomotive depot. Under sunny skies the train threaded the rolling green countryside to Wincanton, with its goods yard crammed with wagons. Then a pause at Cole and over the GW main line to reach Evercreech Junction, the 'Crewe' of the S&D, with a class 2 4-4-0 on the waiting three-coach connecting train for Highbridge across the Somerset Levels.

For the Bath train it was different. At 1 in 50 it began the climb into the Mendips on a ledge in the hillside, with long views across to Glastonbury Tor, rising from the Levels. The viaduct was crossed to reach Shepton Mallet, a valuable pause to raise more steam for the climb to come. In the yard were a north and a southbound freight, each in the charge of a classic S&D 2-8-0, both of which were attaching and detaching wagons. Beyond, the ascent was resumed up the stone-walled hillside, through Winsor Hill Tunnel and through Masbury Halt non-stop to gain the 811ft Summit on the very top of Mendip.

Passengers could feel the train breasting the top as it rapidly gathered speed. Toiling up the reverse curves came a goods with a tall column of exhaust rising from each end, from a 2-8-0 blasting away at the head and a vociferous 'Jinty' 0-6-0T assisting in the rear. From Binegar onward it seemed a traffic watershed had been crossed as well as the physical one. For passengers by the dozen boarded the train at each stop instead of the two or three hitherto, while about forty were waiting on the platform at Shoescombe Halt.

At Midsomer Norton, a village rather less attractive than its name, the 09.55 Bath–Bournemouth stopping train was passed. Then came Radstock with its rail-connected collieries. Beyond Shoescombe a southbound parcels train, headed by yet another 2-8-0, was passed.

After Wellow, with its lovely church tower, the train came to a stand in a rocky cutting and simmered there for ten minutes before entering the single-track section, crossing the viaduct and passing through Midford with its single platform and small goods yard the other side of the short tunnel. Then the train rapidly climbed the valley side above the remains of the already forgotten Limpley Stoke & Camerton line, before plunging into what seemed to be the very hillside, but was the smoke-filled rat-hole of Combe Down Tunnel. Then came a blink of daylight in the secluded Lyncombe Vale before Devonshire Tunnel. Then, as the train squealed through the reverse curves of the 1 in 50, a magnificent panorama of Bath City opened out below. Then, over the Western Region line and past Bath Junction and the engine sheds to reach the cavernous train-shed of Green Park station a few minutes after 10.46. The passengers poured out of the now crowded coaches and it was all over for that day.

A quarter of a century later it is truly all over. It is impossible to re-create that far off, everyday 37 mile journey, other than through the magnificent photographic record of Ivo Peters or the pen of Robin Atthill. Though perhaps it is possible to stand on the B3135 where it crossed over the line at Masbury Summit and imagine the procession of trains toiling up from each side to the windswept summit. Here would come the ten-coach holiday extras double-headed by two Black Fives or a 'West Country' and a class 2 4–4–0; the four-coach stopping trains with a single loco; and the slow-moving heavy freights banked in the rear.

But why single out the Somerset & Dorset here? Readers will have their own favourite forgotten lines and treasured memories; it is left to them to conjure up such scenes and journeys from the past for their own enjoyment.

The forgotten railway. Langstone Viaduct connecting Hayling Island with the main-line at Havant crossed by a 'Terrier Tank'. Only the viaduct piers can now be seen.

233

BRITISH TRANSPORT COMMISSION
BRITISH RAILWAYS
WESTERN REGION

PUBLIC NOTICE

The British Transport Commission hereby give notice that from MONDAY, SEPTEMBER 10th, 1962, the passenger train services operating between Wrexham (Central) and Ellesmere together with certain associated services between Oswestry and Ellesmere will be discontinued and the local freight train service operating between Wrexham (Central) and Ellesmere will terminate at Messrs. Cadbury's private Siding (near Pickhill Halt)

The following Stations and Halts will be completely closed:-

Hightown, Sesswick, Pickhill, Cloy, Trench and Elson Halts
Bangor-on-Dee and Overton-on-Dee Stations

Passenger, Parcels and Freight "smalls" facilities will be withdrawn from Marchwiel Station

The existing facilities for the collection and delivery of parcels and freight "smalls" traffic in the area will be maintained. Facilities for the handing in and or collection of such traffic by the public will be available at Wrexham and Ellesmere stations. Facilities for dealing with freight traffic in full truck loads (including coal and livestock) will be available at Wrexham, Marchwiel and Ellesmere stations.

Regular bus services are operated in the area by Crosville Motor Services Ltd. and these will be augmented where necessary. In addition, Hampson's Luxury Coaches operate between Oswestry and Whittington. Details of these services can be obtained from the respective operators.

Any further information may be obtained on application to :
Mr. O. VELTOM,
District Superintendent
SHREWSBURY STATION

Telephone: Shrewsbury 3614 Extension 42

PADDINGTON STATION
August, 1962

S. E. RAYMOND,
General Manager

Bibliography and Acknowledgements

This book is intended to serve as an introduction to the 'Forgotten Railways' series published by David St John Thomas. The reader is referred to the particular volume covering the area he or she wishes to study in detail. Also useful is the 'Regional History of the Railways of Great Britain' series of the same publisher. There is a good bibliography in each volume. Both series have been drawn on as source material for this book.

I have relied particularly on two publications: 'The contraction of the network of railway passenger services in England & Wales' by J. A. Patmore (*Journal of the Institute of British Geographers*, Vol 38, 1966); and *Disused railways in the countryside of England & Wales*, a report to the Countryside Commission by J. H. Appleton (HMSO, 1970). These authors have generously allowed me to use much material for Chapters 2 and 3 and for Chapter 11 respectively, while Figures 2, 3 and 5 are based on the maps in Prof Patmore's paper. In addition there are: the *Study of disused railways in England & Wales: potential cycle routes*, a survey for the Department of Transport by John Grimshaw and Associates (HMSO, 1982); *The Social Consequences of Rail Closures* by M. Hillman and A. Whalley (Policy Studies Institute, No 587, 1980); and of course *The Reshaping of British Railways* (the 'Beeching Report') by the British Railways Board (1963). *I Tried to Run a Railway* by G. F. Fiennes (Ian Allan, 1967) is one of the few publications by a railway officer which deals with closure policies. Though not directly focussing on closures, M. R. Bonavia's *British Rail: The First Twenty-Five Years* (David & Charles, 1981) provides much background. *Closed Passenger Lines of Great Britain 1827–1947*, by M. D. Greville and Jeoffry Spence (Railway & Canal Historical Society, 1974), *Clinker's Register of Closed Passenger Stations and Goods Depots 1830–1977*, by C. R. Clinker (Avon-Anglia, 1979) and the *Guide to Closed Railways 1948–1975* by R. J. Hill and A. O. McDougall (Branch Line Society) are useful factual sources.

It is impossible here to list fully the vast and rapidly growing bibliography on the history and character of particular forgotten lines. *A Bibliography of Railway History* by G. Ottley (Allen & Unwin, 1965) is an invaluable source for earlier publications.

A few publications are selected here as bringing out particularly strongly the 'atmosphere' of forgotten lines. *The Country Railway* by D. St J. Thomas (David & Charles, 1976) is most evocative. D. L. Smith's reminiscences of south-west Scotland are superb in *The Little Railways of South West Scotland*

(David & Charles, 1969), *Legends of the Glasgow & South Western* (David & Charles, 1980) and *Tales of the Glasgow & South Western* (Ian Allan, no date). *London's Lost Railways* by C. Klapper (Routledge, 1976) deals with the question from an urban viewpoint. *Narrow Gauge Railways of the British Isles* by P. B. Whitehouse and J. B. Snell (David & Charles, 1984) is useful, though Ireland naturally looms large.

The Golden Valley Railway by C. L. Mowat (University of Wales Press, 1964) is a model study of a particularly fascinating line. But a major source is provided by the series of railway histories published by David & Charles. Among them are studies of *The Somerset & Dorset* (R. Atthill, 1967), *The Midland & Great Northern Joint Railway* (A. J. Wrottesley, 1970), *The Severn & Wye* (1963) and *The Great Western Railway in Dean* (1965) (both by H. W. Paar), *The Midland & South Western Junction* (C. G. Maggs, 1967) and *The Royal Deeside Line* (A. D. Farr, 1968). Many of the monographs published by the Oakwood Press are of value, though too numerous to mention here. More recently, Wild Swan Books have produced a series of very detailed branch-line studies which provide a unique photographic record, along with detailed plans of station layouts. Those consulted were *The Wisbech & Upwell Tramway* (C. Hawkins and G. Reeve), *The Severn & Wye* Vol 1 (I. Pope et al), *The Didcot, Newbury & Southampton* (P. Karau et al), *The Wallingford Branch* (P. Karau and C. Turner), and *Branch Lines of the Southern Railway* (G. Reeve and C. Hawkins).

The files of certain journals also contain great quantities of source material, particularly *Railway Magazine*, *Railway World*, *Trains Illustrated*, *Modern Railways* (especially when published as *Trains Illustrated*), *Journal of the Stephenson Locomotive Society*, *Journal of the Railway & Canal Historical Society*, and *British Railway Journal* (founded 1983 and of high quality).

Stone Blocks and Iron Rails by Bertram Baxter (David & Charles, 1966) is the definitive study of pre-steam lines and of their remains. For those wishing to explore forgotten railways on the ground and for those interested in their natural history the following are useful: *Walking Old Railways* by C. Somerville (David & Charles, 1979); *Railway Walks: Exploring Disused Railways* by G. L. Jones (David & Charles, 1983); and *A Walk Along the Tracks* by Hunter Davies (Hamlyn, 1982).

Particular thanks are owed to Professor J. A. Patmore, editor of the 'Forgotten Railways' series, for his unfailing encouragement and helpful comment. I am also deeply indebted to David Thomas for much help and in particular for making his notes on West Country closure events available, and allowing me to use his Dartington Hall Study *The Rural Transport Problem* (Routledge, 1963) and *Lake District Transport Report* (David & Charles, 1961).

Finally, acknowledgement is due to the following for permission to reproduce photographs (page numbers in brackets): H. C. Casserley (41); John Chalcroft (203 top, 205); John Clarke (29, 119, 148–9, 172, 198); Brian Cowlishaw (14,

15, 44 right, 60 main, 63, 161, 179, 180, 181, 225, 234); Stanley Creer (123); Derek Cross (138); Brian Cuttell (187, 188 right, 199, 200); M. Dunnett (101, 171); Tim Edmonds (104, 174 bottom, 177 bottom right); John Goss (title page, 69, 89, 136, 158 bottom, 182, 210, 212, 214, 228, 231); Peter W. Gray (20–1); R. M. S. Hall (26, 68, 82, 139, 233); H. G. W. Household (75); G. D. King (178); R. L. Knight Ltd (174 top); L&GRP (47, 48, 49, 52, 58, 65, 72, 76, 88, 95, 122, 127, 134, 144 bottom, 147, 152, 153, 156, 219); T. Mahoney (half-title); John Marshall (9, 31, 84, 154); Millbrook House (185, 203 bottom); Millbrook House – P. M. Alexander (107); Millbrook House – H. C. Casserley (103); Millbrook House – Eric Treacy (97, 109, 112, 113); Allan C. Mott (77, 131, 191, 206); Allan Patmore (19); Russell Collection (50); J. Sainsbury plc (208); R. J. Sellick (137); A. D. Simpson (207). The remaining photographs were supplied by the author.

Index

Note Lines belonging to major railways will be found under the line name: e.g. the GWR Helston branch will be found under Helston, not GWR. Minor companies are to be found under their own name: e.g. Blackwall Railway. Numbers in **bold** type indicate illustrations.